SECOND SERIES

ANTIQUE COLLECTOR'S DOLLS

by

Patricia R. Smith

Edited by: Karen Penner
Price Guide Editor: Kim McKim of Kimport Dolls

COLLECTOR BOOKS

Published by Collector Books
Box 3009
Paducah, Kentucky, 42001

ANTIQUE COLLECTOR'S DOLLS

Dedication

Dedicated to those, young and old, whose thoughts are reflected in the following poem:

MY IMAGE OF A DOLL

Oh, how the look of yesterday
Is etched in every line;
And just the thought of touching her
Sends your thoughts back into time,
Where fine drawn features were the case
And splendid clothes all trimmed with lace.

A doll could be a girl's escape
A wonderland of dreaming,
Where she could imagine that her doll
Was like her...a human being!

Christina M. Burkard
10806 Langdon Lane
Houston, Texas 77072

COVER DOLLS
18" F.G. and her "brother," 20" unmarked.

All photography by Dwight F. Smith except pictures of Jeanne Gregg, Thelma Flack, Phyllis Houston and Donna Maish.

The author wishes to thank the following for the use of their dolls' pictures: Each picture is credited with owner's name.

Jane Alton, Jean Anderson, Frances and Mary Jane Anicello, Blue Barn Antique Dolls, Alice Capps, Ruth Clark, Barbara Coker, Helen Draves, Cecelia Eades, Helen Faford, Thelma and Joleen Flack, Martha Gonyea, Jeanne Gregg, Bessie Greeno, Ralph Griffith, Margaret Gunnel, Ellie Haynes, Maxine Heitt, Phyllis Houston, Virginia Jones, Elaine Kaminsky, Kimport Dolls, Susan Manos, Marge Meisinger, Mini Things By Suzanne, Jay Minter, Barbara Mongelluzzi, Grace Ochsner, Mary Partridge, Carolyn Powers, Pat Raiden, Jimmy and Faye Rodofos, Julia Rogers, Terri Schall, Jessie Smith. R.H. Stevens, Mae Tetters, Kathy Walter.

Other books by Author:
Modern Collector's Dolls
Armand Marseille Dolls
Modern Collector's Dolls, Second Series
Modern Collector's Dolls, Third Series
Antique Collector's Dolls, First Series
Kestner and Simon Halbig Dolls
The Shirley Temple Story of Dolls

About the Author
PATRICIA R. SMITH

SCHOOLS: Page School for Girls, Los Angeles, California
St. Mary's, Santa Barbara, California
Nevada State, Nevada
St. Theresa, Kansas City, Missouri

DEGREES: Pedogogy
Adult Psychology
Child Psychology
Dogmatic Theology
Apologetics
Literary Methods

OTHER: "Famous Artists" Course, studying art layout and design. A commissioned
artist, who specializes in "faces" and religious art.
Studied with "Famous Writers School" in Connecticut on fiction aspects.

WORK: Has worked in Occupational Therapy Departments in Psychiatric Wards.
As Assistant Advertising Director for large catalog order firm. Member of
Ad Club. Worked as substitute teacher in local school system.

PUBLISHED: Articles and short stories on such varied subjects as: "Teen-age Dating",
"How to Sculpture A Face", "Comparative Religions", "The Art Of Being A
Wife", "Safety Afloat", "That Life-Jacket May Save You", "What It Is All
About (USCGAUX)", "The Day That Tim Drowned", "What Is Religion?",
"The Ins and Outs of Ceramics", "You Can Paint".

HOBBIES: Archery, Boating, Sewing, Collecting dolls.

ORGANIZATIONS: National Field Archers Ass'n, U.S. Coast Guard Auxiliary, Council of
Catholic Women, Lake of the Ozarks Yachting Assn., National Federation
of Doll Clubs.

A MORTIFYING MISTAKE

I studied my tables over and over,
    and backward and forward, too:
But I couldn't remember six times nine,
    and I didn't know what do do,
Till sister told me to play with my doll
    and not to bother my head.
"If you call her "Fifty four" for awhile,
    you'll learn it by heart," she said.

So I took my favorite Mary Ann, though
    I thought 'twas a dreadful shame
To give such a perfectly lovely child
    such a perfectly horrid name.
And I called my dear little "Fifty-Four"
    a hundred times, till I knew
The answer of six times nine as well as
    the answer of two times two.

Next day, Elizabeth Wiggesworth, who
    always acts so proud,
Said "Six times nine is fifty-two",
    and I nearly laughed aloud!

But I wished I hadn't when teacher said:
    "Now, Dorothy, tell if you can,"
For I thought of my doll and — sakes
    alive!...I answered: "Mary Ann!

Taken from Arthur's Home Mag.
March 1893

V

CONTENTS

HOW TO USE PRICE GUIDE

The main and of utmost importance to any doll is the head. The quality of the bisque and that it is not damaged in any way, is the determining factor for which prices should be based. That means no hairline cracks, cracked or broken shoulder plates, eye chips, any mends or repairs, etc. and that the quality of the bisque is very good to excellent.

The most desirable dolls are completely perfect, original, in original boxes and never played with. But prices based on this assumption are unrealistic because the ratio is an overwhelming 6,000 to 1. That leaves 5,999 dolls showing varying degrees of use . . . so the prices are for excellent quality bisque in perfect condition and with no defects.

Body rubs, a missing finger, a crack in a kid body, a minor repair to the foot, etc. (These are minor, not major damages), play no part in the prices in this book and we have not gone into great detail on bodies, because who can say what is original or not. After all, many, many heads and bodies were replaced when the dolls were toys and for various reasons, bisque heads did break and were replaced; bodies broke and were replaced.

The prices in this book were not make-up. They cover a 4 year study from mail order firms, ads, price guides and price lists from all over the United States and Canada. They are the now prices and any changes will be reflected in Series 111 of "Antique Collector's Dolls" at a future date. If a doll is more than I have based prices on . . . that is, all original, in an original box and unplayed with . . . you can add 20% over and above these prices and get it!!

Please let me repeat! The first and foremost importance is the condition and quality of the head of the doll that you are thinking of buying or selling. I will finish this by saying that collectors set their own prices by the amount they are willing to pay for any certain doll.

I have priced all dolls by using the retail dealer's prices except for bisque. Since allowances must be made for the quality of the bisque, I have used a scale method of pricing. For example: 18" M-N would mean that the price of the doll was between $800.00 and $900.00 depending on the quality of the bisque.

A	50.00	N	900.00
B	100.00	O	1,000.00
C	150.00	P	1,050.00
D	200.00	Q	1,100.00
E	250.00	R	1,200.00
F	300.00	S	1,300.00
G	350.00	T	1,450.00
H	400.00	U	1,700.00
I	450.00	V	1,900.00
J	500.00	W	2,200.00
K	600.00	X	2,400.00
L	700.00	Y	2,700.00
M	800.00	Z	3,000.00

A FASCINATION OF DOLLS-WHAT IS AN ANTIQUE?

Value is generally placed on an item because it is an "antique". This value may be in research of period and time, a true appreciation of the art of antiques or it could be relative to monatary value. Some look upon antiques as a means of investment, and others, the investment part is only a side effect to the deep, true meaning of the word "antique".

Antique means, according to Webster, belonging to former times as contrasted with modern, and something belonging to or remaining of ancient times. The world over an item must be over 100 years old or it is not legally an antique, and fairly new collectors may be shocked to know that Europeans showed great distain for bisque dolls during the 1950's and 1960's. Now they would like them back, and are willing to pay tremendous amounts to keep what they have left. During these times the true antiques were dolls of wood, wax and mache and since the "incoming" of bisque into the collection field (those made prior to 1875) these particular dolls have lost their appeal, which is so very unfortunate as the really deep sense of antiques seems to have faded. Since the mid-1960's there has been a great rush

to collect the collectable's: Bisque. Most Americans are not as time conscious as true antiques call for. After all, we have moved from the horse and buggy to landing on the moon in the space of fifty short years. Our European friends took hundreds of years to evolve to the means of mass production and innovation.

Because of the vast and fast pace that Americans have always set for themselves, anything that is old or hard to find is considered, of course wrongly, an antique. In the minds of a lot of collectors all china, parian, bisque, wax, wood, anything is an antique and they draw no lines, no dates to separate the antique with the "collectable," BUT we must all remember that collectables seemingly become antiques! An ANTIQUE has to be more than 100 years old and a COLLECTABLE means anything from 100 years ago to now, this date.

Here is a listing of dates that will help divide antiques and collectables:
1690's: Wood, pressed wax and glazed stoneware.

1700's: Pressed wax. Wood. Queen Anne type woodens (1873), English woodens (1775-1780), Peddler woodens (1780)

1800's: Pápier maché, wood, earthenware, Ball (bald) head chinas, Biedermeir chinas, Parian (1800-1830), 1st sleeping eyes (1820-1830), Pink luster in quanties (1800-1840), Pre-Greiners with glass eyes (1830-1850), "fashion" dolls (1840), Queen Victoria woodens (1840-1860), 1850's: Dolls of wax, porcelain china, gutta percha, rubber, rag re-inforced mache, 1st dolls strung with elastic, glass eyes in porcelain heads, Frozen Charlottes, Oriental babies (Motschmann based his 1857 patent on these) Brown eyed chinas (1840), German Mechanicals (1851). Superior papier mache (1850-1870), First childlike dolls appear (1840) Parian with high neck (1846), Parians with beads, flowers molded on hairdo or shoulders (1846) Pasty white chinas with tight curl hairdos (1840-1860) 1860's: Bisque heads tinted and untinted (parian), Kid lady bodies, Motschmann type babies, papier mache, china, wood, wax over maché, rag, Negro dolls appeared, Dolls prior to 1860 were unable to sit down. Pierced ears came into fashion as did heels (prior to this time they had flat feet), Important patents during 1860's: Swivel, socket type neck (Huret 1861), Autoperipetelikos Walker (1862), ball joints strung with metal or rubber (Lee-1866). Adeline Patti china (1859), Nancy Hanks, Covered Wagon china (1840-1860), Jenny Lind (1840-1860), Pre-Civil War China (1840-1860), 1870's: Wax, rag, rubber, porcelain, china, leather, wood, pápier maché, bisque, Elaborate hairdo untinted bisque (parian), all bisque (1878), Musical dolls created in Paris, Jumeau ladies (1860-1880), Greiners (7 types) (1858-1872), Bru Jun pat'd (1879), Mary Lincoln Todd (1862), 1880's: Bisque, composition heads and bodies, bodies of kid, composition, wood and cloth. Jointed all bisque, the re-appearing of sleep eyes, celluloid, Flat top china, head sizes appeared, German walking dolls (1880-1900), Edison Phonograph doll (1887-1888) Highland Mary and Dotter china (1880), Nellie Bly china (1882), 1890's: Bisque heads on composition or kid bodies, Turned shoulder heads, chinas with bangs, Negros, American Indians, Bonnet Dolls, Flirting eyes, spring joints as well as elastic. Forming of S.F.B.J. (1899).

1900's: Pet name chinas on printed bodies, Introduction of character dolls (1909), Hair parted to side instead of middle (1905), Pierced ears decline, Flapper style bodies (Jointed above knee to allow for shorter dress lengths), Dolls dressed in Military costumes (1904), Rag dolls with photograph faces (1905), All felt dolls (1908), Bent limbs baby bodies (1909), Chase dolls (1910), Kewpie (1913), Gibson Girls (1910), Fulpher (1914) By-Lo (1924).

Some outstanding and highly collectable American made dolls are:

1866: F.E. Darrow obtained a patent for dolls heads of untanned leather. Bristol Conn. until 1877.

1866: Philip Lerch of Philadelphia, Pa. made pápier maché heads that looked much like Greiners. Some are marked Lerch and King. Until 1870.

1873: Izannah F. Walker patented dolls on Nov. 4, 1873. The distinguishing feature about these dolls are the two little curls in front of each ear.

1875: The Hotchkiss Walking Doll was patented Sept. 21, 1875.

1880: The Dotter Doll was patented Dec. 7, 1880.

1880: Bartenstein patented a two faced wax doll, whose head revolved inside a bonnet. The patents were received April, 1880, Dec. 1880 and Sept. 1881.

1882: The Webber Singing Doll with a wax head was patented April 25, 1882. It was made in three sizes, 22", 24" and 26". First on kid and later on cloth bodies. A complicated mechanism made it sing.

1888: The Jacques Phonograph Doll was patented May 22, 1888.

1893: The Columbian Rag Doll was first made by Mariatta and Emma Adams of Oswego, NY in the 1890's. In 1893 it was accepted at the World Fair in Chicago and named Columbia Rag Doll. After Emma Adams death, the doll was made by her younger sister, Marie, from 1906 to 1910. Her sister used her married name of M.A. Ruttan.

1902: The E. U. Steiner Walking Doll was patented March 11, 1902.

1905: The Art Fabric Dolls (cloth) were made from 1905 through 1910.

1909: Hoffman's American Doll and Toy Co. in May 1909 began making Billikens, an animal manikin.

1911: The Schoenhut Doll was patented Jan. 17, 1911.

1914: The Parson Jackson Baby dolls were patented Dec. 8, 1914. Their Trademark is a "stork".

1914: Uneeda Biscuit Doll of composition was made to help sales of Uneeda Biscuit Co.

1917: The Dolly Walker Dolls were patented April 1, 1917 and made until 1921. These dolls were made by Harry H. Coleman.

1919: The Aluminum head doll was patented Nov. 4, 1919 and was actually made 1918 to 1920. They had aluminum hands and feet and were on a German type of jointed, hollow wood body.

This author has mentioned in several places that Armand Marseille dolls with pierced ears are rare and to date we must report that we have now heard of only three. Margaret Wirgaw of Weirton, WV writes that she has a 29" one marked: Made In Germany/Armand Marseille/390n/DRGM 246/1/A. 13 M. and has a 3051/12 stamped in black with this and she has seen a marked Floradora with pierced ears. Mrs. Lee C. Fielden from Conn. has an 18" with pierced ears, who is marked: A.M. Dep./Made In Germany. It is interesting to note that the pierced ear A.Ms are about as scarce as French dolls with double chins!

Also we received a letter from Elizabeth Davis of Campbell, California who has an almost identical doll that is shown on page 206, Antique Collector's Dolls Series 1 (Manufacturers Unknown Section) and hers is also a turned shoulder head which was so popular during the 1890's. Her doll is 32" tall and has fur eyebrows. The doll is marked on the upper rim of the crown: 11X/195 Dep 17/ ♪ Made In Germany. The body is pin jointed kid with the Kestner crown and streamers lable and what reads: Pat. 1895/J.D. Kestner.

ALL BISQUE

There are very few authenticated French, all bisque dolls, and as throughout all other sizes and types, many, many parts or entire dolls were imported to France from Germany. Although the French and German hated each other, especially after the Franco-Prussian War of 1870-71 (Fall of Napoleon and the Empire of France) due to economic necessity, they had commercial and industrial agreements.

Among the All Bisque dolls, ones with swivel necks are the most desirable because they are rarer and MAYBE they are French. Of these swivel heads a few may have the French loop molded onto the base of the head. These loops are easily identified as they look like the tops of bells. ⊌

Many French-Type all bisque are peg strung and a few have painted eyes, but most have glass eyes and well painted lashes. In the small sizes, the eyes are usually set and generally blue with no pupils. As they get larger, they gain the pupils and sleep.

The French-Type legs are much more varied, thinner and more delicate than German made ones. They are mainly barefooted, although many have vertical as well as circular ribbed sockings in many colors, including white, blue, brown, black and yellow. The molded on shoes also can be high top boots with pointed toes, high buttoned ones with four or more painted straps. They may have brown, pink, blue, black one or two strap slippers, with or without heels, some with bows or even plain black with a colored bow.

French-Type dolls generally have good flesh tinted bisque and are artistically painted. Many have kid lined joints so the bisque doesn't squeak. Many have cork pates in the tiny open crowns.

The German swivel heads that are strung without a wooden neck plug have holes at the sides of the necks ⇒ ⊄ and the head is strung with the arm rubber. ⋊ ⊢ These heads will not hold a "turned" position, but will always snap back to face front.

All bisque dolls with molded on clothes are highly collectable and the oldest of these are believed to be the ones with a ruffled one piece underwear in pink or blue.

Germany's Kestner seems to have produced more all bisque dolls than any other manufacturer. Here are a few clues to Kestner dolls: A great, great number have warped out of shape domes to the head, the top lip is painted "squared" off at ends, they have glossy, multistroke eyebrows, upper and lower black eyeliner, many have lower painted lashes only, but few have upper painted lashes also. Kestner liked a blue-grey eyes and used plaster pates. He also liked one strap shoes with a pom pom on the toe. The shoes were generally black with yellowish soles. A great number of his all bisque dolls have white unpainted bisque socks with blue top band, also: Pink vertical ribbed with no top band or, rose or magenta bands. He also used blue circular with no top bands and blue vertical ribbing with dark blue bands.

Some Kestner mold numbers for all bisque dolls are: 112, 130, 142, 150, X150, 151, 152, 164, 192, 208, 257, 307, 310, 314, 600, 620.

The following is a "desirability rating" for all bisque dolls:

French (Identified)
French-Type in original clothes
Slender legs
Glass eye, swivel neck with molded hair
Jointed knees and elbows
Pierced ears

Long stockings (above knees)
Arms not alike (molded in same position)
Free standing thumbs
Peg jointed
Kid in joints
Molded on clothes

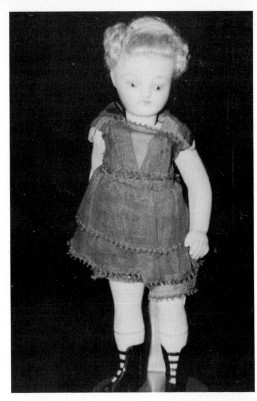

All Bisque--5½". Socket swivel head. Strung arms and legs. Inset glass eyes. Closed mouth, open crown. Painted socks and high top boots. Original. $185.00. (Courtesy Helen Draves)

All Bisque. 4" With socket swivel head and pin jointed arms and legs. Closed mouth. Inset glass eyes. Painted on shoes with white ribbed socks/ red band around top. Original wig & clothes. $115.00. (Courtesy Kimport Dolls)

1

All Bisque--4" All bisque with one piece body and head. Open crown. Glass inset goo goo eyes. One hand closed. Free formed thumbs. Well molded knees. Molded on shoes and socks. Marks: Germany. $295.00. (Courtesy Kimport Dolls)

All Bisque--5" All bisque. Socket swivel head with strung arms and legs (jointed). Inset Decal eyes. Closed mouth. Painted on hose and high top boots. Marks: None. Original. $185.00. (Courtesy Helen Draves)

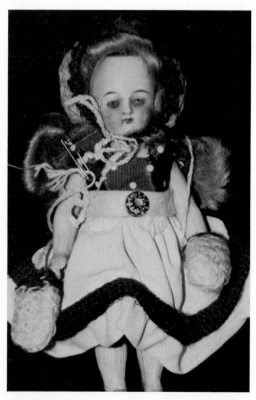

All Bisque--5" All bisque with one piece body and head. Pin jointed arms and legs. Inset glass eyes. Closed mouth. Flat crown slice on top of head. Painted on white ribbed knee hose with light brown painted toe area. Marks: SO 34. $85.00. (Courtesy Helen Draves)

All Bisque--9½" All bisque with jointed neck, shoulders and hips. Brown sleep eyes. Open mouth. Open crown. Beautiful molded hands and feet. Most have molded on high top boots, but also came bare footed. Marks: 4, on head. $495.00. (Courtesy Kimport dolls)

All Bisque--6" All bisque. One piece body and head. Inset glass eyes. Pin jointed arms and legs. Painted on shoes and socks. Marks: None. $75.00. (Courtesy Helen Draves)

All Bisque--4½" All bisque with one piece body and head. Pin jointed arms and legs. Inset glass eyes. Small open mouth. Marks: 237/13/SWC. $75.00. (Courtesy Helen Draves)

All Bisque--6" All bisque with one piece body and head. Painted eyes. Open crown. Painted on socks and boots. Original. Marks: 520/3½. $75.00. (Courtesy Helen Draves)

All Bisque--5½" All bisque with one piece body and head. Has molded bow in side of hair. Original. Marks: P 23, a three leaf clover/Made In Germany. Wire jointed shoulders and hips. $65.00. (Courtesy Helen Draves)

3

All Bisque--7" All bisque with molded on bonnet. Molded on slippers. Not marked. This same head can be seen on a 12" version under "White Bisque." $195.00. (Courtesy Helen Draves)

All Bisque--4" Shirley Temple. All bisque and painted. Marks: Germany. $135.00. (Courtesy Marge Meisinger)

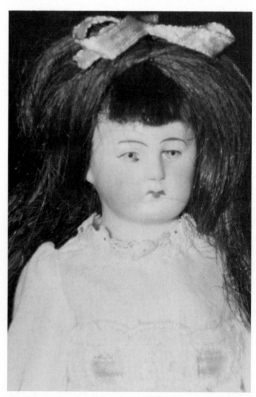

All Bisque--6½" All bisque with one piece body and head. Molded blonde hair. Original. Marks: None. $65.00. (Courtesy Helen Draves)

All Bisque--6" All bisque with one piece body and head. Open crown. Closed mouth. Painted on shoes and socks. Marks: None. $75.00. (Courtesy Helen Draves)

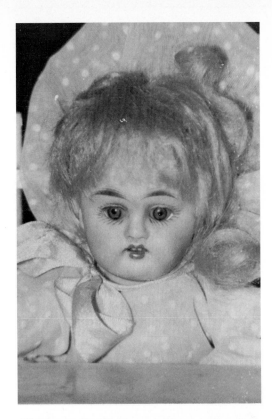

All Bisque--6½" All bisque with one piece body and head. Open mouth. Blue sleep eyes with hair lashes. Open crown. Painted on shoes and socks. Original. $200.00. (Courtesy Kimport Dolls)

All Bisque--7" All bisque with one piece body and head. Blue sleep eyes. Open mouth. Painted on lavender ribbed socks and black shoes. Marks: None. $200.00. (Courtesy Helen Draves)

All Bisque--7½" All bisque. One piece body and head. Sleep eyes. Open/closed mouth. Painted on shoes and socks. This doll is suspected to be a Bonn doll because of the ungainly large feet and mold # of 83/150/18. See "All Bisque and Half Bisque Dolls" by Genevieve Angione for details on Bonn dolls. (Courtesy Kathy Walter)

All Bisque--Close up of suspected Bonn Doll. Painted area between lips with no indication of teeth. Painted lashes over and under eyes. Bisque is nice but not the finest of quality. $125.00.

5

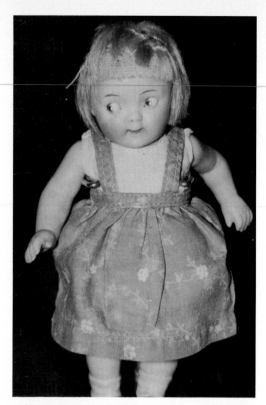

All Bisque--6" All bisque with one piece body and head. Goo Goo eyes to side. Molded on socks and shoes. Free formed thumbs. Marks: None. Original wig and clothes. $295.00. (Courtesy Jane Alton)

All Bisque--5" Googly. Jointed shoulders and hips. Closed mouth, painted on shoes and socks and original wig. Marks: None. $295.00. (Courtesy Kimport Dolls)

All Bisque--8" All bisque boy with side parted modeled pale blonde hair. Dressed in his original Groom (Tux) clothes. $135.00. (Courtesy Kimport Dolls)

All Bisque--7" All bisque girl with side part pale blonde hair and molded in ribbon. One piece body and head. $115.00. (Courtesy Kimport Dolls)

All Bisque--5½" All bisque with swivel head. Set in glass eyes. Closed mouth. Marks: 5 2/3. $100.00. (Courtesy Kimport Dolls)

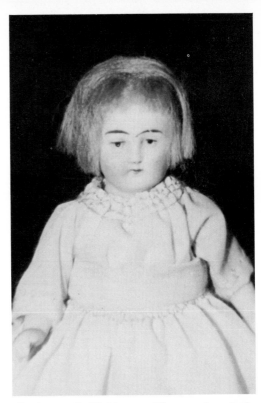

All Bisque--4" All bisque with one piece body and head. Ball (bald) head with wig. Marks: 5000, on head. $75.00. (Courtesy Kimport Dolls)

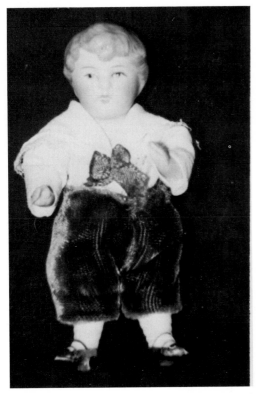

All Bisque--3½" All bisque boy with side parted blonde hair. Open/closed mouth. Painted on two strap, heeled shoes. One piece body and head. Marks: 525-2. $65.00. (Courtesy Kimport Dolls)

All Bisque--3½" All bisque. Pin jointed arms only. Tucked in chin. Marks: Germany. $75.00. (Courtesy Helen Draves)

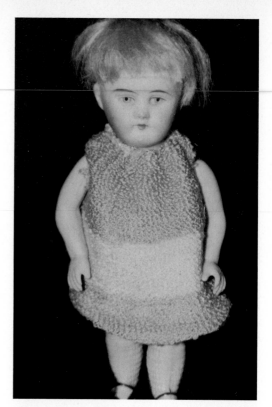

All Bisque--6" All bisque boy and girl in swing. To swing above baby crib. Germany. $115.00. (Courtesy Helen Draves)

All Bisque--8" All bisque with one piece body and head. Open crown with part of original wig. Closed mouth. Painted on socks without upper band and shoes with pom pom on toe. Marks: 6, on back. $75.00. (Courtesy Jane Alton)

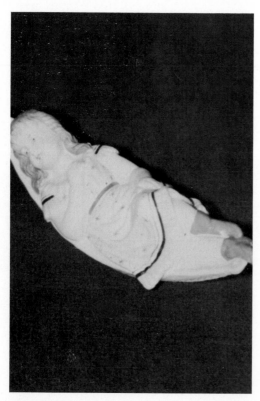

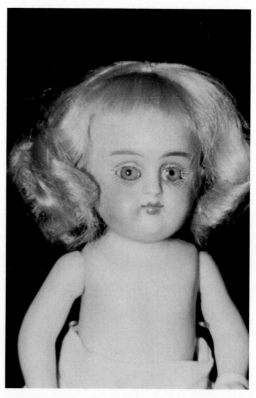

All Bisque--7" long all bisque child in a hammock. Germany. $100.00. (Courtesy Helen Draves)

All Bisque--6" All bisque with one piece body and head. Inset pale blue glass eyes. Closed mouth. Marks: 158. $95.00. (Courtesy Kimport Dolls)

All Bisque--5½" All bisque with molded on underclothes. One piece body and head. Marks: Germany. $150.00. (Courtesy Helen Draves)

All Bisque--3½" All bisque with molded on clothes. Jointed at shoulders only. Marks: None. $110.00. (Courtesy Helen Draves)

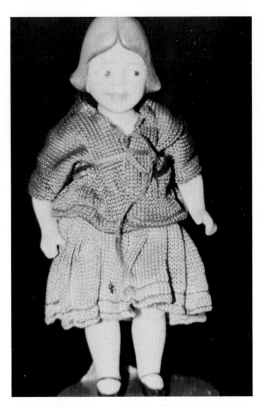

All Bisque--3½" All bisque "Campbell Kid" with molded on clothes. Jointed shoulders only. Molded yellow hair. Pre-World War I. Marks: Germany. $95.00. (Courtesy Helen Draves)

All Bisque--3" All bisque with open/closed mouth with painted teeth. Jointed at shoulders only. Original. Painted on shoes and socks. Unmarked. $115.00. (Courtesy Helen Draves)

9

All Bisque--4" All bisque with one piece body and head. Two molded in bows. Lightly painted on socks and shoes. Original. Marks: Germany. $45.00. (Courtesy Helen Draves)

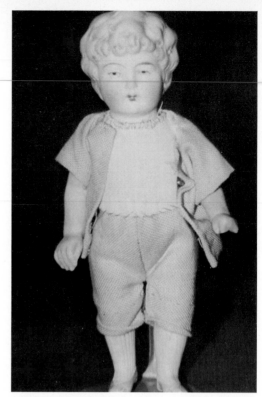

All Bisque--5" All bisque with one piece body and head. Molded blonde hair. Painted on socks with lightly painted over shoes. Marks: Germany/3. $75.00. (Courtesy Jane Alton)

All Bisque--4" All bisque with one piece body and head. Pin jointed arms and legs. Molded blonde hair. Marks: 249. $75.00. (Courtesy Helen Draves)

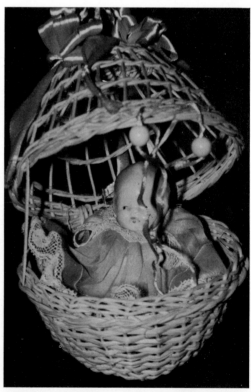

All Bisque--3" All bisque baby in basket. Jointed shoulders and hips. Doll Marks: Germany, on back. Basket: Park Avenue/Phil. Pa./Doll Outfitters. $50.00 complete. (Courtesy Helen Draves)

All bisque--6 3/4" All bisque with one piece body and head. Molded blonde hair. Large goo goo eyes. Excellent quality bisque. Marks: Germany. $200.00. (Courtesy Kimport Dolls)

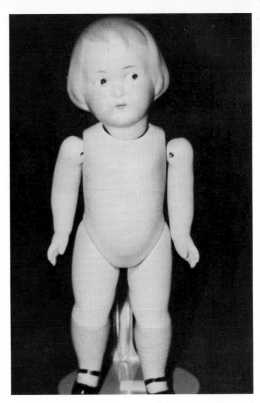

All Bisque--8" All bisque. Painted on shoes and hose with circular ribbing. Molded blonde hair. Side glance goo goo eyes. Marks: 33 11/0. Replaced arms. $165.00. (Courtesy Kimport Dolls)

All Bisque--2" All bisque babies. Jointed hips and shoulders. Molded blonde hair. Original basket and glass bottle with rubber nipple. Germany. $45.00 complete. (Courtesy Helen Draves)

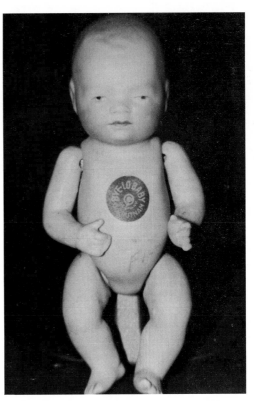

All Bisque--5" All bisque Bye-Lo. One piece body and head. Shows red Bye-lo seal. $225.00. (Courtesy Jane Alton)

11

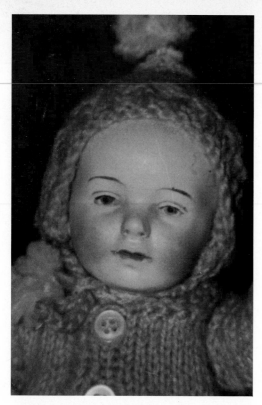

All Bisque--7" All bisque with sweet face. Good bisque with well painted eyes. Full closed mouth. One piece body and head. Bent baby legs. Free formed thumbs. Marks: None. $95.00. (Courtesy Helen Draves)

All Bisque--5½" All bisque with one piece body and head. Heavily painted lower lip. Painted blonde hair. Bent baby legs. Marks: None. $85.00. (Courtesy Jane Alton)

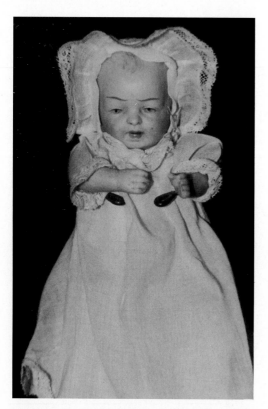

All Bisque--5" All bisque baby. Open/Closed mouth. Brush stroke hair. Frown. Free formed thumbs. One piece body and head. Marks: None. (Courtesy Jane Alton)

All Bisque--4" "Peek-A-Boo". All bisque molded in one piece. Large to side googly eyes. Molded on clothes. Marks: Made In/Germany. Designed by Grace Drayton. $75.00. (Courtesy Marge Meisinger)

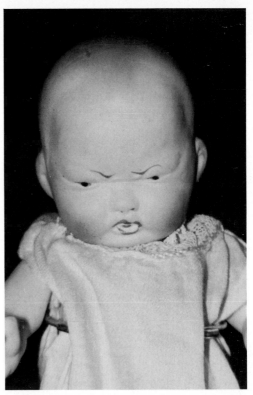

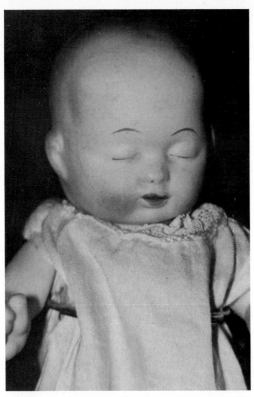

All Bisque--5" Unusual Japanese all bisque baby with two faces. Both hands are curled. Bent baby legs. Marks: Japan. $250.00. (Courtesy Kimport Dolls)

All Bisque--Other side of Japanese two faced baby. Mouth is open/closed.

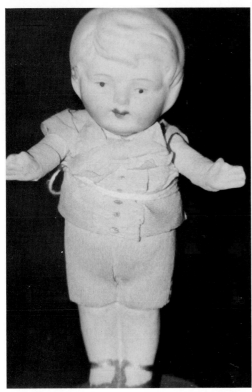

All Bisque--4½" All bisque with jointed shoulders only. Gold painted feet and crepe paper clothes. Pants are glued on. Marks: None. $45.00. (Courtesy Helen Draves)

All Bisque--4 3/4" Baby Darling. All bisque with tucked in chin. Jointed shoulders only. Pink bows with blue ribbon molded in hair. Shield shape seal on stomach: M.B./Baby Darling. Japan, on back. Painted on gold shoes. Crepe paper dress. $75.00. (Courtesy Helen Draves)

13

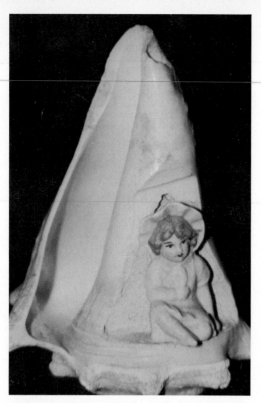

All Bisque--1¾" tall sitting figure of child in cut out part of sea shell. Germany. $18.00. (Courtesy Maxine Heitt)

All Bisque--4" tall box with figure. Marks: None. $35.00. (Courtesy Helen Draves)

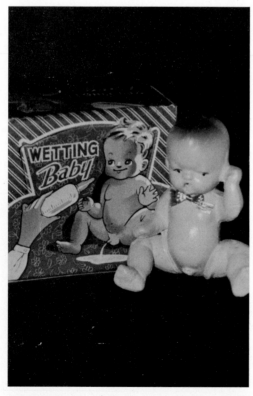

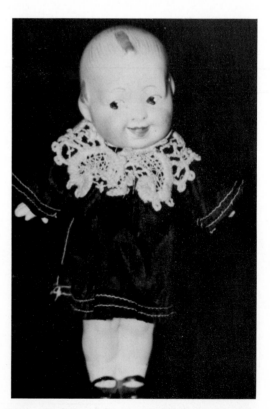

All Bisque--9" "Wetting Baby" One piece (unjointed) head and body. All wood arms and legs. Original. Shackman, Japan. $15.00. (Courtesy B. Mongelluzzi)

Japan--6" Copy of Germany's Wide Awake doll. All bisque with jointed shoulders only. Open/closed mouth, painted eyes, shoes and socks. Marks: Japan. $65.00. (Courtesy Kimport Dolls)

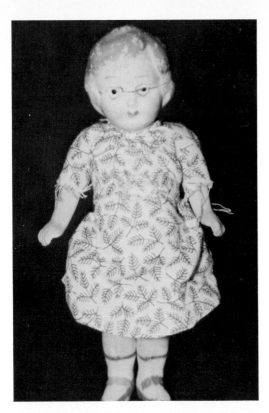

All Bisque--5½" All bisque with painted grey hair and painted on glasses. One piece body and head. Painted on shoes and socks. Marks: Japan. (Courtesy Helen Draves)

All Bisque--7" All bisque. Socket swivel head. String jointed arms and legs. Molded yellow hair. Painted on shoes and socks. Marks: Japan. $28.00. (Courtesy Helen Draves)

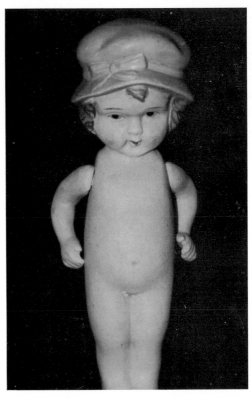

All Bisque--4" All bisque. Jointed shoulders only. Molded blonde hair. Crepe paper and ribbon original clothes. Marks: Made In/Japan. $18.00. (Courtesy Helen Draves)

All Bisque--7½" All bisque with jointed shoulders only. Molded on bonnet. Marks: Made In Japan. $22.00. (Courtesy Helen Draves)

KNOTTERS

All Bisque--Knotters are also referred to as "nodders" because the heads bob and nod. But the earliest reference to them is "knotters" because of the way that they are strung. The stringing is a fine elastic and most are tied with a knot at the tops of the heads if they can be concealed by hair or a hat. If not, they will be strung through two holes in the top of the head and the knot tied inside. Knotters were introduced in the mid 1920's and the majority of them were comic strip or comic characters such as Our Gang, Skeezix, Orphan Annie, etc., but also there were couples for each holiday and ones that represented no one in particular. Knotters were also made by Japan.

All Bisque--3" All bisque Knotter that represents St. Patrick's Day and is marked Germany. $22.00. (Courtesy Helen Draves)

All Bisque--3" All bisque St. Patrick's Day girl. Marked Germany. $22.00. (Courtesy Helen Draves)

All Bisque--3" Indian. All bisque Knotter marked Germany. $25.00. (Courtesy Helen Draves)

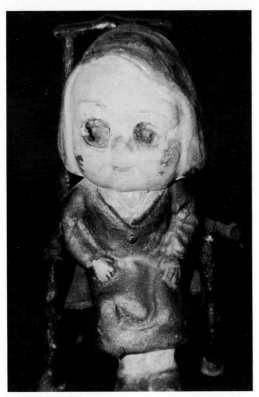

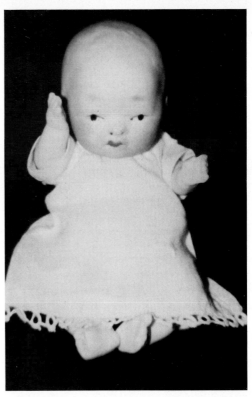

All Bisque--5" All bisque Knotter head in bisque chair (molded in). Large painted eyes. $35.00. (Courtesy Jane Alton)

All Bisque--3½" Bye-Lo copy. All bisque with socket head. Jointed shoulders and hips. Marks: Japan. $65.00. (Courtesy Kimport Dolls)

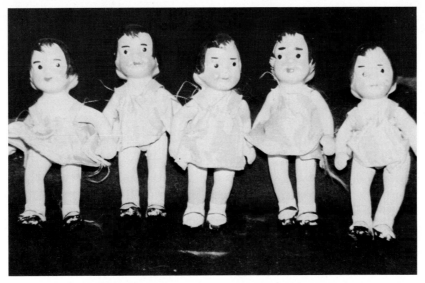

All Bisque--3½" Quints. One piece body and head. Eyes painted to look straight ahead and to each side. Slightly bent toddler legs with painted on shoes and socks. Marks: Japan. $75.00 set. (Courtesy Helen Draves)

17

SNOW BABIES

Snow Babies were first produced by Hertwig and Co. in the late 1800's but they were soon made by many manufacturers. These figures were made as a Christmas or Winter decorations item and the earliest Snow Babies can be identified by their excellent quality bisque and facial expressions and color (artists work). This color is soft and lifelike.

These early Snow Babies are very rare but the most difficult to find of the early ones is the Angels. They have pale pink or blue wings of smooth bisque. Next in rariety is the Snow Children that have the tops of the heads molded with an open crown, these were used as planters, and measure under 5" tall. Along with these would be the Snow Baby Dolls, with jointed shoulders and hips.

Snow Babies came in colors as well as all white. Their clothes were of porcelain sand (grit) and they were molded in just about any position. Some were incised Germany and more were unmarked. They usually range from a tiny 1 1/16" to 6" or 8". The average size is 3½".

As demand grew and production increased these Seasonal items began to become less artistically painted and the bisque took on an orange tint with bright red lips and by 1920 another group of Snow Babies were on the market and are referred to as "Action Snow Babies" . . . although the very excellent first ones also were "action" figures.

The best known ones of these are: Snow Babies on a polar bear, feeding a seal, crawling with other Snow Babies on their backs, pulling a sled with penguins, polar bear on top of a cliff overlooking a crouching Snow Baby, riding a sleigh drawn by dogs, inside an igloo with Santa Claus, Santa leading two Snow Babies, sliding down a snow ledge, on reindeer, pulling a sled, three Snow Babies on one sled, six piece band with different instruments, on a swing, mother with baby carriage, on skis, holding sailboat and many others.

Japan also made Snow Babies but their workmanship is not as good as the German ones. Some Snow Babies were made in the 1940's and are marked "U.S. Zone" Germany. Japan is currently making new Snow Babies (Shackman) and they only bear a small paper label. Snow Babies are a case where doll collectors do not distinguish between dolls and figurines.

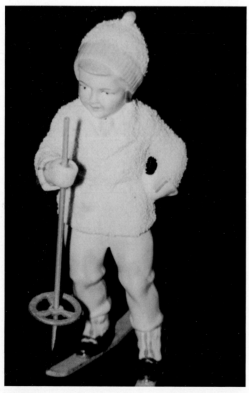

All Bisque--6" Early Snow Baby. Wood skis and pole. Marks: Germany. $165.00. (Courtesy Helen Draves)

All Bisque--5" Early Snow Baby. Excellent quality with pinned jointed arms and legs. $195.00. (Courtesy Helen Draves)

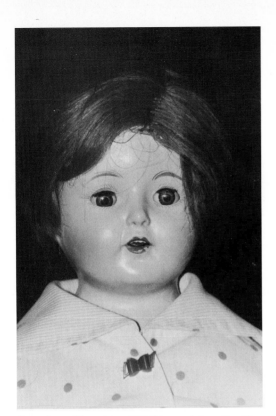

American Character--22" Composition shoulder-head with disc jointed limbs. Open crown. Sleep eyes/lashes. Marks: Petite/American Character Doll, in half Circle. Ca. 1934. $50.00. (Courtesy Alice Capps)

American Doll Co--8" Clown. All composition. Spring strung. Dimples. One piece body and head. Molded, unpainted hair. Original clothes. $45.00. (Courtesy Kimport Dolls)

ALT, BECK & GOTTSCHALCK

Alt, Beck and Gottschalck--Alt, Beck and Gottschalck began with a porcelain factory called Porzellanfabrik Von Alt in 1854. They were among the producers of both the Bonnie Babe and Bye-Lo babies for the George Borgfelt Co. Many of their regular production dolls have pierced nostrils. Known mold numbers used by them are: 1322, 1352, 1353, 1361, 1362, 1366, 1367, 1368, 1373, 1376, 1402, 1432.

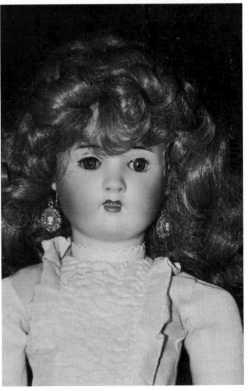

Alt, Beck and Gottschalk--18½" Socket head on fully jointed composition body. Open mouth/4 teeth and molded tongue. Marks: ABG/1362/ Made In Germany/0 3/4. (Courtesy Alice Capps) D-E

19

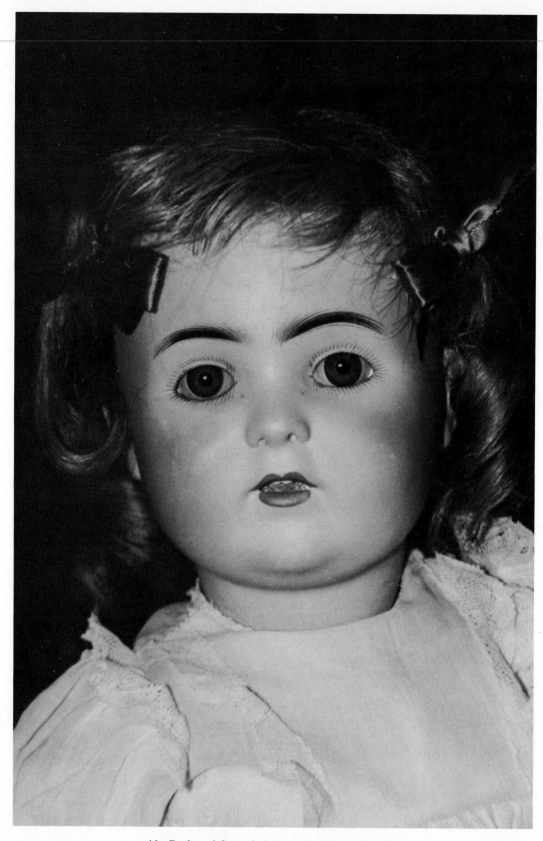

Alt, Beck and Gottschalck--18" Socket head on 5
piece baby body of composition. Open mouth
with two upper teeth. Sleep eyes. Marks: ABG
(in scroll)/1367/45. (Courtesy Kimport Dolls)
E-G

ARMAND MARSEILLE

The following information is excerpts from "Armand Marseille Dolls" by this author.

A greater number of A.M. dolls have survived to be on the current market by the sheer fact of ratio to production. They are the dolls most available and a re-valuation of the Armand Marseille's dolls is important. They must be judged, not because they are Armand Marseille's but on an INDIVIDUAL BASIS OF QUALITY.

The Armand Marseille factory began in 1865 in Koppelsdorf, Thur. It did not fully recover from the World War 1 diversion to defence material and failed altogether by 1928. This factory made entire dolls, and also heads for such firms as Louis Wolf and Co., Maar and Sohn, Max Handwerck and Cuno and Otto Dressel.

The following are mold numbers used by Armand Marseille. It should once again, be noted that "370" on a doll JUST MEANS that it is a SHOULDER HEAD and "390" JUST MEANS it is a SOCKET HEAD:

70, 95, 100, 110, 200, 210, 225, 231, 240, 246, 250, 251, 252, 253, 254, 255, 256, 257, 258, 259, 264, 266, 276, 300n, 301, 310, 320, 320½, 322, 323, 324, 325, 326, 327, 328, 329, 340, 341, 345, 347, 351, 352, 353, 362, 370, 372, 376, 380, 387, 390, 390n, 398, 400, 401, 449, 500, 517, 518, 550, 560, 560a, 580, 590, 600, 620, 640, 700, 701, 750, 753, 760, 800, 917, 925, 957, 966, 970, 971, 975, 980, 985, 990, 991, 992, 995, 996, 1330, 1804, 1890, 1894, 1895, 1897, 1900, 1901, 1914, 1921, 2015, 2549, 2966, 3200, 3500, 3600, 3700, 4008, 83115.

Name dolls by Armand Marseille: Alma, Baby Betty, Baby Gloria, Baby Phyllis, Beauty, Columbia, Darling Baby, Duchess, Floradora, Just Me, Kiddiejoy, Lilly, Mabel, My Companion, My Playmate (body), Nobbikid, Queen Louise, Rosebud, Sadie, Special, The Dollar Princess. The following name dolls are not incised but were sold with paper name tags and/or marked boxes: Little Mary (#225), Dotty (#251), Little Bright Eyes (#252;, Peero (#253), Little Jane (#256), First Steps (#259), May Queen (#300n), Marguerite (#320), Glad Baby (#325), Rosie Baby (#326), Prize Baby (#326), 1st Prize Baby (#326/250), Jason (#327), Baby Bobby (#328), Betsy Baby (#329), My Dream Baby (#341 and 351), Baby Love (#352), Banker's Daughter (#370), Miss Myrtle (370 4830), Banner Kid Doll (372), Little Sweetheart (#380), My Dearie (#390n-246), Patrice (#390n), Pretty Peggy (#390-245), Mimi (#390n-216), Wonderful Alice(#17 377439), Gibson Girl (400 and 401), Infant Berry (#500), Hoopla Girl and Boy (#590), Child Berry (#600), Bernadette (#640), Beatrice (#700), Lady Marie (#970), Minnit (#971) Sadie (#975), Happy Tot (#990) Herbie (#991), Cleonie (#1894), New Born Baby (L.A. and Co. 1914 and 1921).

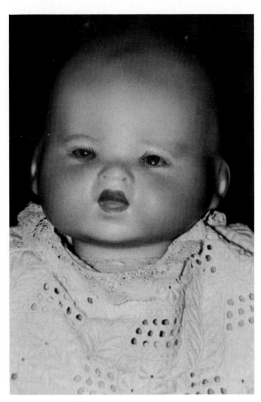

Marseille, Armand--10" Dream Baby. Bisque head on cloth body. Celluloid hands. Sleep eyes. Molded wide open/closed mouth. Marks: A.M./ Germany. (Courtesy Jane Alton) C-D

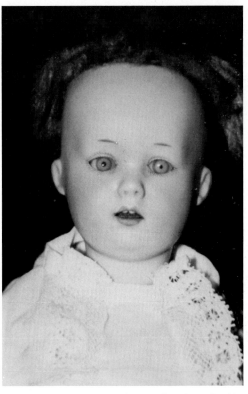

Marseille, Armand. 8" Socket head on 5 piece baby body. Sleep blue eyes. Open mouth/2 upper teeth. Marks: 251/G.B./A. 9/0 M./DRGM/ 248/6. Made for George Borgfeldt and usually this mold number has an open/closed Pouty type mouth. (Courtesy Kimport Dolls) C-D

Marseille, Armand. 12" Just Me. Bisque head on
5 piece composition body. Bent right arm.
Marks: Just Me/Registered/Germany/A 310
3/0 M. Sideglance sleep eyes. Closed "rosebud"
mouth. (Author) M-N

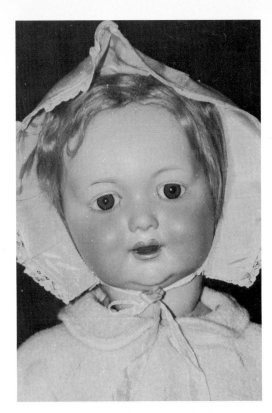

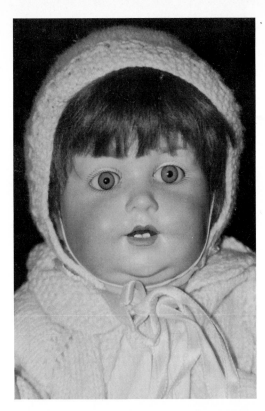

Marseille, Armand. 21" Socket head on 5 piece baby body. Sleep eyes. Open mouth/2 upper teeth. Marks: G.B. 327/A. 12 M./Germany. Courtesy Grace Oschner. F.G.

Marseille, Armand--13" Betsy Baby. Socket head on 5 piece composition baby body. Blue sleep eyes. Open mouth/2 lower teeth. Marks: G.B. 329/A. 2 M. Made for George Borgfelt, 1922. (Courtesy Grace Oschner) A-C

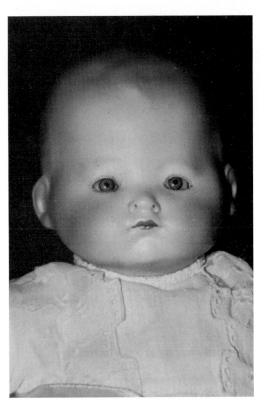

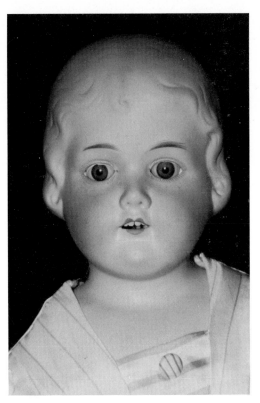

Marseille, Armand--12" Kiddiejoy. Bisque head on cloth body with celluloid hands. Closed mouth. Sleep eyes. Marks: Germany/Kiddiejoy/345/2. Made for Hitz, Jacobs and Kassler, 1922. (Courtesy Kimport Dolls) D-E

Marseille, Armand--24" "Banner Kid Doll" Shoulder head on kid and musling body with bisque forearms. Molded blonde hair. Blue sleep eyes. Open mouth. Marks: Germany/Kiddiejoy/372/A. 2. M., Made for Hitz, Jacobs and Kassler, 1922. (Courtesy Helen Draves) E-G

23

Marseille, Armand--6½" My Dream Baby (mold
#341) Light tawny brown skin tones. Polynesian.
5 piece matching composition body. Made for
Arranbee Doll Company, 1924. Named "Tawny"
by owners Jimmy and Fay Rodolfos. C-D

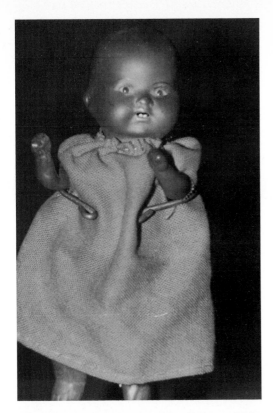

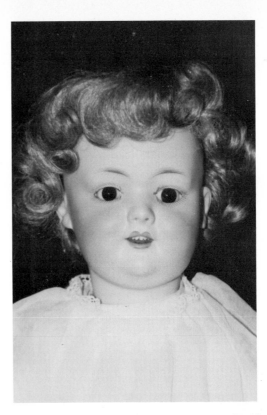

Marseille, Armand--5½" My Dream Baby. Socket head on 5 piece black maché body. Sleep eyes. Open mouth. Marks: A.M./Germany/351/10. (Courtesy Jane Alton) C-D

Marseille, Armand--14" with 10" head circumference. Set brown eyes. Open mouth. 5 piece composition bent leg baby body. Marks: A.M. 560a/DRGM R 232/1. (Courtesy Kimport Dolls) E-F

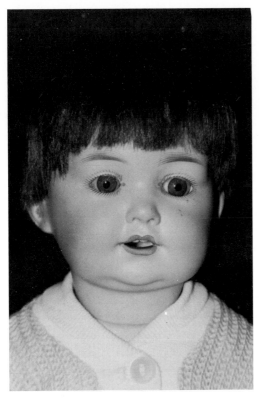

Marseille, Armand--15" Socket head on 5 piece composition baby body. Sleep eyes. Open mouth/2 upper teeth. Marks: Germany/971/A. 4 M. (Courtesy Helen Draves) B-D

Marseille, Armand--14" Socket head. 5 piece composition baby body. Sleep eyes. Open mouth/2 upper teeth. Marks: 971/Germany/A. 2 M. (Courtesy Kathy Walter) B-D

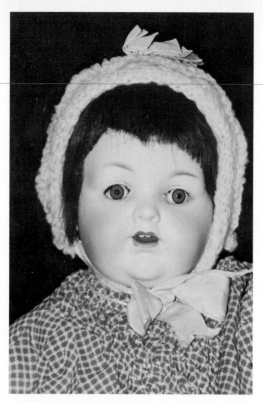

Marseille, Armand--16" Happy Tot Socket head on 5 piece baby body. Sleep eyes/lashes. Open mouth/2 upper teeth. Marks: Armand Marseille/Germany/990/ A. 6 M. Cryer in stomach. Made for George Borgfelt in 1910. (Courtesy Kimport Dolls) C-D

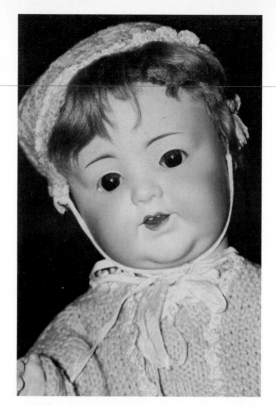

Marseille, Armand--16" Socket head on fully jointed toddler body. Set eyes. Open mouth/2 spaced upper teeth. Marks: Armand Marseille/Germany 996/ A. 3 M. (Courtesy Jay Minter) C-D

Marseille, Armand--21" Socket head on fully jointed toddler body. Sleep eyes/lashes. Open mouth with wiggle tongue. Marks: A.M. Koppelsdorf Germany/1330-A. 12 M. (Courtesy Grace Ochsner) C-D

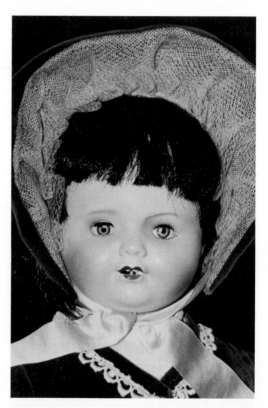

Marseille, Armand--16" Painted bisque head on cloth body. Tin blue sleep eyes/lashes. Dark Grey eyeshadow. Open mouth/two upper teeth. Original. Marks: A.M./2549/9 3/4-3½. (Courtesy Kimport Dolls) A-B

26

Marseille, Armand--8" long, 6½" head circumference. Bisque heads on cloth bodies with composition hands. Large sleep eyes. Closed mouths. Marks: A.M./Germany/83115. (Courtesy Jeanne Gregg) C-D

Marseille, Armand--11" Scowling Indian and baby. Painted bisque heads. Crude maché bodies. Glass set eyes. Baby has un-outlined painted eyes, closed mouth. Open mouth in adult. Original. Marks: A.15/0 M. (Courtesy Helen Draves) D-E

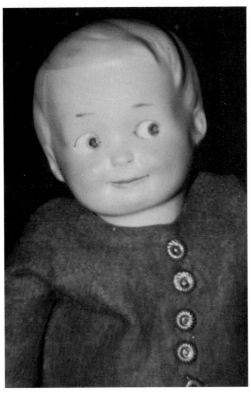

Marseille, Armand--6½" Bisque head on composition body with maché limbs. Indent intaglio eyes. Closed mouth. Molded blonde hair. Original felt clothes. Marks: 254/A.M./Germany. (Courtesy Helen Draves) G-I

Marseille, Armand--6½" Socket head on fully jointed composition/maché body. Brush stroke hair. Indent intaglio eyes. Closed mouth. Marks: 320/ A. 4/0 M. (Courtesy Helen Draves) H-J

27

Marseille, Armand--6½" Bisque head on 5 piece
maché body. Sleep googly eyes. Closed smile
mouth. Original except bonnet. Marks:
A.M./353/ 0½. (Courtesy Kimport Dolls) H-J

Marseille, Armand--14" Socket head on adult
composition/wood body. Closed mouth.
Unpierced ears. Marks: Armand Marseille/400/
A. 2 M. Made in 1913. (Courtesy Blue Barn
Antiques) L-M

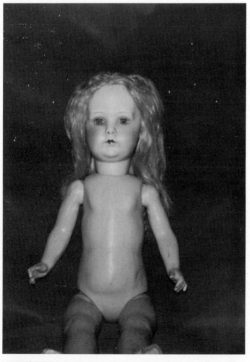

Marseille, Armand--19" Highly colored bisque
head with closed mouth, no painted lashes. Light
brown one stroke brows. Pale blue sleep
eyes/lashes. Cardboard pate and original wig.
Marks: A. 449. M/Germany/0½, with an "x" low
on neck. (Courtesy Jessie Smith, New
Westminster, Canada) B-D

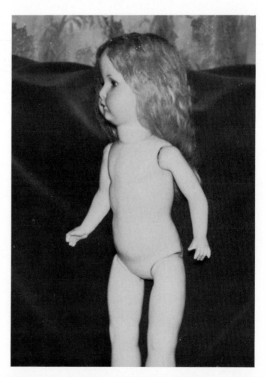

Marseille, Armand--Shows full body on 449 A.M.
Very light weight. Pressed cardboard which is
greyish color inside. Straight legs with very flat
feet. Thin straight arms. (Courtesy Jessie
Smith, New Westminster, Canada) B-D

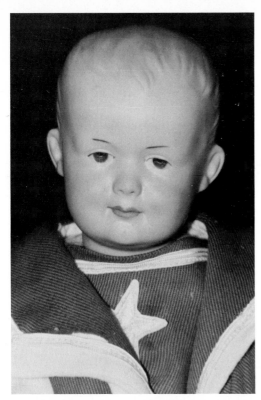

Marseille, Armand--15" Infant Berry. Socket
head on fully jointed composition/wood body.
Closed mouth, intaglio blue eyes, molded blonde
hair. Marks: 500/Germany/A 1 M with DRGM
running vertically down side of mark. Made in
1909. (Courtesy Helen Draves) E-G

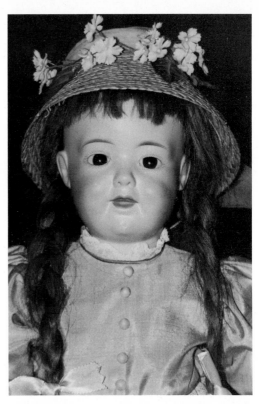

Marseille, Armand--20" Hoopla Girl. Socket
head on fully jointed composition body.
Unpierced ears. Set dark eyes. Wide
open/closed mouth. Marks: 590/A. 5
M./Germany. Made for Hitz, Jacobs and Co.
1916. (Courtesy Jay Minter) G-I

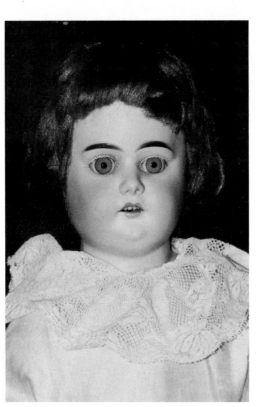

Marseille, Armand--22" Shoulder head on kid
body with bisque lower arms and muslin lower
legs. Sleep eyes, very dark brows and open
mouth. Marks: A.M. 4008 DEP/Made In
Germany 4. (Courtesy Kimport Dolls) C-D

Marseille, Armand--26" Socket head on fully
jointed composition body. Close set large black
sleep eyes. Open mouth. Long "squat" face.
Molded brows. Marks: Made In Germany/Queen
Louise. This doll does not look like any other
Queen Louise the author has seen. (Courtesy
Virginia Jones) D-E

29

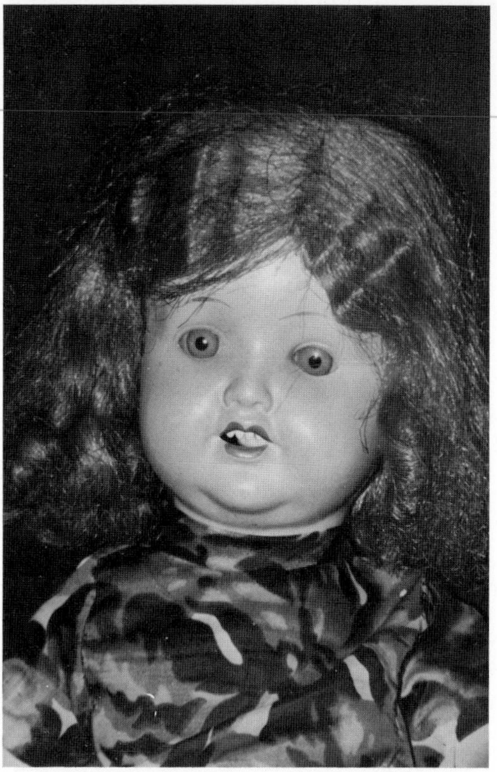

Armand, Marseilles--16" All composition. Open mouth, sleep eyes. Original wig. Marks: ($) 2966/5/0x/2/0x. Made by Armand Marseille for unknown distributor. (Courtesy Virginia Jones) A-B

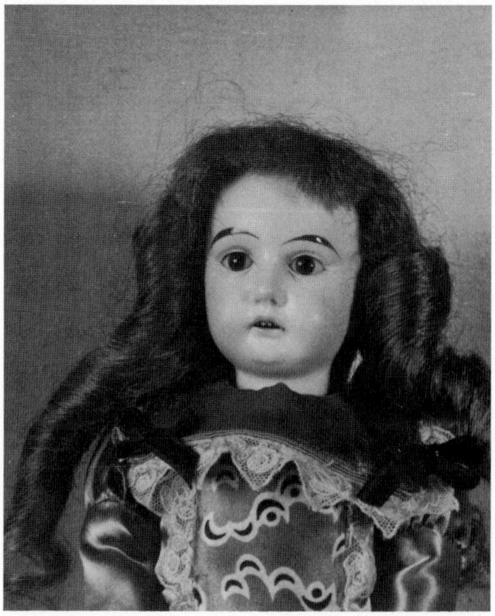

Armand, Marseile--14" Socket head on fully jointed composition body. Open mouth. Single stroke eyebrows. Marks: 2000/AM 4/0 DEP. (Courtesy Mini Things By Suzanne) C-D

Bahr and Proschild operated at Ohrdruf, Thur from 1871 until the first World War. Their marks are: "Buporit," a heart: (BP) and B✝P/O
The following are some of their mold numbers: **535, 585, 604, 619, 624, 678.**

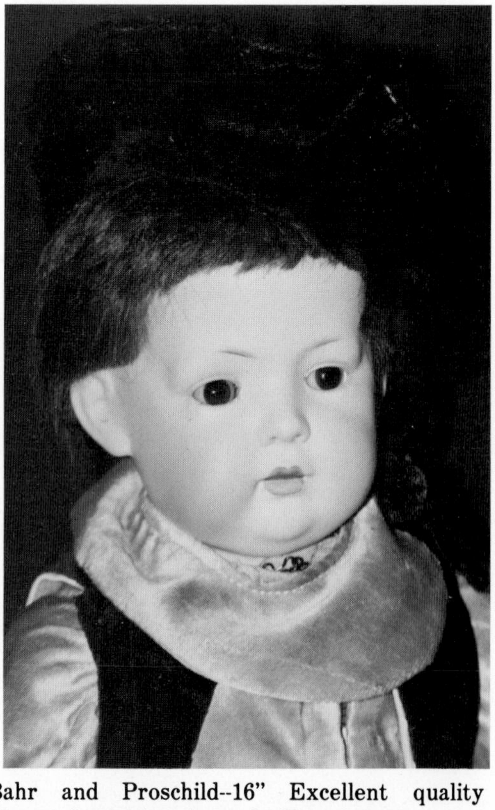

Bahr and Proschild--16" Excellent quality bisque. Open/closed mouth. Sleep brown eyes. 5 piece composition baby body. Marks: B✝P/O (Courtesy Kimport Dolls) L-N

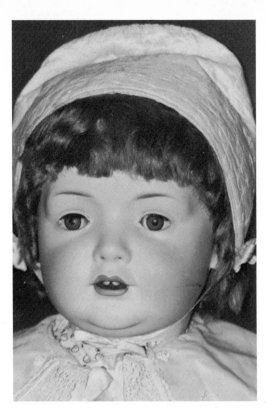

Bahr and Proschild--25" Socket head on 5 piece composition baby body. Sleep eyes with lashes. Open mouth/2 upper teeth. There are more dolls with this mold number available than other molds by this company. Some, like this one, have excellent bisque. Marks: ⚹ /585/16/Germany. (Courtesy Helen Draves) E-G

BELTON

Belton and Jumeau made dolls from 1842 to 1846 and it was in 1844 that they received Honorable Mention for the clothing of their dolls. The address they worked from was 14 Rue Salle au Comte. Belton ran the business alone until he apparently died in 1852. From then to 1855 the Widow Belton continued to operate the doll making business. In 1856, F. Pottier became the successor and only stayed in business one year.

Belton dolls have a concave area on the top of the heads that are solid (no crown slice) with 2 holes for stringing (with wig attached to the stringing material) or 3 holes with the wig attached by a plug in the third hole.

Belton and Jumeau dolls look very much like the later Jumeau's and one wonders if Jumeau carried over the "Belton" heads into his own business. The "Belton" and Widow Belton dolls have almost white bisque with wider open/closed mouths with the space between the lips painted white.

"Dome heads" or "ball or bald heads" are different. The heads are not flat or concave on top but the top of the heads are continued to be round or oval. There may be one to three holes used for the same purpose, that is to string the doll and attach the wigs.

Belton--12" Socket head on composition body with straight wrists. Set eyes, open/closed mouth. Original except necklace. Concave top to head with three holes. Marks: 137/3. Jumeau body. (Courtesy Helen Draves) F-H

Belton--15" Concave head with 3 holes. Socket head on wood/composition fully jointed body. Open/closed mouth. All original. Ears pierced into head. Marks: None. (Courtesy Helen Draves) G-I

Belton--12" Concave head with 3 holes. Socket head on maché/wood body with straight wrists. All original. Open/closed mouth. Ears pierced into head. Marks: 4. (Courtesy Helen Draves) F-H

CHARLES M. BERGMANN CO.

Bergmann, Charles M.--The Charles M. Bergmann Company opened in Germany in 1889. He made doll bodies of composition as well as kid. The heads he used were made by such companies as Kestner, Simon and Halbig, Armand Marseille and Others. His dolls carry either his initials C.M.B. or the full name of C.M. Bergmann along with the maker of the head.

12" All original Belton. For full description see
Belton section. (Courtesy Helen Draves)

Bergmann, C.M. 28" Socket head on fully jointed composition body. Sleep eyes with lashes painted below only. Molded brows. Open mouth and pierced ears. Marks: C.M. Bergmann/Simon and Halbig/13½. (Courtesy Helen Draves) D-E

Bergmann, C.M.--23" Socket head on fully jointed composition body. Open mouth. Sleep eyes/lashes. Unpierced ears. Marks: C.M. Bergmann/BB1/Germany. $165.00. (Courtesy Kimport Dolls) C-D

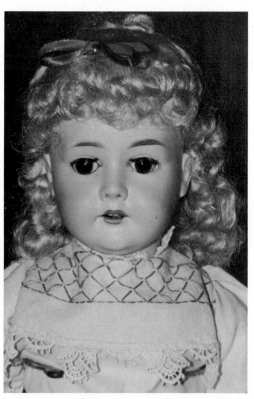

34

Bergmann, C.M.--25" Socket head on fully jointed composition body that is spring strung. Molded eyebrows, open mouth and pierced ears. Original clothes. Marks: C.M. Bergmann/Simon and Halbig/11. (Courtesy Jeanne Gregg) D-E

Bergmann, C.M.--23" Socket head on composition body that is fully jointed. Sleep eyes/lashes. Open mouth. Marks: C.M. Bergmann/Walterhausen/1916/6½a. (Courtesy Helen Draves) D-E

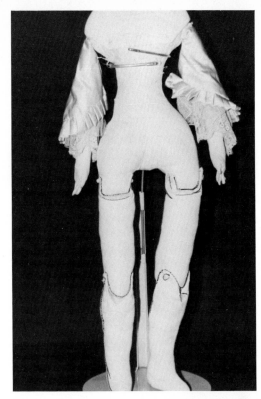

Shows a Sarah Robinson patented body of 1883. The head on this doll is a "Parian". All the stitching is hand done on the joints. The main body parts by machine. There appears to be a thin cardboard bent in a "U" shape that forms the joints.

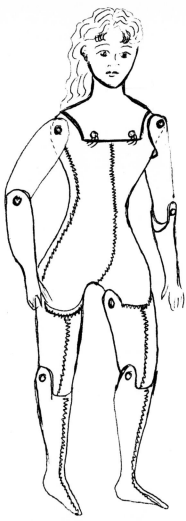

Bodies--Doll's body patented August 21, 1883 (#283,513) by Sarah C. Robinson, Chicago, Ill. Bodies to be of cloth, leather or similar material. Jointed by cords or wire passing through the joints and fastened by buttons or washers. Heads could be any material. (Parian, chian etc.)

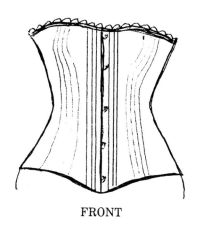

FRONT

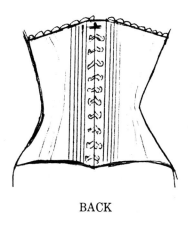

BACK

Bodies--Attached corset by Charles T. Dotter. Patented Dec. 7, 1880. U.S. ⅓ 235,218.

15" all original E.J. Jumeau. See Jumeau section
for full description. (Author)

All original 17" Bru Jne with wood over kid and
wood lower legs. See Bru section for full
description. (Author)

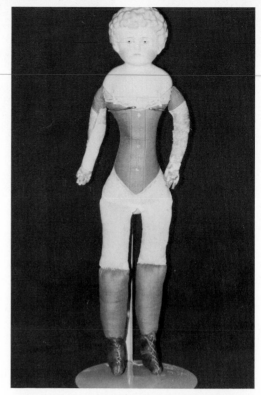

Bodies--Attached corset by Phillip Goldsmith. Patented on Dec. 15, 1885. U.S. #332,248.

Bodies--This is a Phillip Goldsmith body with attached corset. The corset, upper arms and lower legs are of bright red Chinz type material. Where the corset is attached at the top is stamped "Pat. Pend." The thin leather boots are also sewn on. (Courtesy Kimport Dolls)

FASHION BODIES

The term "French Fashion" has been so widely used and accepted that all lady dolls seem to fall into this category by collectors. It is important to remember that the majority of "French Fashions" are actually and correctly called "Parisiennes", which were play dolls and meant for children whose parents could afford them. Because the clothes of the period (1860-1900) were so elaborate, collectors refer to them as "French Fashions", which actually confuses the issue of the first and earlier courriers of fashions sent out to show the current fashions that were available in France, before papers and magazines were available to show these fashions.

The most common (majority) of these doll's bodies are made of kid, with slender waists, full hips, individually wired fingers and generally stitched toes. Of the minority and rather rare are bodies that are all wood and fully articulated (jointed). Some include joints at the wrist, waist and ankles. A very few even have a second joint at the upper arm or upper leg. There is a rare wood body like this that is also covered with a tight skin of kid. The limbs can be bisque or wood.

Also considered rare is the Gesland stockennette covered over a wire armature body. It also is fully articulated. The hands are usually bisque and the feet also, with some that are bisque to the knee joint.

The two rarest of these style dolls would be the Huret and Rohmer. The Huret body, generally, was of Gutta Percha which is a rubber like substance. The body was articulated when found and with broken fingers or a leg broken in two, the Gutta Percha is jet black. The Rohmer used both china and bisque heads on their dolls and had beautifully arched arms that extend well above the elbow and of the finest quality china (luster). The upper arms are usually wood and sometimes covered with kid and jointed to a kid stuffed body. Some have carved lower legs and feet.

There were endless combinations used by the French doll makers. When the all kid bodies came into general usage, a few makers still used the bisque hands and in some areas, bisque hands and arms with the upper arms section kid over wood. About the time the French doll industry began to decline, some of these Fashion dolls were made with cloth bodies, which at times, had leather arms, sometimes even leather feet and were sawdust filled. Some of the very late Fashions by Limoges has metal feet with bisque heads on cloth bodies.

Fashions and so called Fashions are in the "Ladies Of Fashion" section of this book.

38

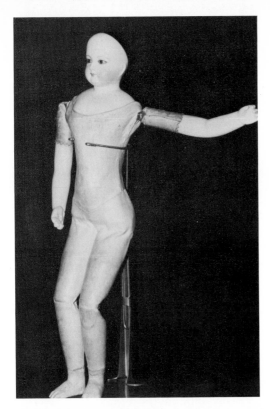

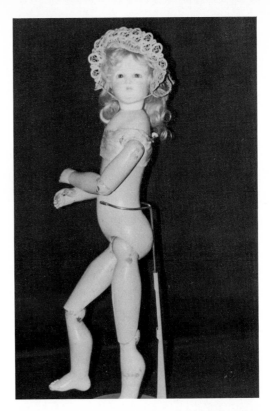

Bodies--This is an 18" kid over wood body with metal "ball" jointed shoulders. Wood covered with kid and jointed hips and knees. Head is marked: E G-32. Stamped on back: E. Gesland. It is not known if Gesland made or just repaired the body. (Courtesy Jay Minter and Kimport Dolls)

Bodies--Shows 18" fully articulated wood fashion body. Some are even jointed at waist and ankles.

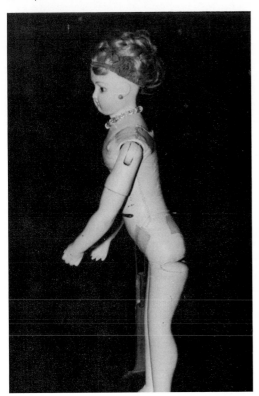

Bru--Shows body of Circle-dot Bru fashion. Straight formed legs. Stitched toes. Arms are hinged by kid over wood at the shoulders. See Bru section for full face picture. (Courtesy Kimport Dolls)

15" Belton head with oriental bisque. Marked
220. See Kestner section for full description.
(Courtesy Helen Draves)

27" See Manufacturer unknown section for full description. Marks: Dep./12. (Courtesy Helen Draves)

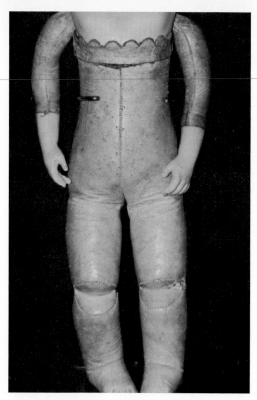

Bodies--All kid Bru body. Stitched toes and scolloped edging.

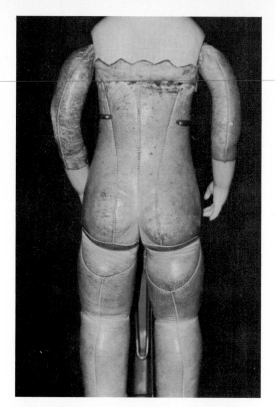

Bodies--Shows back view of all kid Bru. Three seam gusset.

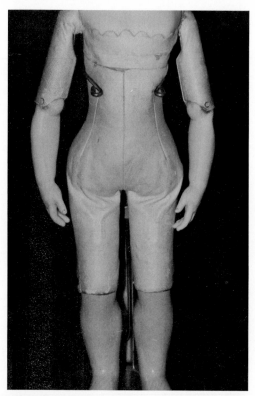

Bodies--Bru. Wood lower and upper legs. Upper covered with kid. Attached at hips with screws. Detailed toes. Wood upper arms covered with kid. Bisque lower arms. Bisque shoulder plate attached to body with nails, 2 in front and back then piece of kid with scolloped edging applied.

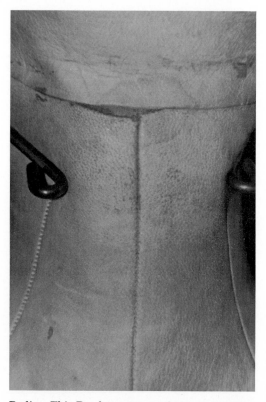

Bodies--This Bru has a stamp that is unreadable but this picture will show the tiny scolloped edging on the scolloped edging.

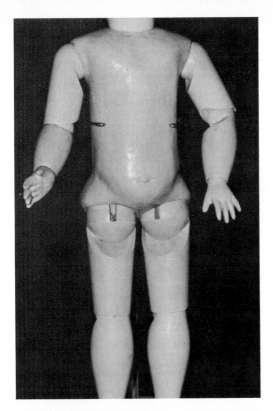

Bodies--Typical Gesland body used on F.G. dolls. Maché torso with "flared" hip. All wood legs with attached maché feet. Wood arms with mache hands.

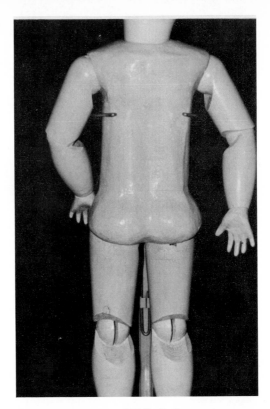

Bodies--Back view of F.G. Body.

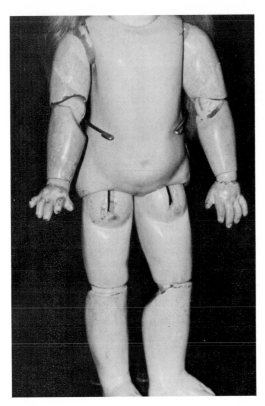

Bodies--Typical Jumeau marked body. Wood ball set in maché lower leg. Same with arms.

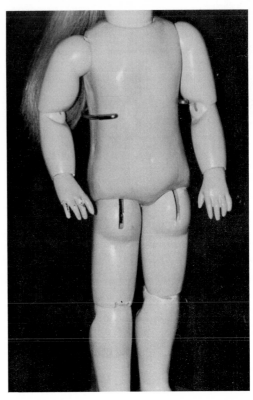

Bodies--Typical Jules Steiner body. Wood upper leg and pressed maché lower leg with indication of individual big toe. Wood upper arms and pressed maché lower. Mache torso.

25" Tete Jumeau Open mouth. Sticker on body: Bebe Jumeau/Diplome d Honneur. (Courtesy Kathy Walter)

24" only marked 15. See Manufacturer unknown
for full description. (Courtesy Helen Draves)

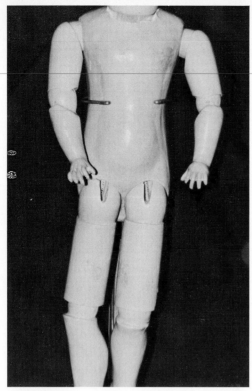

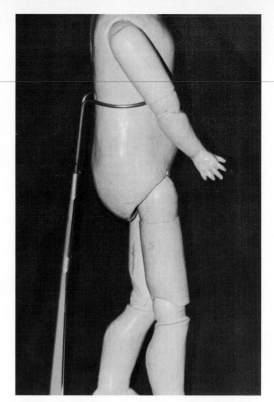

Bodies--Simon and Halbig. Wood upper leg with wood ball sealed into it. Maché lower leg. Same with arms. Wood plug embedded into maché body at neck opening.

Bodies--Shows side view of Simon and Halbig body.

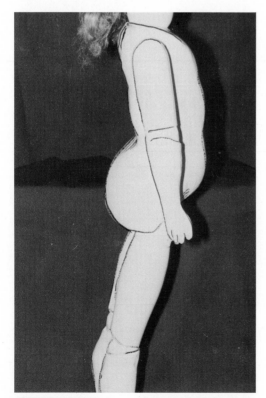

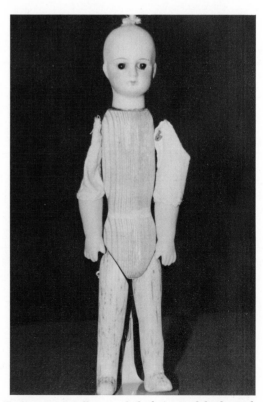

46

Bodies--This body shows the sway back style of the 1890's. The body is German and marked Heinrich Handwerck and has a marked Hch-H head.

Bodies--7½" tall turned (lathe) wood body and legs. Wire jointed cloth arms with bisque lower arms. Flange neck on bisque head. Ball (bald) head with two stringing holes. Marks: 1½, on head.

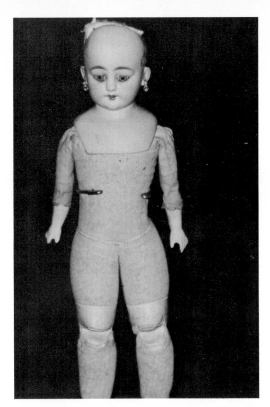

Bodies--This is an all canvas type material body with kid inserts at the knee sewn joints. The hands are bisque and this bisque head was made by Kestner.

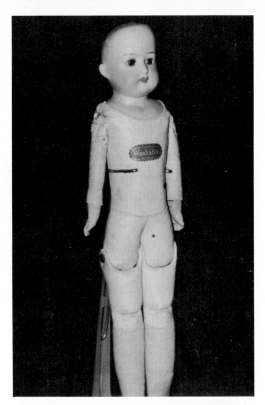

Bodies--This is a marked "WASHABLE" kid body with an Armand Marseille head. The upper legs are Universal jointed and the lower legs are muslin.

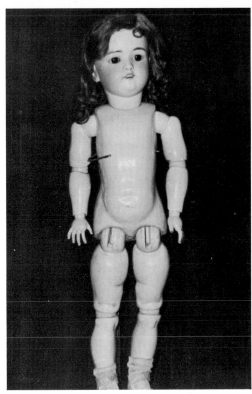

Bodies--This is a typical German body of composition and wood ball joints. There is a space between the upper and lower legs. The Germans enjoyed making knee detail.

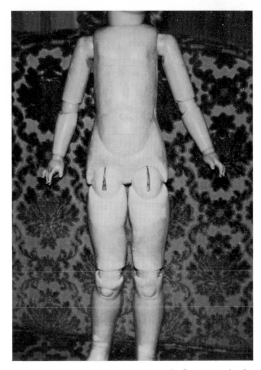

Bodies--This is another typical German body with small molded breasts, round, protruding stomach and ball joints. Much knee molding. (Courtesy Jessie Smith, Canada)

47

22" French lady. See Ladies of Fashion section
for full description. (Courtesy Kathy Walter)

Bodies--Armand Marseille's Floradora seal: Top seal reads: FLORADORA/THIS DOLL HAS/REAL HAIR EYEBROWS/WHICH WILL NOT DROP OUT NOR CAN THEY BE PULLED OUT/US PAT. 952716 Mch. 22/1910. Lower seal: ½/CORK/STUFFED. Doll has kid body with bisque lower arms.

Bodies--This Floradora seal is on kid body doll with marked Floradora head but she does not have fur eyebrows. FLORADORA/GERMANY in streamer. Half/Cork/Stuffed.

Bodies--This seal is on kid body doll with A.M. 370 bisque head. Top seal: Non Plus Ultra/picture of a crown. Lower seal: Real Hair.

Bodies--Seal on kid body with bisque head marked: Germany/370/ A. 5. M. with Non Plus Ultra jointed hips. Seal: Sunshine, picture of sun,/Copyright 1919 By Sears Roebuck and Company/Germany.

49

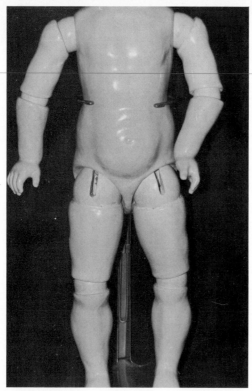

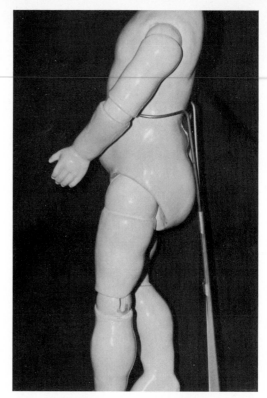

Bodies. Marked Schmitt body. Stands "bull-legged." Independent wood balls at knees and on arms. Upper wood balls attached to composition upper leg section.

Bodies. Side view of marked Schmitt body shows "sway" back and wide flat lower back section. All fingers are together with free standing thumb.

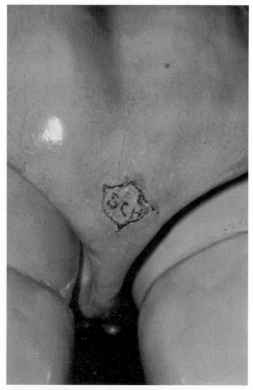

Bodies. Mark on Schmitt body. The crossed hammers are missing.

Bodies. 21" Socket head on marked Schmitt French body with straight wrists. Blue lined eyes, full closed mouth, unpierced ears, cork pate and very "square" ridge to nose. Bisque is almost white with light pink wash over eyes. Marks: none. (Author)

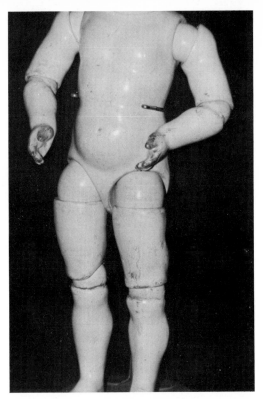

Bodies. This is also a marked Schmitt body but all ball joints are independent. Head on this one is marked x1.

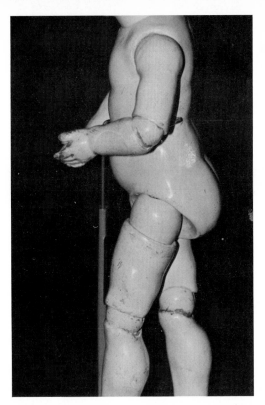

Bodies. This shows side view. Fingers are all molded to gether with free standing thumb. Mark is shield/crossed hammers & SCH.

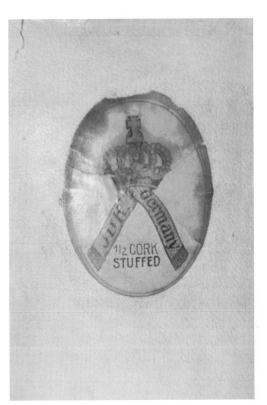

Bodies. Kid body with beautiful molded full celluloid legs & arms. Seal on chest: Kestner's crown & streamers marked J.D.K./Germany on streamers./½ Cork/Stuffed.

THE DOLL'S WOOING

The little French doll was a dear little doll
Tricked out in the sweetest of dresses,
   Her eyes were of hue
   A most delicate blue
And dark as the night were her tresses;
Her dear little mouth was fluted and red,
And this little French doll was so very well bred
That whenever accosted her little mouth said
    "Mamma! Mamma!"

The Stockinet doll, with one arm and one leg,
Had once been a handsome young fellow,
   But now he appeared
   Rather frowzy and bleared
In his torn regimentals of yellow:
Yet his heart gave a curious thump as he lay
In the little toy cart near the window one day
And heard the sweet voice of that French dolly say;
    "Mamma! Mamma!"

He listened so long and he listened so hard
That anon he grew ever so tender,
   For it's everywhere known
   That the feminine tone
Gets away with all masculine gender!
He up and he wooed her with soldierly zest
But all she's reply to the love he professed
Were these plaintive words (which perhaps you have guessed)
    "Mamma! Mamma!"

Her mother..a sweet little lady of five
Vouchsafed her parental protection.
   And although stockinet
   Wasn't blue-blooded yet
She really could make no objection!
So soldier and dolly were wedded one day,
And a moment ago, as I journeyed that way,
I'm sure that I heard a wee baby voice say:
    "Mamma! Mamma!"

Written by Eugene Field-1894

51

BRU

Bru--Leon Casmir Bru and his wife founded the Bru company in 1867. Casmir Bru, Jeune (Junior) and Cie took out several patents by 1873. H. Chevot took over the Bru firm in 1883 and kept the Bru name. From 1880 to 1899 the Bru firm moved into the hands of Paul Eugene Girard. After 1899, the firm became part of the Société Française de Fabrication de Bébés et Jouets (S.F.B.J.) Marks: ⊙ ⌒ Bru: Bru Jne: Bru Jne R: Bébé Brevette. Refer to Series 1, page 73 for more information.

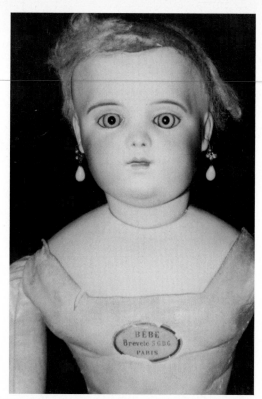

Bru--20" Bisque swivel head on bisque shoulder plate. All kid body with bisque lower arms. Set eyes. Closed mouth. Pierced ears. Original remains of Caricul fur hair. Marks: Bébé/ Brevette S.G.D.G./Paris. (Courtesy Kimport Dolls) Z+

Bru--17" Bisque socket head on bisque shoulder plate. Kid over wood body with bisque lower arms and wood lower legs. Open/closed mouth. Pierced ears. All original. Marks: Bru Jne, on head. Bru Jne-5 and No. 5 over shoulder plate.(Author) Y+

Bru--Shows original clothes on 17" Bru Jne. Shoes are marked: Bru Jne/Paris, in an oval.

BUSCHOW & BECK

Buschow and Beck--Vischer and Co. established a U.S. trademark of "Minerva" in 1894 and this same trademark was registered by Buschow and Beck in Germany the same year, although it was for both metal and celluloid dolls heads. This type of metal head was actually first patented by Joseph Schon in 1886. All types of metal were used, including brass and tin. The "MINERVA" mark is a helmet:

Buschow & Beck--20". One piece metal head and shoulder plate. Open mouth/2 upper teeth. Deep dimple/right cheek. 2 sew holes front/back. Cloth body, twill lower legs/leather feet. Bisque lower arms. Open crown/wig.Inset glass eyes. Marks: Minerva/helmet, on front/Germany, on back of shoulder. $75.00. (Courtesy Bessie Greeno)

Buschow and Beck--19" Metal head with painted eyes and open mouth. One piece shoulder and head. Cloth body with bisque lower arms. Sewn on black boots. Molded red/blond hair. $75.00. (Courtesy Kimport Dolls)

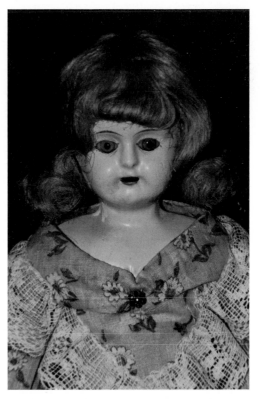

Buschow & Beck--12". One piece metal head and shoulder plate. Solid dome/wigged. 2 sew holes front/back. Inset glass eyes. Open mouth/2 upper teeth. Pink cloth body/dark green lower legs/black sewn on "boots." Cloth arms. Marks: Minerva/helmet, on front, Germany on back of shoulder. $45.00. (Courtesy Bessie Greeno)

53

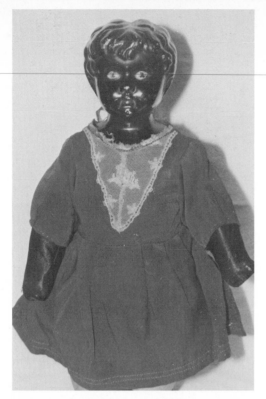

Buschow and Beck--12" Black metal head. One piece head and shoulder. Molded hair and painted eyes. Closed mouth. Body and arms are stuffed "sateen" with pink muslin lower legs with sewn on black boots. Marks: Minerva/helmet, on front and Germany, on back of shoulder. $115.00. (Courtesy Helen Draves)

Cameo--4" Bisque Kewpie with molded on hat, belt, sword and gun. Shown with all bisque figure made in Japan. 4" Kewpie $95.00. 4" Japan $25.00. (Courtesy Helen Draves)

Cameo--4" all bisque Kewpie with jointed shoulders. Glued on original felt clothes. $75.00. (Courtesy Helen Draves)

Cameo--4" Bisque Kewpie with jointed shoulders. Glued on original felt Band Leader outfit. $75.00. (Courtesy Helen Draves)

Cameo--This is the lid from an all bisque Kewpie box. (Courtesy Helen Draves)

Cameo--4" Soap Kewpie. Marks: In a heart: Kewpie/Reg U.S./ Pat. Off and underneath: U.S. Des. Off./43680. $45.00. (Courtesy Helen Draves)

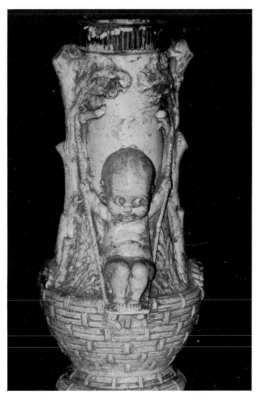

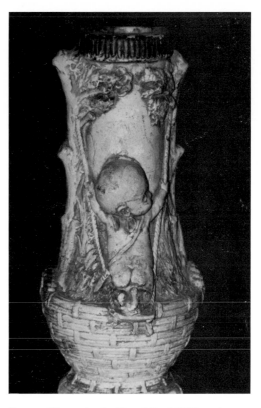

Cameo--14" tall chalk type material vase and/or lamp base. Kewpie on a swing. $235.00. (Courtesy Helen Draves)

Cameo--Shows back side of the 14" Kewpie vase belonging to Helen Draves.

Cameo--2" Celluloid Kewpie with no joints. High gloss enameled black tux coat and glued on crepe paper hat. $35.00. (Courtesy Kimport Dolls)

Cameo--17" "Bandy" Wood and composition.Advertising doll for General Electric. Marks: Sticker on Back: Art Quality Manu./By Cameo Prod. Inc/Port Allegany, Pa./Des. and By Jlk. On hat: Ge/General Electric!/Radio. $100.00. (Courtesy Alice Capps)

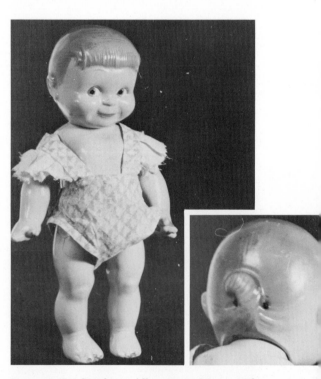

Cameo--15½" "Joy" Composition and wood jointed boyd and limbs. Composition head with painted eyes, molded hair and head band. Closed mouth with painted teeth. All original $75.00. (Courtesy Helen Draves)

Cameo--14" Giggles. All composition with molded hair with hole for ribbon in back and painted blue eyes. Designed by Rose O'Neill. Same body as Skootles. Jointed shoulders and hips. Original. $185.00. (Courtesy Phyllis Houston)

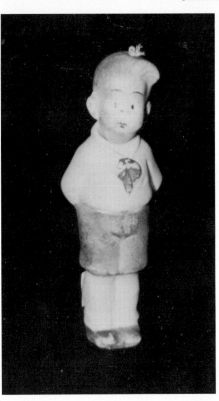

Cartoon Characters--4" all bisque. Jointed shoulders only. Molded on clothes. Original blonde hair in braids. Original red felt hat. Marks: Germany/Little Annie Rooney/Reg. U.S. Pat. Off./Copr. By Jack Collins. $95.00. (Courtesy Jeanne Gregg)

artoon Character--13½" All leather Skeezic ith individual stitched legs. (Courtesy Barbara oker)

Cartoon Characters--2½" All bisque knotter with nodding head. Marks: Skeezic. $35.00. (Courtesy Helen Draves)

Cartoon Characters--3" All wood Mickey and Minnie Mouse. Marks: Mickey/Mouse/Copyr. By/Walt Disney. $25.00 each. (Courtesy Helen Draves)

Cartoon Characters--9½", 4½", 4" Composition and wood Mickey Mouse. One on far right is a 4½" felt Mickey. 9½" $55.00. 4½" $65.00. 4" $35.00. 4½" Felt $22.00. (All Courtesy Marge Meisinger)

57

Cartoon Characters--3½" Knotter all bisque. Nodding head with body and limbs in one piece. Marks: Rachel/Germany. $35.00. (Courtesy Helen Draves)

Cartoon-14" Comic character of the 1930's. Cloth body, arms and legs. Composition feet, hands and head. Marks: None. $55.00. (Courtesy Helen Draves)

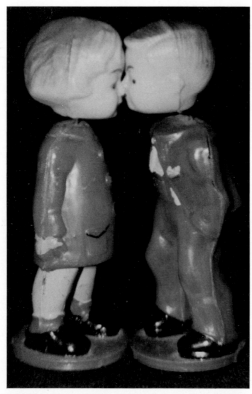

Celluloid--3" "Nodding Kissers" All celluloid. Heads are on springs and have small magnets that make the dolls "kiss". Marks: Made in Hong Kong/HKL, in a circle. 1961. $6.00 pair. (Courtesy Maxine Heitt)

Celluloid--4" All one piece celluloid. Not marked. $3.00. (Courtesy Helen Draves)

CELLULOID

Celluloid--Celluloid was invented in England in 1855 by Alexander Parkes, who dubbed it Parkesine. It was in 1863 that the brothers, John and Isiah Hyatt "discovered" the substance and called it by the trade name of "Celluloid". They submitted it as a replacement for ivory in the manufacturing of Billard balls. France, the U.S., Germany, Poland and Japan were among countries which produced celluloid dolls. The dolls were, at times, a by product to other items such as celluloid collars and making dolls were a way to use up the scraps. Celluloid is very flammable as it has a nitric base and should never be kept near extreme heat or open flames. Because it became apparent that celluloid was a dangerous substance, it's use was discontinued in the mid 1940's. Most celluloid dolls are charming and indeed should be a welcome addition to any fine collection.

Century Doll Co.--16" "Betty" Excelsior filled cloth body and pin jointed legs. Gauntlet composition hands. Composition head with yellow molded hair. Painted eyes. Marks: Century Doll Co. $45.00. (Courtesy Barbara Coker)

Celluloid--23" Celluloid girl. Jointed neck, shoulders and hips. Sleep eyes/lashes. Closed mouth. Molded brown hair. Marks: France/ ◇ $125.00. (Courtesy Kimport Dolls)

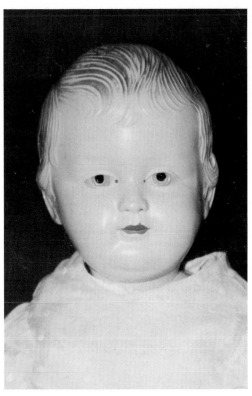

Celluloid--13" Celluloid with painted pale blue eyes. Molded hair. Jointed shoulders, neck and hips. Celluloid toddler body. Marks: France, on head. $85.00. (Courtesy Kimport Dolls)

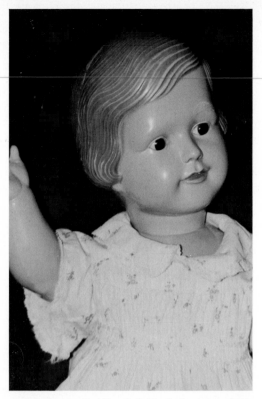

Celluloid--17½" All celluloid of the late 1920's. Molded light brown hair. Inset glass brown eyes. Open/closed mouth with two painted upper teeth. Marks: Head of animal in shield/45/46. $85.00. (Courtesy Barbara Coker)

Celluloid--13" All celluloid Buddy Lee by H.D. Lee Co. Jointed shoulders only. Painted on black shoes. $125.00. (Courtesy Helen Draves)

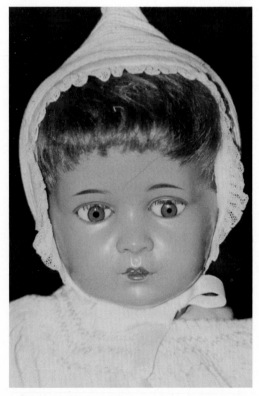

Celluloid--12" Celluloid character baby. Sleep eyes/lashes. Open mouth/2 upper teeth. Open crown/wig. Socket head on composition baby body. $125.00. (Courtesy Grace Ochsner)

Celluloid--13" Celluloid shoulder head on cloth body. Molded hair and painted eyes. Open/closed mouth. Marks: Amer./Indian head. Redressed during World War II. $85.00. (Courtesy Phyllis Houston)

60

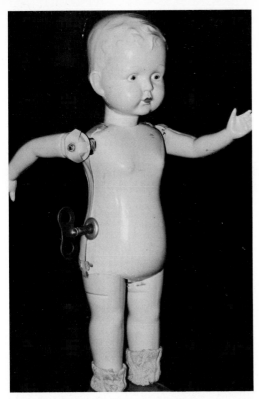

Celluloid--13½" Walking boy. Head and arms moves as he walks. Celluloid arms, legs and head. Tin body and upper arms. Tin, non-removable shoes. Rollers on botton of feet. Key wind. Marks: Japan Ca. 1930. $35.00. (Courtesy Kimport Dolls)

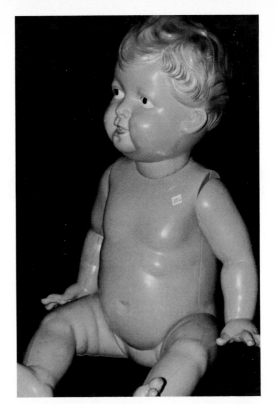

Celluloid--25" All celluloid. Molded red hair. Open/closed mouth with two upper teeth. Excellent molding. Marks: ⇑ 70/Made in Japan. $150.00. (Courtesy Helen Draves)

Celluloid--5" All celluloid. Jointed necks, shoulders and hips. All original costumes. Marked Germany. $8.00 each. (Courtesy Helen Draves)

Celluloid--9" Celluloid with jointed hips and shoulders. Bent baby legs with extra nice molded feet. Molded in head band. Painted eyes. Marks: $12.00. (Courtesy Phyllis Houston)

61

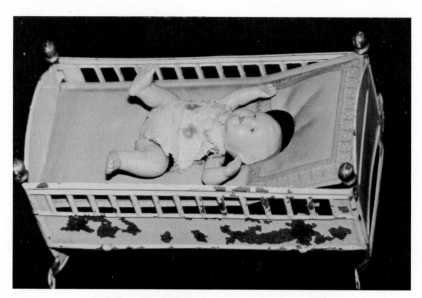

Celluloid--3" Celluloid baby in tin crib. Four
weights control arms, legs and head. Rocking
the crib makes the baby move. Germany $95.00.
(Courtesy Helen Draves)

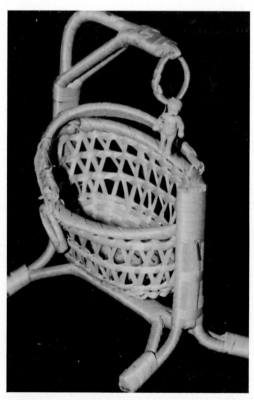

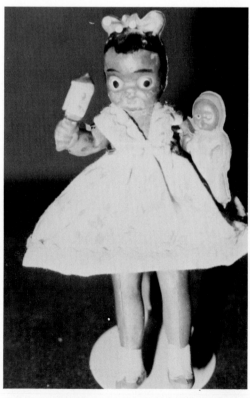

Celluloid--1½" celluloid doll hanging on wicker
swing basket. $25.00. (Courtesy Helen Draves)

Celluloid--5" Black celluloid girl with molded doll
in one hand and rattle in other. Jointed
shoulders and hips. $35.00. (Courtesy Kimport
Dolls)

Celluloid--8" Black celluloid googly with jointed shoulders. Marks: Scroll in Circle/Made in Japan. $35.00. (Courtesy Jane Alton)

Celluloid--7" All celluloid with jointed shoulders and hips. Holds baby and baby bottle. Original. Marks: Japan. $28.00. (Courtesy Maxine Heitt)

Celluloid--10½" Heavy celluloid all original Valentine girl. Jointed at shoulders. Marks: Fethalite/U.L. Co. $8.00. (Courtesy Margaret Gunnel)

Celluloid--4" Celluloid with jointed shoulders. Molded on clothes. Not marked but likely to be Japan. $10.00. (Courtesy Helen Draves)

Celluloid--4" Celluloid boy, molded all in one piece. Made about the time of the Kewpies. $18.00. (Courtesy Helen Draves)

Celluloid--2½" Celluloid half doll with jointed shoulders. May have been a "pop apart" doll or part of a rattle. Marks: Japan. $6.00. (Courtesy Helen Draves)

Celluloid--4" Celluloid girl and lamb. Molded all in one piece. $18.00. (Courtesy Helen Draves)

CHASE, MARTHA

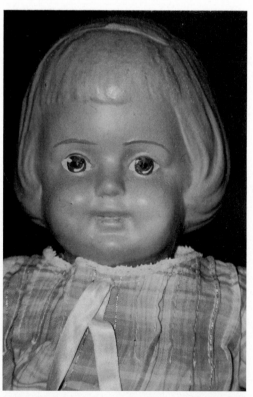

Celluloid--22" Cloth with celluloid face mask. Molded hair and painted features. Ca. 1942. $12.00. (Courtesy Mrs. J.C. Houston)

Chase, Martha--16½" Chase play doll. Blonde molded hair and green painted eyes. Marks: J.J.C. Stockinet Doll. Ca. 1950's. (Courtesy Jay Minter) D-E

CHINA

There are various grades of china. The two main divisions, depending on the clay, are soft paste and hard paste. The soft paste heads usually show more wear, and appear to be more porous than the hard paste heads. Pink china, which is the hardest, is also the best preserved. Some will actually look "new". These pink heads were once called "Chelsia" by collectors, but are now known as "pink luster". The method to obtain this luster, before 1830, was a film of gold applied over a coating of rose iridesense. This process perhaps warranted the name "Pink Luster" because the result is truly a thing of beauty. Flesh toned china was made as late as 1900, but the earlier ones are the finest in tone, paste and design. Even if Pink Luster is a wrong term, it has been so widely accepted that it is most difficult to convince a collector not to use it.

During what is called the Parian Period (1850 to 1875) the same moulds used for unglazed "Parian" dolls were used to make china heads so chinas with elaborate hairdo, etc. can be dated. Some styles were used for many years, even after the style was dropped by women of the time, so there is really no foolproof way to date a china, but we can come close.

Here are a few dates:

Ribbons, bows and bands: 1870's and 1880's
Snoods: 1860's
Curls in front: 1890's
Bangs: 1870's
Coronet Braids: 1850's
Top rolls: 1820's to 1850's
Puffs: 1850's
Flowers: 1860's
Combs: 1850's and 1860's

All the china heads listed above are considered unusual or rare and added to these are the ball head china or "Biedermeir" as collectors call them. Biedermeir china heads have no molded hair at all and there is a small black spot on the top of the head for gluing on the wig. The Biedermeir dates from 1820 to 1830. Here is a list of RARE china heads:

Beads interwined in hair (1832)
Eyes painted to side (flirty)
Swivel necks
Unset eyes or sleep eyes
Brown eyes
Turned heads
Bonnet china
Applied flowers, combs, etc.
Stipple or brush marks around face
Boy with side parts
Blonde china heads

Some additional ways to date china:

Hair rolled or plain at side with back bun: 1820-1850
Long curls falling over shoulders: 1830
Corkscrew curls with all curls ending away from shoulders: 1830 to 1860
Braids around exposed ears (Queen Victoria) 1837
Corkscrew curls on either side of a knot: 1840
Braided bun: 1950
Braids over both ears: 1850
Draped at side and caught in comb in back under a double puff: 1850
Looped in back and called "waterfall": 1860
Under as a "page boy": 1860
Comb marked back from the forehead and falling in ringlets: 1850-1870

Pointed rolled curls running vertical: 1868
Child: curl in center of forehead, long hair over shoulders; bangs or ribbons: 1870
Short curls over entire head: 1880
Short curly hair with ribbon and top bow: 1880
Colored glass jewelry embedded into glaze: 1890

Right or wrong, some "name" dolls will be listed. Some of the names may be correct but here again the collector has dubbed that a certain doll be called a certain "name," and it has stuck, even if known to be incorrect. Collectors constantly refer to that particular head as "so and so," and we are pretty well stuck with it! Queen Victoria; Mary Lincoln Todd; Empress Eugenie; Jenny Lind; Sophia Smith; Dolly Madison; Covered Wagon Child; Covered Wagon; Countess Dagmar; Currier and Ives; Adelaine Patti; Curly Top.

Most all early china are unmarked and in 1860 size numbers began to be used. Many of the great porcelain and china head manufacturers may have used a "mark" but it is found inside the shoulder rather than on the outside. The following are some marks that have been found on early porcelain and china:

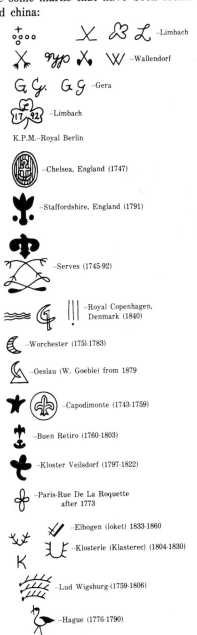

X ℬℒ --Limbach

W --Wallendorf

G G. G G --Gera

17 92 --Limbach

K.P.M.--Royal Berlin

--Chelsea, England (1747)

--Staffordshire, England (1791)

--Serves (1745-92)

--Royal Copenhagen, Denmark (1840)

--Worchester (1751-1783)

--Oeslau (W. Goebel) from 1879

--Capodimonte (1743-1759)

--Buen Retiro (1760-1803)

--Kloster Veilsdorf (1797-1822)

--Paris-Rue De La Roquette after 1773

--Elbogen (loket) 1833-1860

--Klosterle (Klasterec) (1804-1830)

K

--Lud Wigsburg-(1759-1806)

--Hague (1776-1790)

--Nyon (1781)1813)

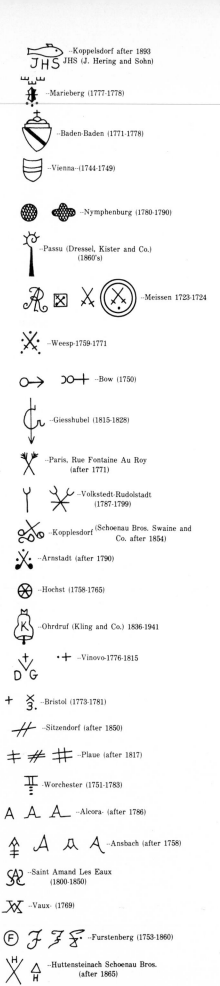

--Koppelsdorf after 1893
JHS JHS (J. Hering and Sohn)

--Marieberg (1777-1778)

--Baden-Baden (1771-1778)

--Vienna--(1744-1749)

--Nymphenburg (1780-1790)

--Passu (Dressel, Kister and Co.)
(1860's)

--Meissen 1723-1724

--Weesp-1759-1771

--Bow (1750)

--Giesshubel (1815-1828)

--Paris, Rue Fontaine Au Roy
(after 1771)

--Volkstedt-Rudolstadt
(1787-1799)

--Kopplesdorf (Schoenau Bros. Swaine and
Co. after 1854)

--Arnstadt (after 1790)

--Hochst (1758-1765)

--Ohrdruf (Kling and Co.) 1836-1941

--Vinovo-1776-1815

--Bristol (1773-1781)

--Sitzendorf (after 1850)

--Plaue (after 1817)

--Worchester (1751-1783)

--Alcora- (after 1786)

--Ansbach (after 1758)

--Saint Amand Les Eaux
(1800-1850)

--Vaux- (1769)

--Furstenberg (1753-1860)

--Huttensteinach Schoenau Bros.
(after 1865)

China--17" Exceptional china of 1779. The hair is a beautiful golden blonde that blends to brown. Cloth body with wooden limbs. Marks: $\mathcal{G}$ of the Gera porcelain factory of the Griener family. See next photo for the snood detail. $1,500.00. (Courtesy Kimport Dolls)

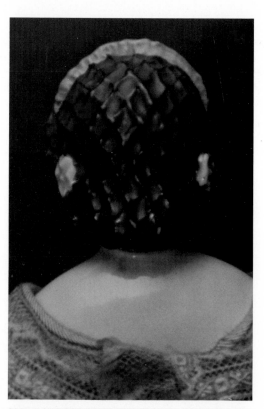

China--17" Gera Porcelain Factory china to show the detail of the snood.

The following are the various marks of Meissen (Dresden)-Royal Berlin-(Konigliche Porzellan Manufaktur). Established in 1751 by William Wegeley, these marks; are the early specimens. In 1761 the factory was purchased by Gottskowski. After the occupation of Dresden by Fredrick the Great, he moved the Meissen factory lock, stock and barrel to Berlin, that is the raw materials, moulds and workman. ⚬ ᵂᴱ ᵂ ↧ ❅ was the mark of Charlottenberg founded by Pressel (1760) and was abosrbed by the Royal Berlin works. A special mark for soft paste porcelain by Royal Berlin was:   is a late mark.

Marks and Dates:

H.P.F --Meissen-1723

K.P.M --Meissen-1724

✕ → 𝓰 𝓰 --J.E. Golzkowsky 1761-1763

--Royal Berlin-(Konigliche Porzellan)- 1823-1832 KPM

KPM ↥ -Royal Berlin (Konigliche Porzellan)- 1837-1844

1844-1847 same as 1823-32 except it looks like one foot is holding an umbrella rather than rod.

KPM -Royal Berlin (Konigliche Porzellan) from 1857

China--22½" China of the 1830's. Long slender neck and face. Brown eyes. Pink luster china. Hair pulled back into braided bun. Marks: ↥ₖₚₘ Made by Royal Berlin (Konigliche Porzellan Manufaktur). $2,500.00. (Courtesy Kimport Dolls)

China--18½" boy with brown eyes and pink luster. Brush mark hair. Old clothes. Ca. 1779 to 1820. Marks: 𝒢.𝐹. The "F" is most likely an artist symbol. Made by Gera Porcelain between 1779-1820 as mark is of J.G. Ehwaldt and J. Gollbrecht and was later acquired by the Greiner family. $1,200.00. (Author)

China--10½" Early china with long neck and back swept hairdo which is held in place with a molded comb. Deep shoulders. Stipple painted at temples. Ca. 1820-40. $550.00. (Courtesy Kimport Dolls)

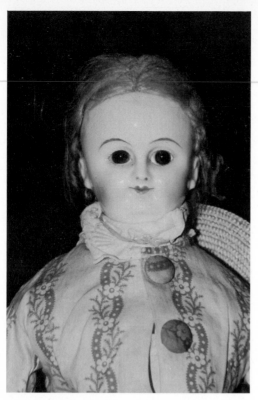

China--18" China with open crown and large glass brown eyes. She has a "squat" neck, molded ears and a smirky smile. A real character! Ca. 1840's. $2,500.00. (Courtesy Kimport Dolls)

China--11" Biedermeier bald head china with underglaze painted black dome where wig is glued on. Cloth body with leather limbs. Dated 1840 to 1860. $450.00. (Courtesy Helen Draves)

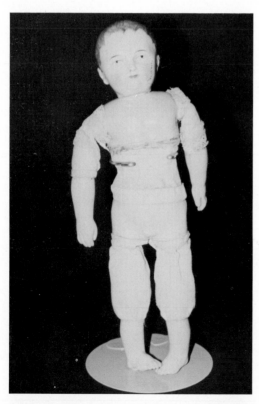

China--12" china baby with pink luster china and brush stroke brown hair. Enigma Motschmann style body. Has squeeker in stomach area. Ca. 1850's. $1,395.00. (Courtesy Kimport Dolls)

China--19" china of the 1850's. Black painted snood with side drapped scarf over pale blonde hair. Paper stuffed in head is dated 1858. Cloth body with leather arms. $1,500.00. (Courtesy Kimport Dolls)

China--16½" Side part hair china man. Brush strokes at temples. Cloth body with leather arms. Old clothes. Ca. 1850's. $650.00. (Courtesy Kimport Dolls)

China--20½" Man of the 1850's. Side part hair. Flaw or "beauty mark" on cheek. Cloth body with leather arms. Old clothes. $750.00. (Courtesy Kimport Dolls)

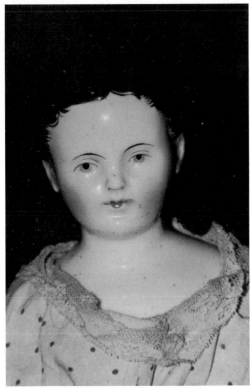

China--14" China with molded ears, off center part and very short curly hair. Ca. 1850's. $400.00. (Courtesy Helen Draves)

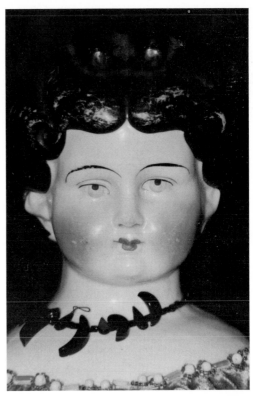

China--24" very unusual china of around 1850. The hair is molded with a large coronet braid over the top of the head. She has very large ear lobes and full lips. $350.00. (Courtesy Helen Draves)

JENNY LIND

It was in 1850 on Sept. 1st, when Jenny Lind first came to America. The "Swedish Nightengale" was famous on the Continent and England and, perhaps, if it had not been for Phineas Taylor (P.T.) Barnum, she may never have reached America and the popularity she did.

Because of Barnum's great showmanship personality, the desire to see and hear Jenny Lind was more than "enthusiastic", it was wild. Over thirty thousand people lined the dock of Manhattan's Canel St. to catch a glimpse of the singer, and as the 29 year old descended the gang plank, hundreds of people were injured in the crush that resulted.

Her first American tour was a sell out and lasted through 137 cities with the first in the "Battery" area of New York at the Castle Gardens.

Johanna Maria Lind was born in Stockholm, Sweden in 1920. She was a blonde. All the Jenny Lind dolls the author has seen have been black haired and there is a reason for this. Jenny, herself, requested the dolls, that were made under the direction of P.T. Barnum, have black hair. Barnum demanded the head to be made in China. It is a well known fact that Jenny Lind was "plain" and much ado was made about her looks because of how her looks actually transformed when she was singing and acting.

Once at a musical party given for the Princess of Prussia, Lady Westmorland remarked, on seeing the singer for the first time, "Why--she is not only pale, thin and plain-featured, but awkward and rather nervous. Exactly like a schoolgirl! It is preposterous." When asked afterward about the performance, Lady Westmorland exclaimed, "She is simply an angel . . . when she began to sing her face shone like an angel. I never saw or heard anything the least like it."

It is known Jenny Lind's interest in music was evident from the age of three. It is also a recorded fact that her parents home, when she was nine, was on the busy street leading to St. Jacobs Church and Jenny often sat at the window, holding her cat and singing almost constantly. People moving up and down the street would stop and listen to her. One of these people was the maid for the famous Swedish dancer, Mademoiselle Lundberg, who decided to see if the reports of the maid were true. She was amazed as she listened to the outstanding voice of the 9 year old.

Mme. Lundberg visited Jenny's mother and attempted to convince her that Jenny's was a great voice that only needed training. Jenny's mother was a very bitter woman, her father a "failure" who moved from job to job. The mother had what she considered more important things for Jenny to

do...work and more work. Finally the mother was convinced that it was her "duty" to get the child training and a Master by the name of Herr Berg was hired. As the training progressed, the expense was taken over by the Swedish Government.

At age 12, Jenny's voice broke and voice exercises stopped but she did not, for she devoted herself to the study of harmony and composition. With time, of course, her voice "returned" and at age 16, Jenny had become the pupil of the Swedish composer, Lindblad, who undertook to instruct her in the fullest knowledge of music known up to that time.

By 21, she had moved to Paris, under the tutorage of the celebrated singer Signor Garcia. It was from Garcia she learned the true Italian style of singing. She was recommended to the Director of the Academic of Music in Paris, after being heard by the composer Meyerbeer.

A meeting was arranged with the Director of the Academic of Music and other important and great French musicians but the Director did not appear to hear her sing. The Director, a most important man of his times in the world of music, was kept away by the very jealous lady singer of the hour, Mdlle. Rosina Stolz, and as a consequence, Jenny Lind was not offered a singing engagement in Paris. This unfair treatment so impressed Jenny Lind, that she resolved never to sing in Paris and she never did, although she later had many tempting offers. Jenny Lind counted among her friends, Queen Victoria, Mendelsshon, Chopin, and Hans Christian Anderson. She married her accompanist, Otto Goldschmidt in 1852 in Boston, Mass. They had three children, Walter Otto born in 1853, Jenny M.C. in 1857 and Ernst S.D. in 1861. Jenny Lind died on Nov. 2, 1887, in their home in Malvern, England, among the hills of Glouceshire.

Because of P.T. Barnum's campaign for Jenny Lind, all types of items carrying the Jenny Lind name were sold, these included such items as stoves, lamps, beds, medals, buttons, clocks, trivets, sofas, caps, chairs, shawls, combs, dolls and all sorts of bric- a brac. One such article was a tea kettle that was advertised that is "commenced to sing in a few minutes."

In recent years, the Madame Alexander Doll Company has issued a doll called Jenny Lind and her Listening Cat. This doll represents Jenny as a nine year old, with long blonde hair. The following is the true portrait doll that was authorized by P.T. Barnum. It is supposed that Jenny Lind requested she be of black hair because it looked good with the paleness of her face and this combination reproduced well in the china media.

China--This is the original Jenny Lind button that is attached to the top of her dress. It shows her name and a child holding a doll. This Jenny Lind is marked: 6, on front. 50/X(red)/3 M, inside shoulder plate.

China--19" Jenny Lind. All original. Cloth body. China limbs. The original clothes are that of Agathe in "The Freischutz" This opera was Jenny's first great success and was written by Carl Maria Von Weber with words by Fredrich King. After the performance, even the orchestra laid down their instruments to applaud the 18 year old girl. On the original dress, she wore a small rose where the button is. $950.00. (Courtesy Kimport Dolls)

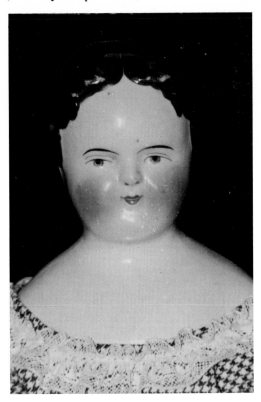

China--23"Portrait china with flowing hair in a snood. Sloping slender shoulders. Stippled hair around face. Ca. 1850's. Marks: ꙅ $650.00. (Courtesy Jane Alton)

China--18" Brown eyed china with flat top hair do. White center part. 3 sew holes front and back. Down cast eyes. Ca. 1850's. $495.00. (Courtesy Grace Ochsner)

71

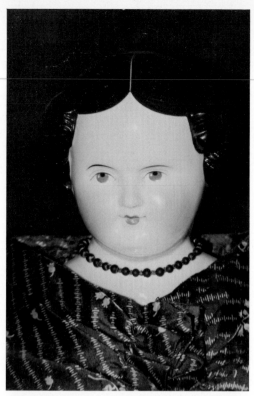

China--22" Brown eyed china of the 1850's. White center part. Slightly turned head. Cloth body with leather limbs. Marks: Germany. $495.00. (Courtesy Helen Draves)

China--17" China with partly exposed ears. Stippled hair completely around face. Snood with gold luster head band. Ca. 1860's. $595.00. (Courtesy Kimport Dolls)

China--20½" Portrait china. Brush marks around face. See next photo for back hair style. $1,050.00. (Courtesy Kimport Dolls)

China--Profile of 20½" unusual portrait china.

China--15" China with cloth body and china limbs. Applied porcelain flowers. Ca. 1860. Marks: 12, on back. $595.00. (Courtesy Kimport Dolls)

China--10½" China with a "waterfall" hairdo. Cloth body with china limbs. Black bow in back of hair. Ca. 1860. $375.00. (Courtesy Kimport Dolls)

China--18" Brown eyes china. Cloth body with china limbs. Ca. 1860. $495.00. (Courtesy Kimport Dolls)

China--10" China with a snood that has a white band trimmed in gold. Blue flowers are in the center. She has deep sloping shoulders. Cloth body with slender china limbs. Ca. 1860. $500.00. (Courtesy Kimport Dolls)

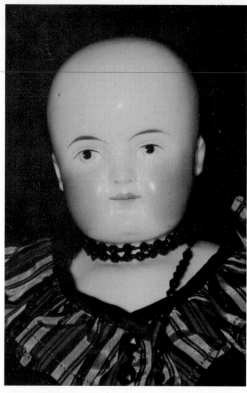

China--22" Bald china of the 1860's. Blue eyes and detailed ears. Cloth body with china limbs. $350.00. (Courtesy Helen Draves)

China--18" Curly Top china of the year 1868. Down cast eyes. Rare because majority of these dolls were done as blondes. Emma Clear made a black hair version in the 1940's and they are all signed "Clear", and they do not have the stipple marks at the end of each curl. $475.00. (Courtesy Helen Draves)

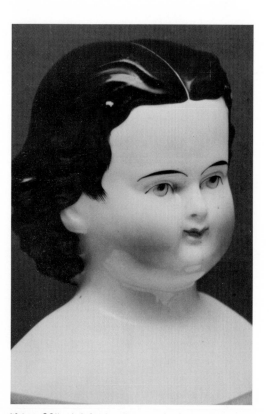

China--23" Adelaide Patti of the 1870's. 10 sausage curls and brush strokes over ears. Cloth body with china limbs. $450.00. (Courtesy Kimport Dolls)

China--14½" Pierced ear china of the 1870's. Short curls around head. Cloth body with china limbs. $395.00. (Courtesy Kimport Dolls)

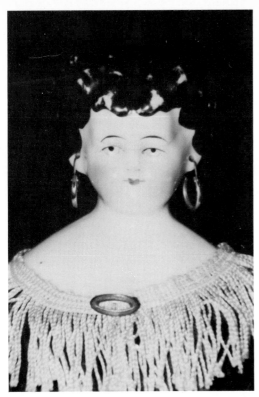

China--12" Pierced ear china of the 1870's. Center part with mass, short curls. Cloth body with china limbs. $350.00. (Courtesy Kimport Dolls)

China--25" China boy of the 1870's. Has brush stipple marks around hair. Nicely molded ears. Cloth body with china limbs. $475.00. (Courtesy Kimport Dolls)

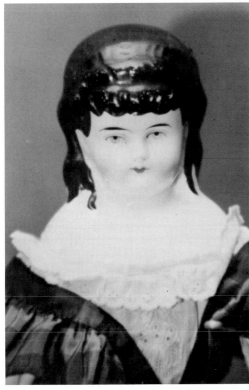

China--15" Currier and Ives china with long spill curls on shoulders. Full bangs. Ears exposed. Cloth body with leather arms. Ca. 1970's. $400.00. (Courtesy Kimport Dolls)

China--12" China of the 1870's. Cloth body with china limbs. $135.00. (Courtesy Kimport Dolls)

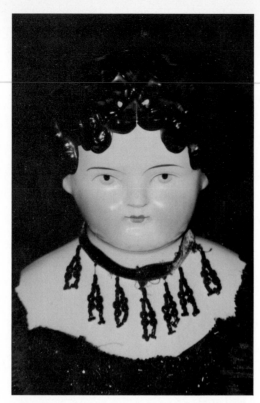

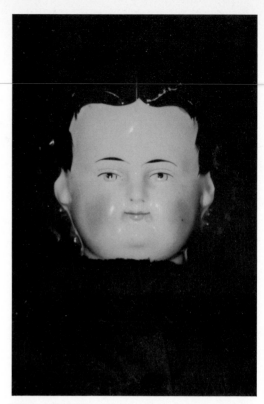

China--24" China called Dolly Madison. Has molded bow in front and black band in back. Ca. 1880's. Many of these were made in blonde "parian". $250.00. (Courtesy Helen Draves)

China--23" China of the 1880's. Partly exposed ears. Stipple painted on forehead. Smile mouth. Cloth body with china limbs. $395.00. (Courtesy Helen Draves)

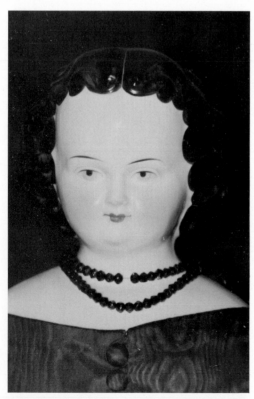

China--28" China of the 1880's. Cloth body with china limbs. $285.00. (Courtesy Helen Draves)

China--24" Light brown haired china of the 1870's. Gold band molded in hair. Ears partly exposed. Cloth body with china limbs. $425.00. (Courtesy Helen Draves)

China--28" Blonde china of the 1890's. Exposed, nicely molded ears. Short, curly hair. This doll is usually found dressed as a boy. $295.00. (Courtesy Kimport Dolls)

China--38" A hugh china of the 1860's. Cloth body with leather limbs. $595.00. (Courtesy Helen Draves)

China--38" another hugh china of the 1860's. Cloth body with limbs of leather. $595.00. (Courtesy Helen Draves)

China--12" Blonde, pierced ear china from Japan. Made in the 1920's. $65.00. (Courtesy Kimport Dolls)

China--19" Rare hairdo china of the 1850's. Stipple painted around face. Two puffs at sides, pulled back into one large puff. Cloth body with china limbs. $750.00. (Courtesy Kimport Dolls)

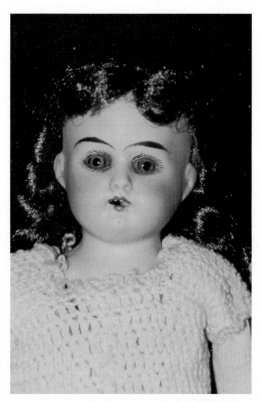

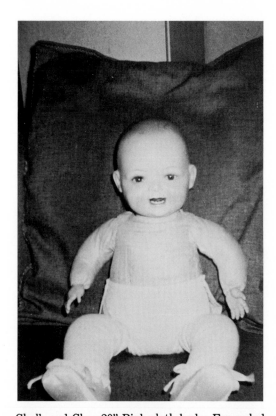

Cissna, W.A.--The W. A. Cissna and Co. were distributors located in Chicago in 1898 and were importers and jobbers for many doll makers. It is known they imported a doll with this description. 14" Shoulder head. Set eyes and open mouth. Marks: Ruth/18/0. (Courtesy Helen Draves) A-B

Chalk and Clay--20" Pink cloth body. Enameled red clay flanged neck. Open mouth/2 rows teeth. Sleep eyes. Celluloid hands. Marks: Germany/ 1431/45. May have been made by J.J. Orsini. $1,000.00. (Courtesy Martha Gonyea)

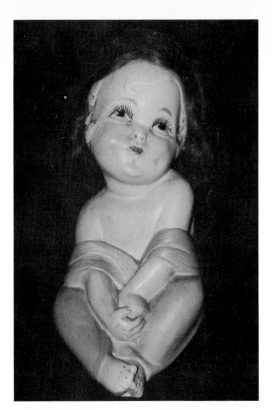

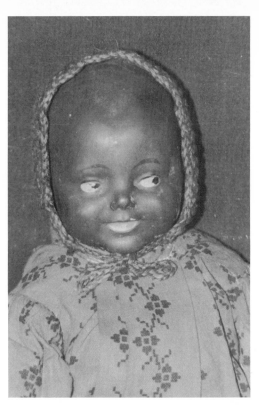

Chalk and Clay--5" tall chalk figure "Tiss Me". Mohair over molded hair. Has mold hole in top of head. $35.00. (Courtesy Virginia Jones)

Chalk and Clay--11" Clay material head. Painted eyes. Open/closed mouth. 5 piece composition black body of a baby. $50.00. (Courtesy Helen Draves)

Chalk and Clay--20" tall wood with chalk head. Used as display piece for hat, gloves and tie. Ca. 1932. $18.00. (Courtesy Helen Draves)

Chalk and Clay--15½" Chalk carnival figure. Marks: None. $22.00. (Courtesy Maxine Heitt)

Cloth--25" "Merrie Marie" all lithographed cloth. Marks: Patent Feb. 13,1900/Art Fabric Mills. $175.00. (Courtesy Kimport Dolls)

Cloth--8" A tiny all cloth lithograph. Was given by Imperial Granum Foods in 1914. There is another rag doll given by them also that has a different face than this. She is blonde, a child, has eyes to side and a smile. $35.00. (Courtesy Helen Draves)

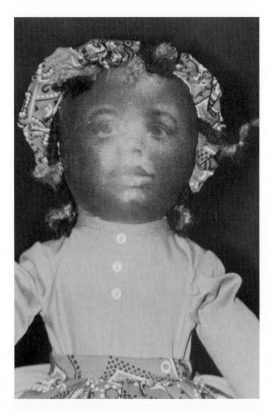

Cloth--26" Life Size Doll of 1904. All printed cloth. Marks: Art Fabric Mills/New York/Patented Feb. 13th, 1900. $145.00. (Courtesy Maxine Heitt)

Cloth--12" Double end cloth doll with photographic faces. One of white girl and other of black. $300.00. (Courtesy Maxine Heitt)

Cloth--12" This is the "white" side of the double end doll, which has turned dark with play.

Cloth--18" Bottle Doll. Black cloth "Mammie" with glass bead eyes. Original clothes. Cloth hands sewn around broom handle. Stands on old bottle. $65.00. (Courtesy Barbara Coker)

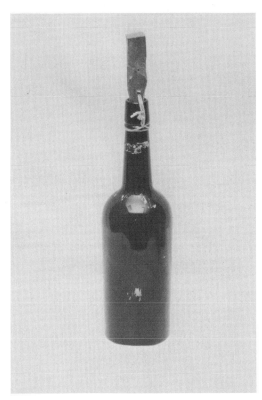

Cloth--Show old deep amber bottle that doll stands on.

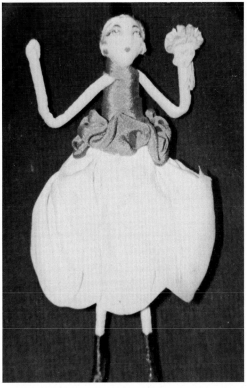

Cloth--6" Flower Girl. Silk covered wire armature. Holds silk flowers. Painted features. Silk thread hair. Silk skirt in form of a flower and underneath is net and pissels that represent a flower. $25.00. (Courtesy Phyllis Houston)

Cloth--32" tall with molded cloth face mask. Painted features. Mohair wig. All cloth body with long arms and legs. Bed doll. $32.00. (Courtesy Maxine Heitt)

Cloth--17" Buchram face mask with oil painted features. Cloth body with celluloid hands. Original. Marks: None. $45.00. (Courtesy Marge Meisinger)

Cloth--12" All felt with molded face. Long lashes. Original. Sewn on wig. Tag: Made in/Austria/Vienna. $22.00. (Courtesy Helen Draves)

Coleman--26" Dolly Walker. Composition head and lower arms. Wood body covered with cloth. Wood arms and legs. The Harry Coleman Walking Doll. $110.00. (Courtesy the Flacks)

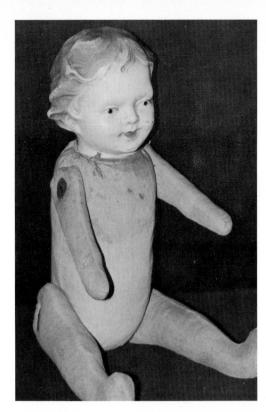

Composition--25" German composition with unusual hairdo. Cloth body the composition arms and jointed wrists. Wood legs. Re-painted features. $200.00. (Courtesy Kimport Dolls)

Composition--18" Excelsior stuffed. Pin jointed limbs. Composition head with deeply sculptured hair. Painted blue eyes. Marks: None. $75.00. (Courtesy Barbara Coker)

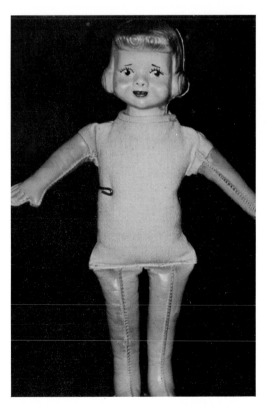

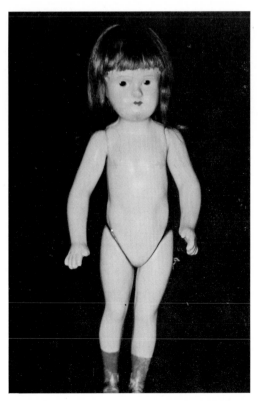

Composition--12½" Pressed composition head. Heavy canvas body with leather limbs. Stitched fingers. Composition head is stapled together halfs. Painted eyes and smile mouth. Marks: None. $50.00. (Courtesy Pat Raiden)

Composition--10" All solid composition with one piece body and head. Painted brown socks with gold shoes, over bare toe detail. Peg strung. Mohair over molded hair, which is low on forehead. Painted blue eyes. Was a gift to Pat Raiden's mother. Marks: None. $50.00.

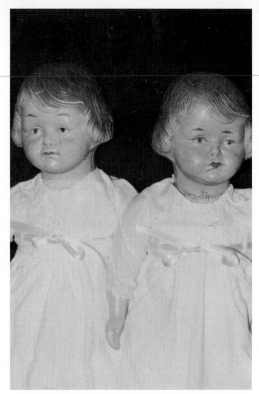

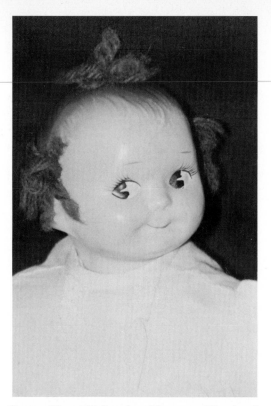

Composition--18" Twins. Cloth body with composition head and limbs. Pouty. Different camera angle and different artist work on lips make them look different. Marks: None. $65.00 each. (Courtesy Helen Draves)

Composition--11" Googly with composition head and full composition arms and legs. Cloth body. 3 tuffs of red yarn hair. Marks: None. $150.00. (Courtesy Barbara Coker)

84

Composition--17" French composition with floss hair over molded hair. Cloth body and limbs. Ca. 1930's. Original. $27.50. (Courtesy Kimport Dolls)

Composition--8" Shirley Temple. All composition. Fully jointed. All original. Marks: Japan. $65.00. (Courtesy Helen Draves)

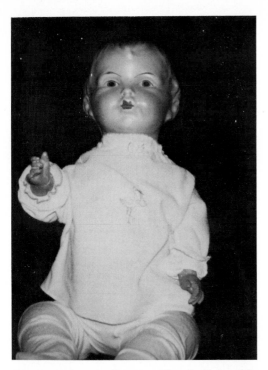

Composition--20" Heavy painted composition over mache head. Cloth body stuffed with excelsior. Cloth legs. Painted blue eyes. Composition arms. All four joints are pin jointed. Legs are bent. Not marked. $55.00. (Courtesy Carolyn Powers)

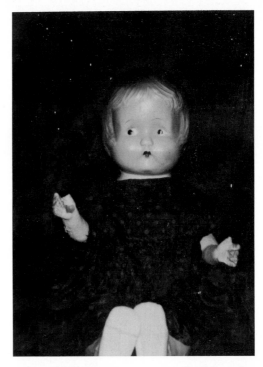

Composition--22" Composition shoulder plate head. Molded reddish hair. Painted blue eyes. Cloth body filled with excelsior. Composition arms and legs. Not marked. $45.00. (Courtesy Carolyn Powers)

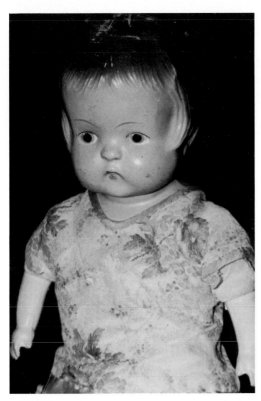

Composition--19" Judy. Muslin body and upper arms. Sewn on excelsior filled legs with sewn on brown cloth boots. Short lower composition arms. Molded red hair. Painted blue eyes. Head is a composition shoulder head. Marks: The Judy . . . company or child. Ca. 1926. $30.00. (Courtesy Mary Partridge)

Composition--12" Bottletot. Composition head with molded blonde hair. Tin sleep eyes. Open mouth/nurser. Composition body with bent right arm. Jointed wrist with celluloid hand. Original including basket. Marks: Arranbee/ Aug. 10, '26, on bottle. $45.00. (Courtesy Teri Schall)

85

Creche Figures--15" man and 14" woman. Wood heads and hands. Gesso finish legs with attached sandles. Molded hair and inset eyes. Original. $285.00 each. (Courtesy Kimport Dolls)

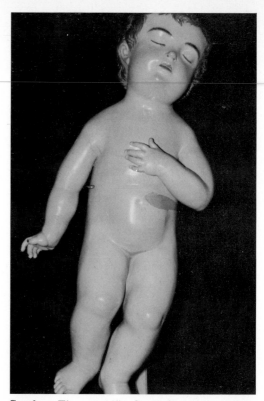

Creche Figures--18" Spanish style infant. Molded one piece of maché. Open mouth and pierced nostrils. $295.00. (Courtesy Kimport Dolls)

Creche Figures--21" Wooden Creche figure. Inset glass eyes. All original. $795.00. (Courtesy Kimport Dolls)

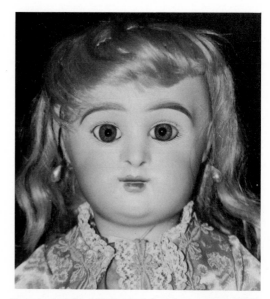

Danel and Cie-19" Socket head on composition and wood body. Fully jointed. Open/closed mouth. Pierced ears. Marks: Paris Bébé/Tête Deposé/9. Eiffel Tower stamp on body. (Courtesy Kimport Dolls) O-Q

Danel and Cie--Danel and Cie operated in Paris from 1889 to 1895. They registered (in France) "Paris Bébé" with a picture of the Eiffel Tower stamped on the body in 1889. In 1891 they registered "Bébé Francais." Jumeau had already registered this name in 1896, so may have had control of this company by 1891.

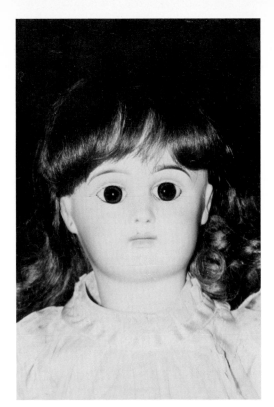

Danel and Cie--16½" Socket head on fully jointed composition/wood body. Open/closed mouth. Pierced ears. Marks: Paris Bébé/Tête Depose/7, stamped in red on head. Stamped Eiffel Tower on lower back. (Courtesy Kimport Dolls) N-P

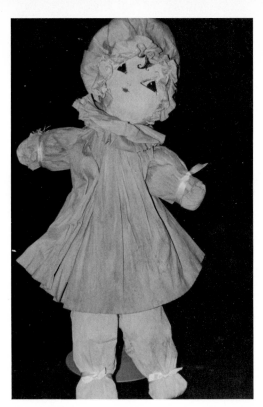

Dennison--20" Dennison Mfg. Co. crepe paper doll. India ink features. All original. Ca. 1890. $25.00. (Courtesy Maxine Heitt)

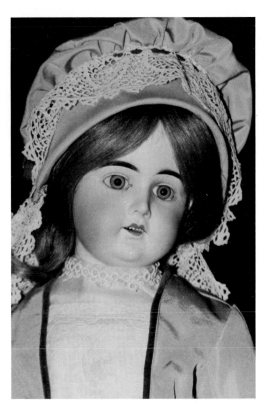

Doliac and Cie--22" Socket head on composition/wood body. Straight wrists. Set blue eyes. Pierced ears. Open mouth. Marks: LD/DEP./9. L. Doliac and Cie operated in Paris from 1881 to 1908. (Courtesy Mae Teters) G-H

DRESSEL, CUNO & OTTO

Dressel, Cuno and Otto--Cuno and Otto Dressel were listed as toymakers in 1873. They registered the Holz Masse mark in 1875. They often bought heads from other companies to use on their bodies. They made dolls in bisque, wax, maché, composition. They began using the "Jutta" trademark in 1906. Refer to page 99, Series 1 (Antique Collector's Dolls) for more complete information on this company. Sample marks of the Cuno and Otto Dressel company:

HOLZ MASSE   DRESSEL

C&O
DRESSEL   DRESSEL

Following are some of their mold numbers: 50, 93, 1348, 1349, 1469, 1912, 1914.

87

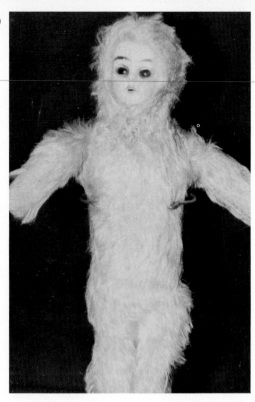

Dressel, Cuno and Otto--9" Polar Bear. Excelsior filled plush one piece body and limbs. Bisque half head with holes top and bottom for attaching. Set glass eyes. Open mouth. (Courtesy Helen Draves) B-C

Dressel, Cuno and Otto--9" Admiral Byrd Plush covered 5 piece maché body with molded on top boots. Bisque head with set eyes and open mouth. All original. (Courtesy Jane Alton) C-D

Dressel, Cuno and Otto--12" Bisque shoulder head on kid body with bisque forearms. Set eyes, unpierced ears and open mouth. Marks: Holz Masse (see introduction)/12/0. A-B

Dressel, Cuno and Otto--18" Shoulder head on kid body with bisque lower arms. Open mouth, unpierced ears and large sleep eyes. Marks: Holz Masse (see introduction)/3/0. (Courtesy Jay Minter) C-D

88

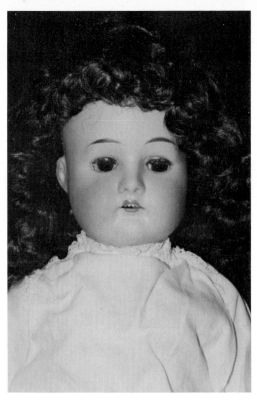

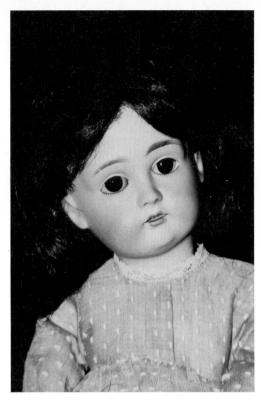

Dressel, Cuno and Otto-23" Socket head on fully jointed composition body. Sleep eyes/lashes. Open mouth. Marks: Made In/ Germany/ 1912-4. (Courtesy Helen Draves) C-D

Dressel, Cuno and Otto--20" Socket head. Fully jointed composition body. Open mouth. Marks: 1349/Jutta/S&H, on head. Body stamped: (Courtesy Jay Minter) C-D

Dressel, Cuno and Otto--20" Socket head on composition fully jointed body. Open mouth, pierced ears and molded brows. All original. Marks: 1349/Dressel/S&H/7. (Courtesy Jay Minter) C-D

89

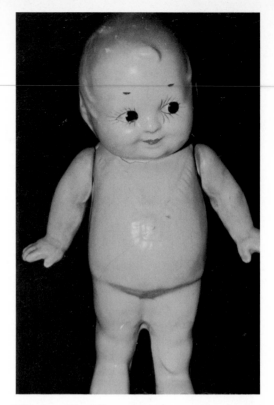

EFFANBEE

Effanbee--Hugo Baum and Bernard Fleischaker started this company in 1910. The company has been sold several times and/or changed hands at least twice but has always kept the Effanbee name. About 1920 the Lenox Pottery made bisque doll heads for Effanbee and these are considered rare items today by collectors. The quality of the old F&B (Effanbee) composition dolls is generally above average. More complete information is on page 101, Ser. 1.

Effanbee--7" All composition with jointed shoulders. Molded on shirt top. Marks: Effanbee, on back. $65.00. (Courtesy Jane Alton)

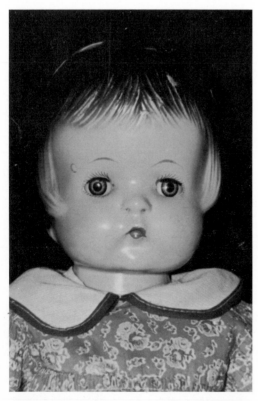

Effanbee--18" Pasty Ann. All composition. Green sleep eyes/lashes. $65.00. (Courtesy Kimport Dolls)

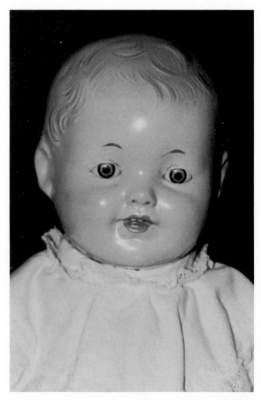

Effanbee--16" Lovums. Cloth with composition head and limbs. Sleep blue tin eyes. Open/closed mouth with two painted upper teeth. Yellow molded hair. Marks: Effanbee/Lovums, on shoulder. $45.00. (Courtesy Kimport Dolls)

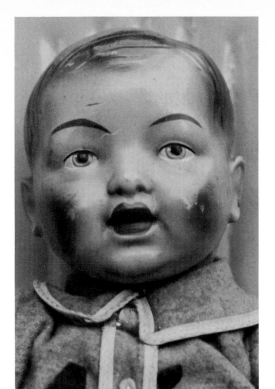

Elektra--32" tall. Composition head with painted eyes. Rest of doll is hard stuffed cotton. Ca. 1915. Marks: Elektra. T.NC.NY./Copyright, with all "N's" backward. AL, on front of baseball uniform. $75.00. (Courtesy Phyllis Houston)

FROZEN CHARLOTTE

Frozen Charlotte--The dolls that collectors call "Frozen Charlotte" (the ballad for this unfortunate young lady is on page 107 of Series 1) have been called by different names over the times. The New England Ballad attached itself to the doll or the other way around and is most popularly called Frozen Charlotte. But there is stories that were once used as "Tea Cup" dolls and placed in the thin cups to keep them from breaking when hot tea was poured in. They have been known as "stuffs", "Twin". One name they have been called stuck almost as much as the Frozen Charlotte and that is "Piller" dolls . . . also a product of the New England states . . . to denote a graphic example to young minds that if not obeyed, they too might turn "into a pillar of salt!"

Frozen Charlotte--7" Frozen Charlotte. All one piece china. She has 13 sausage curls around this little head. Marks: None. $125.00. (Courtesy Grace Ochsner)

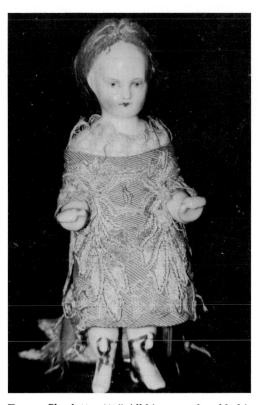

Frozen Charlotte--4½" All bisque and molded in one piece. Bald head with original wig. Molded on gold boots. Remains of original dress. $150.00. (Courtesy Helen Draves)

91

Frozen Charlotte--5" White bisque Frozen Charlotte with jointed shoulders. Blonde molded hair. Marks: 240, on back. $125.00. (Courtesy Jane Alton)

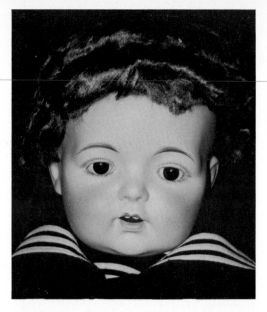

Fulpher--31" Socket head on a fully jointed composition body. Open mouth. Marks: (Courtesy Helen Draves) F-G

Fulpher--The Fulpher Pottery Co. began in 1805 but only made dolls heads for a short time between 1918 and 1921. These heads were developed, first, for the Horsman Doll Co. Fulpher also made some all bisque "Kewpies" in 1920 and "Peterkin", an all bisque, in 1919. Marks:

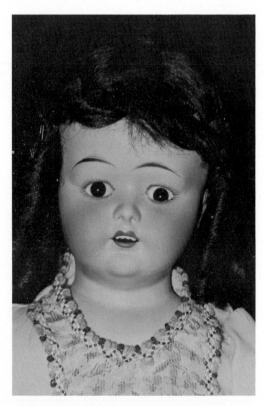

Fulpher--26" Shoulder plate. Sleep eyes. Open mouth. Marks: (Courtesy Helen Draves) D-F

Gans and Seyfarth--22" Gans and Seyfarth socket head on fully jointed composition body. Open mouth. Marks: G & S 3/Germany. Gans and Seyfarth operated from 1909 through the early 1930's. They use their full name on marks and also G.S. and G.&S. (Courtesy Jay Minter) C-D

92

GAULTIER, FERNAND

Gaultier, Fernand--The company of Fernand Gaultier has been accepted as the maker of the "F.G." heads but it is my own personal belief that one day we shall find that they were made by the company, whose bodies they are frequently found on, the Gesland et Fils/ Gesland Freres. It is known that these brothers had the first names of "E". AS WELL AS "F". These dolls are placed under Gaultier by the acceptance of the collectors.

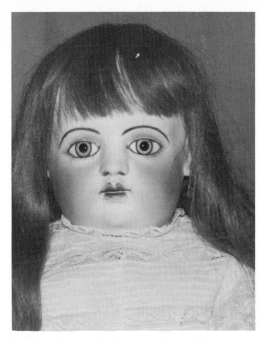

Gaultier, Fernand--25" socket head with portrait eyes. Pierced ears and straight wrists. Open/closed mouth. Pink wash over the dark rimmed eyes. Marks: F 5 G, on Jumeau marked body. (Courtesy Jeanne Gregg) N-Q

Gaultier, Fernand--17" Socket head. Closed mouth. Set eyes. Marks: F.G., in scroll. (Courtesy Jay Minter) N-Q

Gaultier, Fernand--17" Socket head child. On fully jointed composition/wood body. Marks: F.G., in scroll. Is on marked Jumeau body. Closed mouth. Set eyes. $1,295.00. (Courtesy Kimport Dolls) N-Q

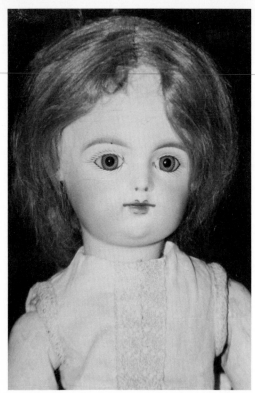

Gaultier, Fernand--13" Socket head. Closed mouth and set eyes. On fully jointed composition body. Marks: F.G., in scroll. (Courtesy Kimport Dolls) M-O

Goebel, William--15" Socket head on fully jointed composition body. Open mouth and unpierced ears. Marks: 60½. William Goebel operated from 1879 to 1960's. (Courtesy Grace Ochsner) A-B

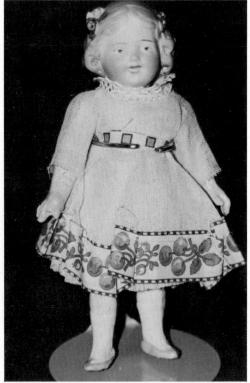

Goebel, William--6" Bisque head on 5 piece composition body. Painted on slippers. Twin bows in hair. Wide open/closed mouth. Marks: 38/1 3/0. All original. $125.00. (Courtesy Helen Draves)

GUÉNOT, P.

Guénot, P.--The doll that is marked with P.G. has begun to be referred to as a Paul Girard Bru. There is NO FOUNDATION to base this on and it is much more likely that the dolls were made by one P. Guénot and made about 1873, this is based on the dolls looks to an "F.G." and Gesland, Guénot and Gaultier all operated in the same close area. It has been reported to this author that a doll marked with P.G., on the head also has the body mark of MLLE GAUDINOT and POPINEAU. This firm operated from 1865 to 1870.

94

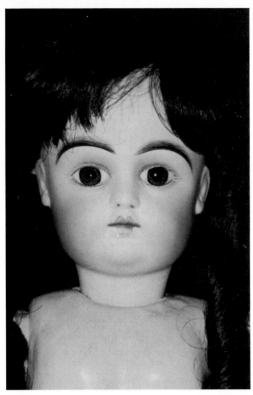

Guénot--20" Socket head. She has a pink wash over the eyes. "F.G." style lips. The ears are not pierced. Marks: 8/P. 10 G. (Courtesy Jay Minter) Q-S

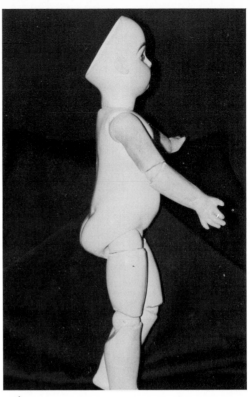

Guénot--This shows the side view of the P.G. doll. She has straight wrists.

Guicherd, Mon. 27" Socket head on fully jointed composition/wood body. Pierced ears and open/closed mouth. See following photo for seal on body. Marks: Paris Bébé/Tête Depee/ 12 17/ V. (Author) N-Q

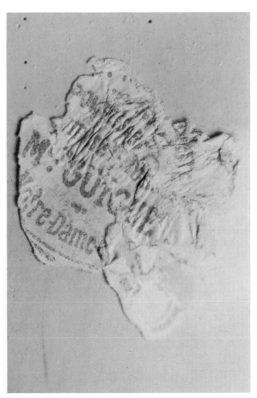

Guicherd, Mon.--This is seal on Paris Bébé body. Can be seen: Poupees et Bébés/Brevette and Mon. Guicherd, plus part of an address on Notre Dame.

95

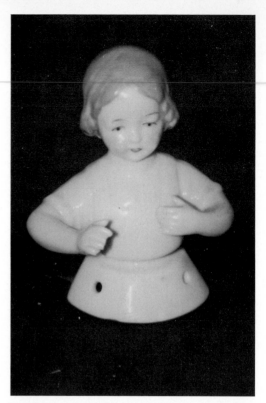

Half Dolls--18" Has tall wire frame for skirt that is covered with lace/silk. Half doll sits on top of frame. Jointed at the shoulders. Was used to cover telephone. $195.00. (Courtesy Elaine Kaminsky)

Half Dolls-2½" Child with both arms away from body. Marks: Germany. $60.00. (Courtesy Helen Draves)

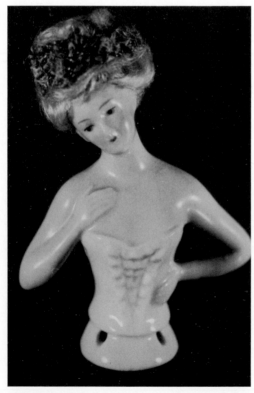

Half Dolls--3" Ball (bald) head with original wig. Molded on corset. Marks: Germany (Courtesy Mary Partridge)

Half Dolls--3" Grey hair. White dress that is pale blue around the bottom. Marks: 16931/Germany. $15.00. (Mary Partridge)

Half Dolls--3" Light brown hair. Blue dress with white sleeves Red rose. Marks: 8544/Germany. $18.00. (Mary Partridge)

Half Dolls--3" and 8" with bottle. Half doll with cork as stopper. Marks: 3380/Germany. $65.00. (Courtesy Kimport Dolls)

Half Doll--2" Child with fan. Marks: None. $27.50.

Half Dolls--4" Celluloid head inside pincushion. 2 sew holes front and back. Marks: None. $12.00. (Courtesy Marge Meisinger)

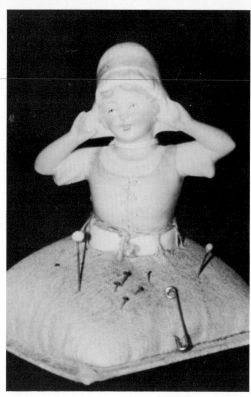

Half Dolls--3" child. Marks: Stamp on bottom of cushion; Germany. $60.00. (Courtesy Kimport Dolls)

Half Dolls--2½" White and green dress and hat. Pink flower. Light brown hair. Marks: 14803/Germany. $35.00. (Mary Partridge)

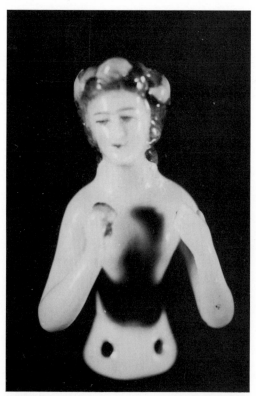

Half Dolls--3" Black hair. Red dress and pale yellow scarfing. Marks: Made in France, sidewards up back. $40.00.

Half Dolls--2 3/4" Both arms away from body. Nude. Light black hair with garland of pink/green flowers in hair and hand. Marks: 76, inside. $45.00. (Mary Partridge)

Half Dolls--2½" Pink dress. Gold trim with blue sash. Marks: Germany. $40.00. (Mary Partridge)

Half Dolls--3" White dress. Deep red necklace. Excellent skin tones. Marks: Germany. $35.00. (Mary Partridge)

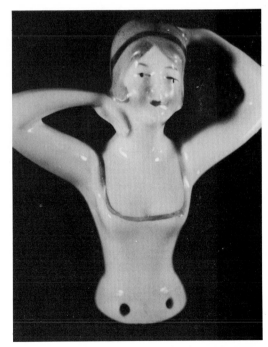

Half Dolls--2½" Yellow hair with blue and white dress/bonnet. Other has brown hair with orange and white dress/bonnet. Marks: 73, at angle/2 . . . (can't read) 30. $27.00. (Courtesy of Mary Partridge)

Half Dolls--3" Very light brown hair. All white with no skin tones. Rose trim and ribbon in hair. Marks: 6102/Germany. $35.00. (Courtesy Mary Partridge)

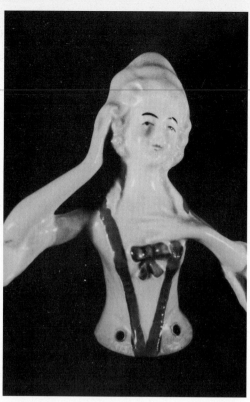

Half Dolls--2½" Arms are in different locations and both away from body. One has pink dress with white bonnet and a blue band. The other has orange bonnet with a black ribbon. Both are marked: 22480. $40.00. (Courtesy Mary Partridge)

Half Dolls--3" Pale blue with orange trim. White sleeves. Blue ribbon. Grey Hair. Marks: 1640/Germany. $27.00. (Courtesy Mary Partridge)

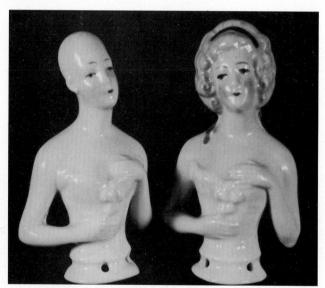

Half Dolls--3" Same doll with ball (bald) head and molded on hair. Both marked: Germany. Left $40.00. Right $25.00. (Courtesy Mary Partridge)

Half Dolls--2½" Light blue dress with pink and gold front. White sleeves and collar. Pink bow and flower. Both arms away from body. Dark blonde hair. Marks: 22612. $28.00. (Courtesy Mary Partridge)

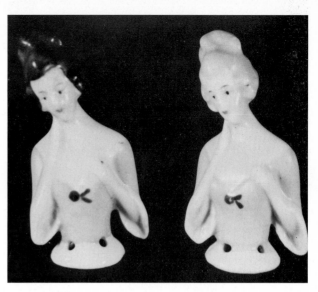

Half Dolls--2¼" Same doll with blonde and brown hair. Blue dress with white sleeves. Flower in front. Marks: 7215/Germany. $25.00. (Courtesy Mary Partridge)

Half Dolls--3" White dress. Light brown hair. Blue/dark red trim in hair. Marks: 6099/Germany. $35.00. (Courtesy Mary Partridge)

HALF DOLLS

Half Dolls--2 3/4" Black hair. White dress with green trim. Yellow rose flowers. Marks: Germany/8310. $18.00. (Courtesy Mary Partridge)

Half Dolls--2" White dress. Pink necklace. Marks: 5331. $20.00. (Courtesy Mary Partridge)

Half Dolls--3 3/4" Pale blue collar. Pink flower. Brown hair. Marks: 12404, on back. Germany, on front. $22.00. (Courtesy Mary Partridge)

Half Dolls--2 3/4" Blue eyes. Painted lashes under only. Rust/green/blue hat. Black hair. Rust/yellow earrings. Marks: 25071. $35.00. (Courtesy Mary Partridge)

102

Half Dolls--2¼ White dress, red rose and green/white fan. Light brown hair with red hair band. Marks: Germany/5737. $30.00. (Courtesy Mary Partridge)

Half Dolls--2 3/4" Nude with both arms away from body. Black hair. Gold earrings. Brown eyes with black eyeshadow. Marks: 23099 and 115, inside. $45.00. (Courtesy Mary Partridge)

Half Dolls--2¼" Blue dress and bonnet. Pink ribbon and rose. Blonde hair. Marks: Germany 6. $18.00. (Courtesy Mary Partridge)

Half Dolls--3" Rust dress. Black hair. Marks: 5119. $18.00. (Courtesy Mary Partridge)

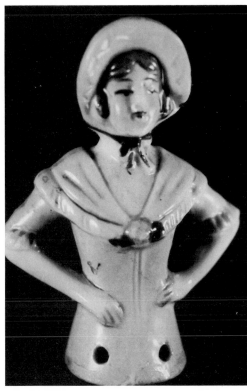

Half Dolls--2½" Orange bonnet with black ribbon. Marks: 22480. $30.00. (Courtesy Mary Partridge)

Half Dolls--2½" Dark blue dress. White sleeves and collar. Pink bows. Light brown hair with pink bow. Hands and arms away from body. Marks: 21122. $15.00. (Courtesy Mary Partridge)

103

Half Dolls--2¼" White with orange trim with blue bows. Grey hair. Green/brown flowers. Marks: Germany/11370. $15.00. (Courtesy Mary Partridge)

Half Dolls--2½" Pink dress. Rust bow. Blue hat. Yellow/rust/green feather in hat. Marks: 46, inside. $20.00. (Courtesy Mary Partridge)

Half Dolls--2 3/4" Blue dress with dark green trim. Dark pink roses and tie. Yellow bonnet. Blonde hair. Unable to make out mark. $18.00. (Courtesy Mary Partridge)

Half Dolls--2¼" Blonde with pale blue dress. White sleeves. Red necklace. Marks: None. $15.00. (Courtesy Mary Partridge)

Half Dolls--1½" Green bonnet. Light brown hair. Marks: S242/Germany. $15.00. (Courtesy Mary Partridge)

Half Dolls--3¼" Blonde hair. Rose dress with blue hat and collar. Red tie. Marks: Made In/Japan, high on head. $8.00. (Courtesy Mary Partridge)

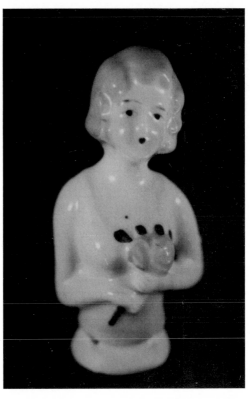

Half Dolls--3½" White with rose checks on dress. Orange bow and hat: Blue feather, cuffs and collar. Marks: Japan. $8.00. (Courtesy Mary Partridge)

Half Dolls--2 3/4" Yellow blonde. White and lime green dress. Pink flowers. Marks: Japan. $7.00. (Courtesy Mary Partridge)

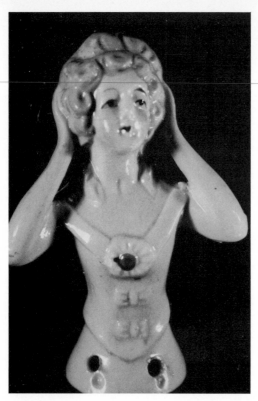

Half Dolls--3½" Yellow hair. Pink dress with orange center to bow. Marks: Made in Japan. $12.00. (Courtesy Mary Partridge)

Half Dolls--2½" White dress. Blue trim. Pink sash and flowers. Grey hair. Pink flower in hair. Marks: Japan. $8.00. (Courtesy Mary Partridge)

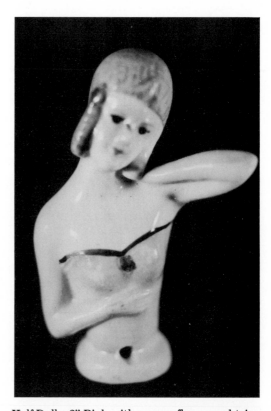

Half Dolls--2" Bathing Doll. Pink skin tones. Orange suit and cap. Marks: None. $22.00. (Courtesy Mary Partridge)

Half Dolls--2" Pink with orange flower and trim. Blue cap with green tassel. Marks: None. $12.00. (Courtesy Mary Partridge)

Half Dolls--8" Stuffed satin body. Glazed head. Marks: Japan. $12.00. (Courtesy Maxine Heitt)

Half Dolls--9" Stuffed silk with glazed head. Original. Marks: Japan. $12.00. (Courtesy Kimport Dolls)

Half Dolls--2½" Pink dress and hat. White scarf and cuffs. Dark brown hair. Marks: None. $12.00. (Courtesy Mary Partridge)

Half Dolls--3¼" Pink dress. Yellow hair. Marks: Japan, inside. $12.00. (Courtesy Mary Partridge)

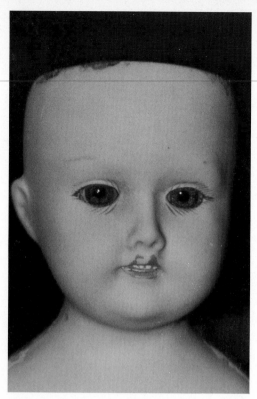

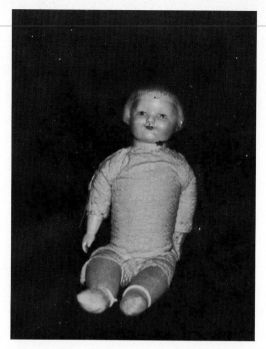

Hancock--17" Shoulder head on cloth body with bisque arms and legs. Open closed mouth with painted teeth. Set eyes. Marks: H½/Hancocks, on head. Stamp on body: Made in England. (Courtesy Kimport Dolls) A-B

Hamley Bros. 15" Buster Brown. Molded hair, painted blue eyes. Closed smile mouth. Cloth body with composition lower arms. Marks: HBº. Hamley Bros. were based in London. (Courtesy Flacks) A-B

HANDWERCK

Handwerck, Heinrich--This company began in 1876 and was located at Gotha, near Waltershausen. They made entire dolls and doll's bodies but a great many of their doll heads were made by Simon and Halbig, plus others. The Heinrich Handwerck marks are an eight point star (see first photo in this section) Other marks:

Hch-H

It is almost certain that Max Handwerck is a member of this family but his dolls are listed separately until absolute proof is forthcoming. The following are some of Heinrich Handwerck's mold numbers: 12x, 19, 69, 79, 99, 100, 109, 119, 124, 139, 152, 199, 1290.

Handwerck, Heinrich--Shows the eight point star that is registered to Heinrich Handwerck. This is the end of a box that a baby doll came in. (Courtesy Jay Minter)

Handwerck, Heinrich--15" Shoulder head on kid body with bisque forearms. Set paperweight eyes. Open mouth. Very Large ears. Marks: HcH 🕸 H. (Courtesy Kimport Dolls) B-C

Handwerck, Heinrich--18" Shoulder head on kid body with bisque forearms. Open mouth. Sleep eyes. All original. Marks: Made in Germany/🕸 HCH 5/0 H. (Courtesy Helen Draves) B-C

109

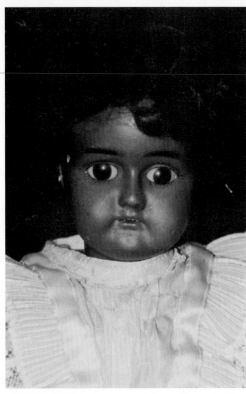

Handwerck, Heinrich--14" Socket head on fully jointed composition body. Sleep eyes. Open mouth. Marks: Germany/Heinrich/Handwerck/Halbig. (Courtesy Jane Alton) B-D

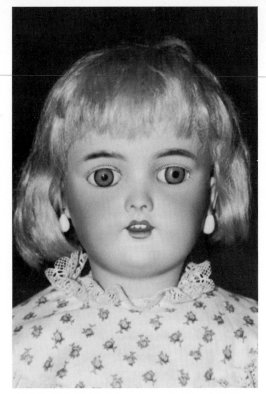

Handwerck, Heinrich--17½" Socket head on fully jointed composition body. Open mouth, pierced ears and sleep eyes. Marks: Germany/Handwerck/Halbig/1. Actually this doll could have been made for either Heinrich or Max Handwerck. (Courtesy Kimport Dolls) C-D

Handwerck, Heinrich--32" Socket head on fully jointed composition body. Sleep eyes. Open mouth. Embedded fur eyebrows. Marks: Germany/Heinrich Handwerck/Simon and Halbig. (Courtesy Helen Draves) H-I

Handwerck, Heinrich--18" Socket head on fully jointed composition body. Molded brows, sleep eyes and open mouth. Marks: Germany/Heinrich Handwerck/Simon and Halbig. (Courtesy Helen Draves) C-D

110

Handwerck, Heinrich--33" Socket head on fully
jointed composition body. Sleep eyes/lashes.
Open mouth. Marks: Germany/Heinrich
Handwerck/Halbig. (Courtesy Jay Minter) H-I

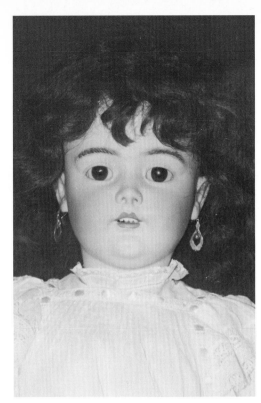

Handwerck, Heinrich--39" tall with an 18" head
circumference. Socket head on fully jointed
composition body. Molded brows, open mouth
and pierced ears. Marks: Germany/Heinrich
Handwerck/Halbig/8. (Courtesy Helen Draves)
H-J

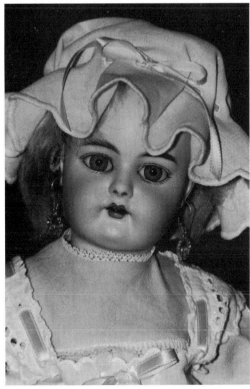

Handwerck, Heinrich--18" Socket head on fully
jointed composition body. Sleep eyes, open
mouth and pierced ears. Marks: 79/10/Ger-
many. Ca. 1899. (Courtesy Helen Draves) C-D

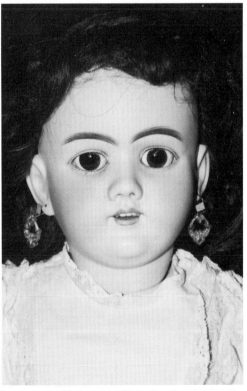

Handwerck, Heinrich--26" Socket head on fully
jointed composition body. Sleep eyes, open
mouth and pierced ears. Marks: 14/Germany/
99/Dep./Handwerck/5½". This is another doll
that may have been made for Max Handwerck.
(Courtesy Helen Draves) D-F

111

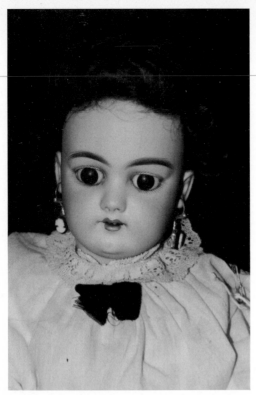

Handwerck, Heinrich--17 Socket head on fully jointed composition body. Open mouth, sleep eyes and pierced ears. This doll was made after Kammer and Reinhardt purchased the Heinrich factory, and made for the French trade. Marks: 109-7½/H/1. (Courtesy Helen Draves) C-D

Handwerck, Heinrich--27" Socket head on fully jointed composition body. Pierced ears, sleep eyes and open mouth. Marks: 119 15/Handwerck/Germany. (Courtesy Kimport Dolls) E-G

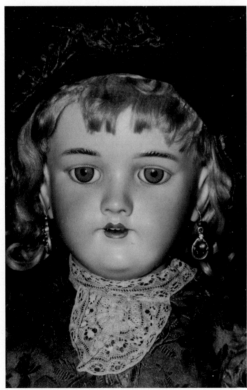

Handwerck, Heinrich--27" Socket head on fully jointed composition body. Sleep eyes, open mouth and pierced ears. Molded brows. Marks: 119 13/Handwerck/5/Germany. (Courtesy Helen Draves) E-G

Handwerck, Heinrich--15" Turned shoulder head. Full closed mouth. Set eyes. Unpierced ears. Marks: HcH ⚬ H. (Courtesy Jane Alton) D-F

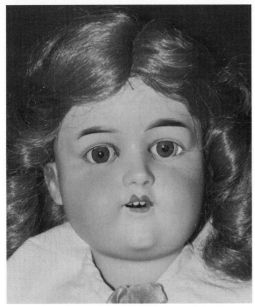

Handwerck, Max--22" Socket head. Sleep eyes. Open mouth. Unpierced ears. Marks: M.H./6½. (Courtesy Kimport Dolls) D-C

HANDWERCK

Max Handwerck started his factory in Waltershausen in 1900. He registered "Bébé Elite" in 1901, heads made for him by William Goebel. As for his marks, they generally have his full name or: M. Handwerck, M.H. Some of his mold numbers: 22, 28, 29, 30, 90, 136, 139, 185, 283, 286, 287, 436. Bebe Elite.

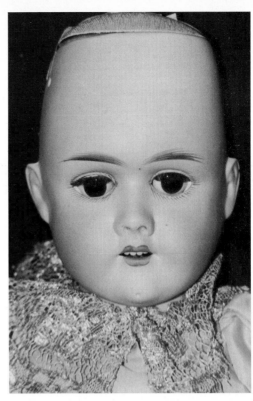

Handwerck, Max--24" Socket head on fully jointed composition body. Sleep eyes/lashes. Open mouth. Unpierced ears. Has odd shape to head. Marks: Max Handwerck/Germany12½. (Courtesy Helen Draves) D-E

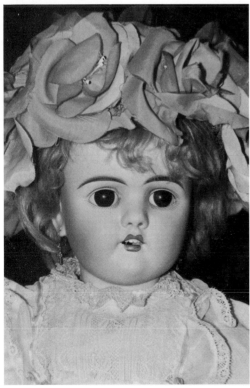

Handwerck, Max--25" Socket head on fully jointed composition body. Sleep eyes, open mouth and pierced ears. Marks: Germany/M. Handwerck/4½. (Courtesy Helen Draves) D-E

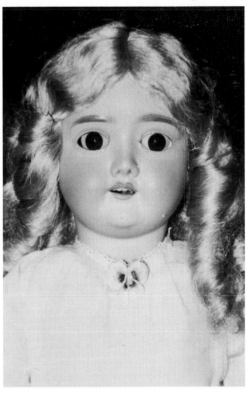

Handwerck, Max--24" Socket head on fully jointed composition body. Sleep eyes, open mouth and unpierced ears. Marks: Max Handwerck/Germany/7½. (Courtesy Kimport Dolls) D-E

113

HANDWERCK,
MAX

HELLER,
ALFRED

HENDREN,
MADAM

Handwerck, Max--23½" Socket head on fully jointed composition body. Sleep eyes, open mouth and pierced ears. Marks: 136. (Courtesy Kathy Walter) D-E

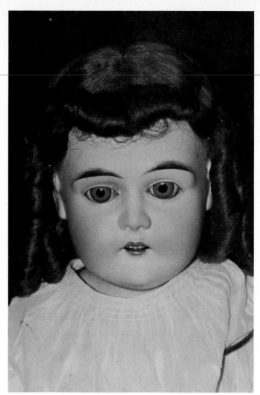

Handwerck, Max--32" Shoulder head on kid body with muslin lower legs and bisque forearms. Sleep eyes and open mouth. Marks: 139/31-5. (Courtesy Helen Draves) F-G

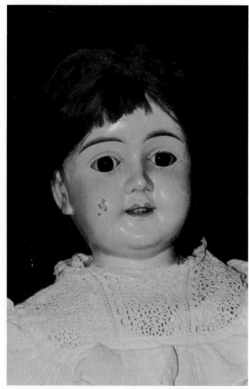

114

Heller, Alfred--22" Metal head on all cloth body with stitched fingers. Sleep eyes, open mouth with four teeth. Applied ears. Marks: ⌐HALL⌐Alfred Heller made dolls from 1902 to 1907. He worked in Meiningen, Thur and registered the "Diana" trademark in the U.S. and Germany in 1903. $75.00. (Courtesy Teri Schall)

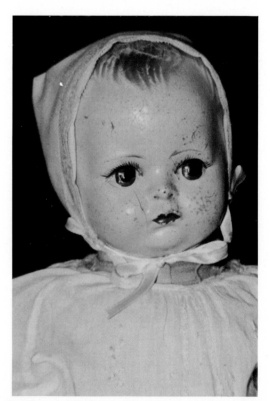

Hendren, Madam--17" Cloth body with composition head and limbs. Very large blue painted eyes. Marks: Madam Hendren/Life Like Doll/Patented June 11, 1918, on body (Stamp): 🍀 , on head. "Madam Hendren" was a mark used by The Georgene Averill Mfg. Co. in the U.S. and Brophy Doll Co. of Canada. $65.00. (Courtesy Kimport Dolls)

Herwig, Bruno--22" Maché head on fully jointed felt stuffed body. Limbs are pin jointed. Painted features. Original wig and clothes. Ca. 1921. Marks: ⊞ $85.00. (Courtesy Barbara Coker)

ERNST HEUBACH OF KOPPELSDORF

Ernst Heubach of Koppelsdorf--This company began in 1887 and by 1895 had over 100 people working for them. Ernst Heubach was the brother-in-law of Armand (Herman) Marseille and it is suspected that he was a cousin of Gebruder (brothers) Heubach. Some Ernst Heubach marks:

The following are some of Heubach of Koppelsdorf mold numbers:

27X, 99, 230, 235, 236, 237, 238, 242, 250, 251, 267, 271, 273, 275, 277, 283, 300, 302, 312, 317, 320, 321, 342, 367, 399, 407, 438, 444, 450, 458, 616, 1310, 1900, 1901, 1902, 1906, 1909, 2504, 2671, 2757, 3027, 3412, 3423, 3427, 7118, 32144.

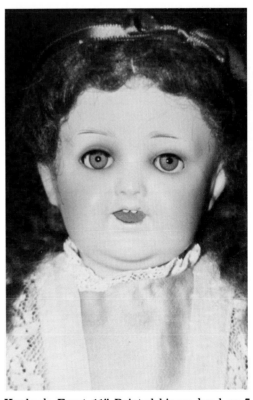

Heubach, Ernst--25" Shoulder head on kid body with bisque lower arms. Open mouth and set eyes. Marks: X/Made In Germany/ Welsch. Made for Welsch Co. (Courtesy Helen Draves) C-D

Heubach, Ernst--11" Painted bisque head on 5 piece bent leg baby body. Original wig. Sleep eyes/lashes. Open mouth. Marks: Heu. Kopp./242-14/Germany. (Courtesy Kimport Dolls) A-B

115

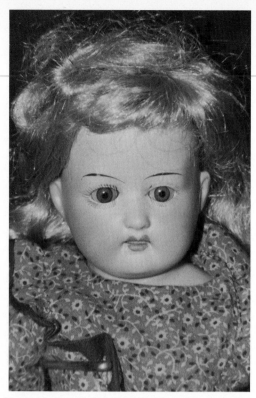

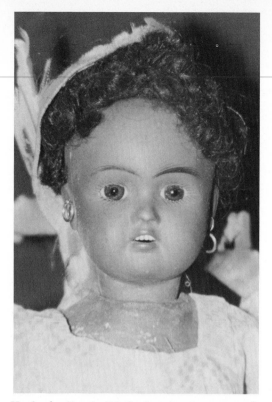

Heubach, Ernst--15" Shoulder head on kid body with composition forearms. Sleep eyes. Open mouth. Marks: Heubach Koppelsdorf/275. (Courtesy Kimport Dolls) A-B

Heubach, Ernst--12" Socket head on maché/composition body with "stick" legs. Straight wrists. Open mouth set eyes and pierced ears. Marks: 277/Dep. (Courtesy Kimport Dolls) C-D

Heubach, Ernst--10½" Bisque socket head on 5 piece composition baby body. Blue sleep eyes/lashes. Open mouth/2 teeth. Marks: Heu. Kopp./300.12/0/Germany. (Courtesy Kathy Walter) B-C

Heubach, Ernst--25" Socket head on 5 piece baby body. Brown sleep eyes. Open mouth/2 upper teeth and "tremble" tongue. Marks: Heubach-Koppelsdorf/300-8/Germany. (Courtesy Grace Ochsner) D-E

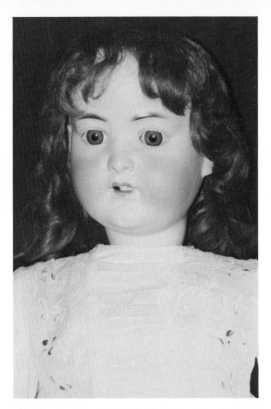

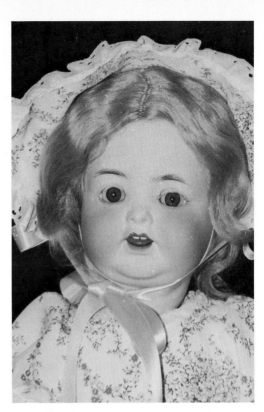

Heubach, Ernst--37" Socket head with fully jointed composition body. Sleep eyes, open mouth and unpierced ears. Marks: Heubach Koppelsdorf/312 ⊕ 15/Germany. (Courtesy Helen Draves) F-G

Heubach, Ernst--18" Socket head on 5 piece Toddler body. Sleep eyes, open mouth with teeth and "tremble" tongue. Marks: Heubach Koppelsdorf/342-d. (Courtesy Grace Ochsner) E-F

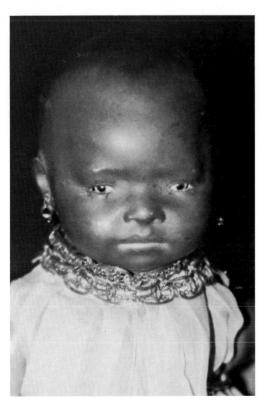

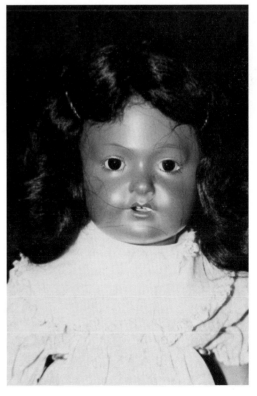

Heubach, Ernst--8½" Dark brown bisque head on 5 piece brown baby body. Set glass eyes, closed mouth and pierced ears. Marks: Heubach Koppelsdorf/399.14/0 D.R.G.M./Germany. (Courtesy Kimport Dolls) D-E

Heubach, Ernst--13" Socket head on 5 piece toddler body. Set black eyes. Open mouth/2 upper teeth. Marks: Heu. Kopp./ 458-10/0Germany. (Courtesy Kimport Dolls) F-H

117

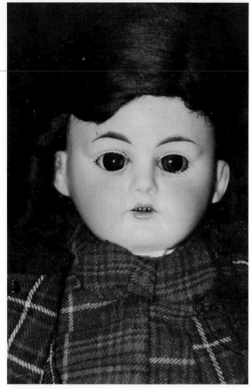

Heubach, Ernst--20" Shoulder head slightly turned. Sleep eyes and open mouth. Kid body with bisque lower arms. Original clothes with replaced wig. Marks: /1902-0. (Courtesy Helen Draves) C-D

GEBRUDER HEUBACH

Gebruder Heubach--The Heubach Brothers (Gebruder) made dolls from 1863 into the 1930's. Their factory was at Lichte, Thur. They made "general" type dolls until 1909 or 1910 when they began to make "character" dolls. Sample Gebruder Heubach marks:

The following are some of Gebruder Heubach mold numbers. 28, 30, 37, 43, 45, 56, 58, 60, 63, 66, 68N, 69, 70, 71, 73, 74, 76, 77, 77G, 78, 79, 81, 83, 86, 87, 90, 91, 92, 93, 94, 95, 101, 122, 165, 750, 892, 0716, 0746, 1063, 1602, 3774, 4660, 5777, 6662, 6692, 6773, 6789, 6836, 6894, 6969, 6970, 7043, 7054, 7066, 7072, 7118, 7143, 7246, 7345, 7602, 7604, 7650, 7802, 7856, 8004, 8192, 8193, 8232, 8306, 8578, 9558, 9573, 10542, 10633, 96643.

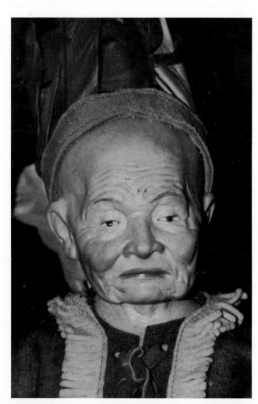

Heubach, Gebruder--13" Portrait Indian with bisque head. All original. Marks: 94 [HEU BACH] 57/1. There is also a matching "squaw" that goes with this "chief". (Courtesy Kimport Dolls) V-W

Heubach, Gebruder--9" Socket head with molded on bonnet. Holes in sides for ribbon. Marks: Heubach, in square. (Courtesy Helen Draves) G-I

118

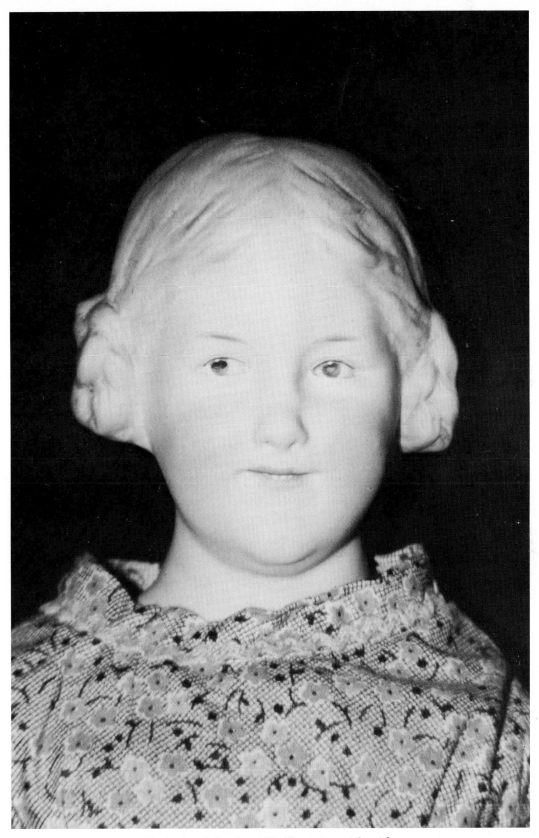

Heubach, Gebruder--16" Character girl with molded braids over ears and wisps of hair at nape of neck in back. Intaglio eyes and open/closed mouth with painted teeth. Shoulder head on cloth body with leather arms. Marks: 119, blue stamp. [HEU BACH] Germany 1867. (Courtesy Kimport Dolls) N-O

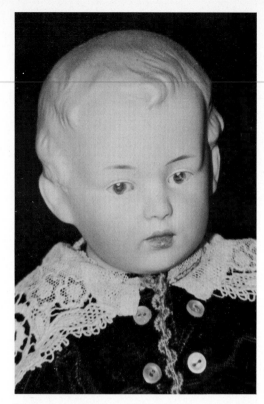

Heubach, Gebruder--15" Socket head on fully jointed composition body. Intaglio eyes and molded hair. Closed mouth. Marks: 4/Germany. (Courtesy Grace Ochsner) E-F

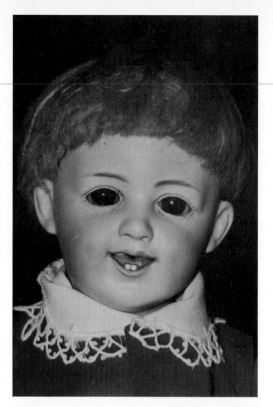

Heubach, Gebruder--19" Socket head on 5 piece mache body. Sleep eyes. Open mouth with 2 lower teeth. Marks: 6½ 🌣 Germany. (Courtesy Helen Draves) I-K

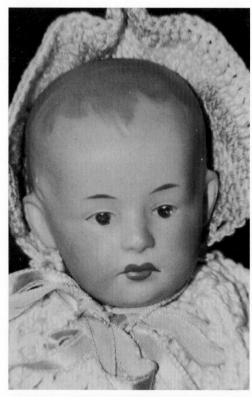

Heubach, Gebruder--8½" Socket head on 5 piece mache baby body. Painted eyes and closed mouth. Marks: 3/2/76/ [HEU BACH] /6. (Courtesy Helen Draves) C-E

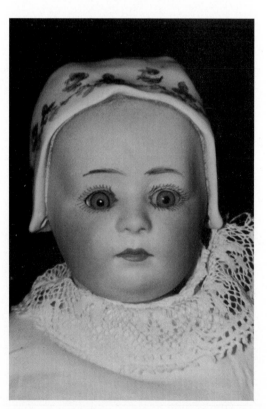

Heubach, Gebruder--9¼" "Baby Stuart" Molded on removable bisque bonnet. Holes in sides for ribbon. Blue sleep eyes. Closed mouth. Marks: 18 🌣 /76/Germany. (Courtesy Kimport Dolls) G-I

120

18" F.G. fashion. Dressed by Bessie Greeno. (Courtesy Kathy Walter)

18½" Pink luster, early china boy. For full description see china section. All original. (Author)

14" Ball (bald) head fashion with kid body. Unmarked. (Courtesy Helen Draves)

18" Kid over wood fashion with gutta percha feet. See Ladies of Fashion section for full description. (Courtesy Jay Minter)

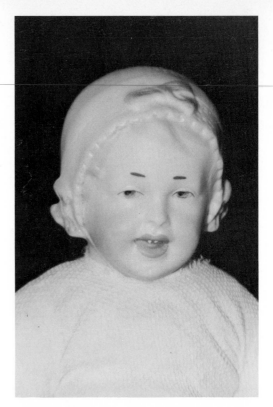

Heubach, Gebruder--12" "Coquette" Tilted bisque shoulder head on kid body with bisque forearms. Molded in ribbon and bow. Blonde hair. Intaglio eyes. Closed smile mouth. Marks: 3/0/78 [HEU BACH] /50/Germany. (Courtesy Helen Draves) E-F

Heubach, Gebruder--8" Socket head on jointed body. Molded on hair and bonnet. Open/closed mouth. Marks: 22-126. A probable Heubach. (Courtesy Helen Draves) C-D

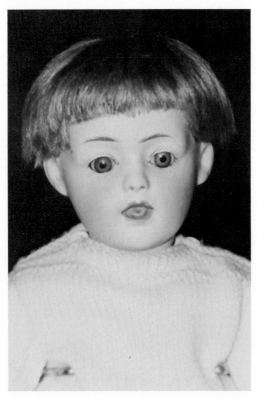

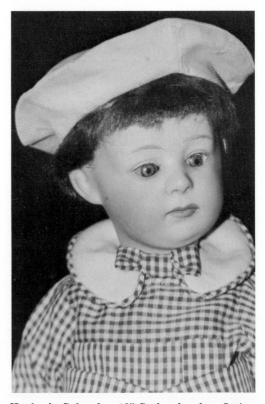

122

Heubach, Gebruder--12" Excellent quality bisque head on 5 piece baby body. Original wig. Blue sleep eyes and a wide open/closed mouth. Marks: 1560/4/Germany. (Courtesy Kimport Dolls) I-K

Heubach, Gebruder--10" Socket head on 5 piece baby body. Sleep eyes and closed, slightly "pouty" mouth. Marks: 6960/Germany/2. (Courtesy Helen Draves) D-E

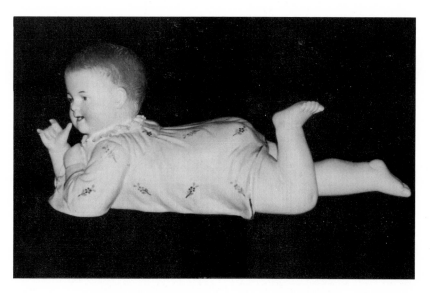

Heubach, Gebruder--11" long "Piano" baby. Brown painted eyes. Exceptional quality porclain. Marks: Heubach, in square. (Courtesy Helen Draves) A-C

Heubach, Gebruder--12" Double Jester. Maché and wood body. Jointed shoulders. Bisque shoulder heads. Set glass eyes and open mouths. All original. Marks: Heubach, in square. (Courtesy Grace Ochsner) D-E

Heubach, Gebruder--19" Shoulder head on kid body with bisque forearms. Open mouth. Marks: 64/5. (Courtesy Jay Minter) C-D

21" on marked Schmitt (and Fils) body. See
manufacturers unknown section for full
description. (Author)

17" Unmarked Schmidt and Fils. See Schmidt
section for full description. (Author)

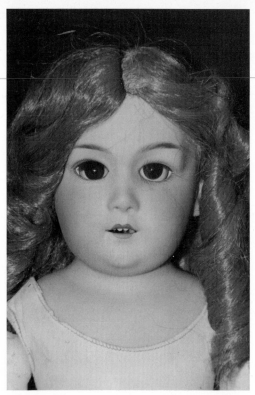

Heubach, Gebruder--25" Dainty Dorothy. Open mouth. Sleep eyes/lashes. Marks: 10633/S/ Gebr. Heubach/Germany/ [HEU BACH] Has seal on chest. See following picture. C-E

Heubach, Gebruder--Seal/Dainty Dorothy/ Copyright 1910 by Sears Roebuck and Co./Germany.

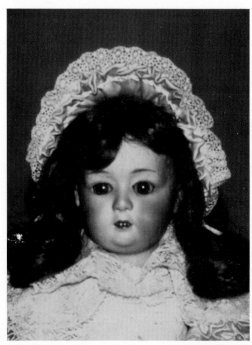

Heubach, Gebruder--14" Socket head on 5 piece baby body. Sleep eyes and open mouth. Marks: 8192/ ⊕ /66/ Germany. (Courtesy Jeanne Gregg) C-D

Horsman--16" Pouty girl. A beautiful quality composition with open crown, set blue eyes and closed mouth. On fully jointed composition and wood body. Marks: E.I.H./Co. (Courtesy Barbara Coker) B-C

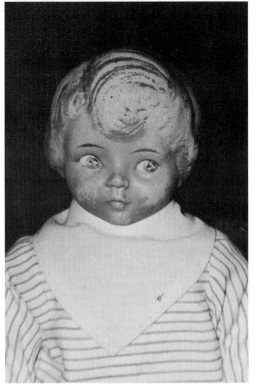

Horsman-13" "Carl" Cloth body and limbs with composition gauntlet hands and head. Patented Nov. 23, 1911 (#G39112). Marks:E.I.H. 1911. By artist Trowbridge. $85.00. (Courtesy Marge Meisinger)

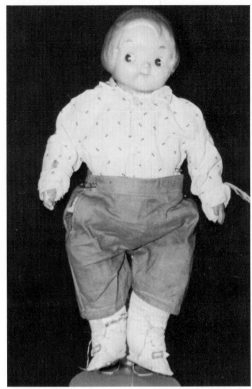

Horsman--13" "Campbell Kid" of 1911. Cloth body with part composition limbs and shoulder head. $65.00. (Courtesy Kimport Dolls)

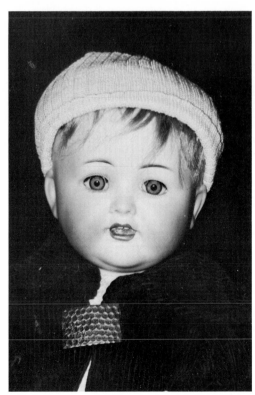

Hulss, Adolf--14" Socket head on 5 piece baby body. Sleep eyes/lashes and open mouth. Marks: Simon and Halbig/ ⦿ /Made in Germany. This mark has been identified with Adolf Hulss but is actually registered to A. Reich of Colburg, Thur in 1911, who made dolls for Louis Wolfe. D-E

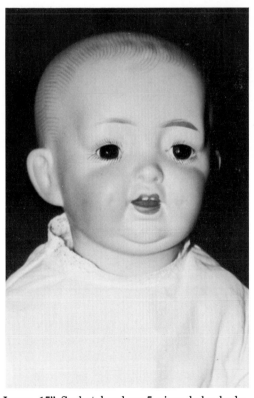

Japan--15" Socket head on 5 piece baby body. Cheek dimples. Open mouth with 2 painted upper teeth. Marks: Nippon, in a circle. (Courtesy Kimport Dolls) B-C

127

17" Socket head marked: S.F.B.J./301/Paris/6.
(Courtesy Kathy Walter)

JAPAN

Japan--The center for celluloid, metal and rubber dolls was at Tokyo. Porcelain dolls were made at Kyoto and Osaka was where the dolls of cotton and paper were made. As in Germany, the dolls of Japan were largely made/constructed as part of the household industry. During World War 1 when bisque dolls stopped coming to the US from Germany (because of war) the Japanese increased production and tried to fill the demand. In 1918 an embargo was placed against Japan to stop the "flooding of the market" but the dolls continued to flow in. The main reason for this was that the large companies doing the importing were American companies and actually designed most of the dolls they distributed. (Re: Morimura Brs., Hager, Tajimi, Yamato, etc.)

Japan--17" Socket head on fully jointed composition body. Open mouth, blue sleep eyes with lashes painted below eyes only. Marks: ✳ /Japan. Made for Morimura Bros. N.Y. (Courtesy Jay Minter) C-D

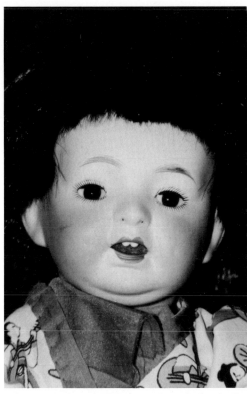

Japan--12"Socket head on 5 piece baby body. Open mouth/2 upper teeth. Ca. 1918. Marks: ✳ /Japan. Made for the Morimura Brothers of New York. (Courtesy Kimport Dolls) B-C

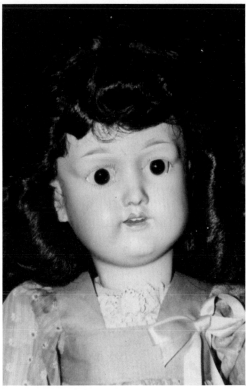

Japan--22½" Socket head with set brown eyes. Open mouth and pierced ears. Fully jointed composition body. Marks: FY/Nippon/405. Made for Yamato Importing Co. 1919. (Courtesy Kimport Dolls) C-D

129

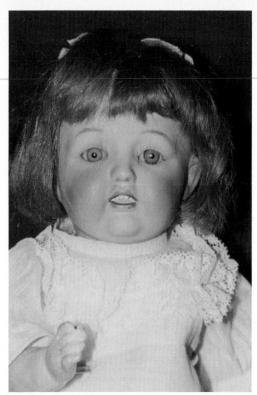

Japan--13" Socket head on 5 piece baby body. Open mouth/upper teeth. Sleep eyes. Marks: ℱ/03601/Nippon/600. Made for Yamato Importing Co. 1919. (Courtesy Kimport Dolls) C-D

Japan--12" Socket head on 5 piece baby body. Open mouth with molded tongue and painted upper teeth. Marks: Nippon. (Courtesy Grace Ochsner) B-C

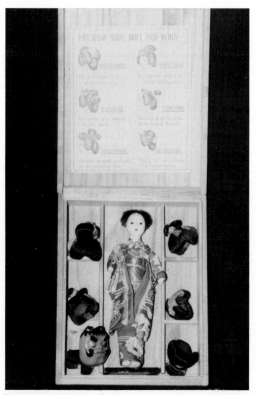

Japan--18" Fan Doll. Wooden fan is painted on one side, doll on the other. Carried by actors in Japan to indicate role being played. Doll has painted silk face and brocade clothing. $27.00. (Courtesy Phyllis Houston)

Japan--6½"Bisque head, hands and feet. 6 wigs for girls of different age and marital status. Second set has male doll with 6 masks for Japan's Traditional Mask Dances. Marks: Katsuraxingyo. Sticker on wooden box. Nishi ◇ Doll/Nishi and Co. Ltd/Made in Japan. $55.00. (Courtesy Phyllis Houston)

Japan--7" All heavy rubber with one piece body and head. Painted eyes. Closed mouth. Marks: 75/Japan/Perfection/Baby. $27.00. (Courtesy Phyllis Houston)

Japan--6½" Black "Carnival Girl" Marks: Made in Occupied Japan" All celluloid. Top hat is silvered paper and carries a cane. $12.00. (Courtesy Phyllis Houston)

JULLIEN JEUNE

Jullien Jeune--Jullien operated his business from 1863 to 1904 and in 1904 he became a part of Société Francaise de Fabrication de Bébé et Jouets (S.F.B.J.). Jullien dolls are generally marked with letters "J.J." or the full name of Jullien.

Jullien--21" Socket head on fully jointed composition/wood body. Open mouth, pierced ears and has pull strings that operate a cryer. Marks: Jullien/Jullien/6. (Courtesy Grace Ochsner) P-R

131

HISTORY OF JUMEAU

The Jumeau family first exhibited dolls in 1844 at London's Crystal Palace Exposition. They were given recognition for the beautiful doll clothes, but not for the dolls themselves. Since the sewing machine had not yet been invented, these clothes were all hand sewn.

It is fairly certain that all the French dollmaker's heads of bisque and porcelain were made in Germany and it was not until the 1860's that Jumeau started to manufacture his own bisque heads which would be more beautiful and artistic than the German heads.

The early Jumeau bodies were built over metal frames and by 1850 these early bodies were all sawdust-stuffed sheepskin. These beautifully made bodies also had sheepskin hands and feet and were gusseted at the hips, elbows and knees. The larger dolls had their fingers and toes stitched separately. Not all these sheepskin bodies were white, some were pink and a few were cream colored. These metal framed and kid covered bodies fit very snuggly into the bisque shoulder plate. Too much handling prevented the dolls to stand erect due to the shift of the sawdust.

Jumeau attempted to overcome the problem of the dolls becoming "ungainly" by having a cloth body with all the joints inside a loose kid overgarment. The joints were supposed to function inside the kid. This body didn't work out at all and is considered the rarest of the Jumeau bodies by today's collectors.

The next body from Jumeau may have been the "Walking Jumeau", the fourth type was a body and limbs of wood covered with kid with the kid being shrunk onto the joints before assembling. Fifth type was all wood and jointed at the waist, wrists and ankles. The sixth type was Jumeau's son Emiles design, composition and strung with elastic. The first are strung with the elastic looping out and in through two holes in the sole of each foot. Each leg and head also, are fastened onto a bar in the body.

It is not known exactly what year Emile Jumeau took out his first registration of "Bébé Jumeau" but we know that during the 1870's he created his Bébés on composition ("'unbreakable"), jointed bodies. The use of Tete Jumeau became very popular and the words means "Head Jumeau".

The heads of the Bébés were of a porcelain paste made of a substance called Kaolin. The paste was kneaded just like bread dough, then rolled out to the correct thickness for the head and cut into squares which was moulded into plaster casts that were mae intwo halves. After these casts (molds) were used fifty times, they were discarded. After setting up, the heads were removed from the casts (molds) and the eye sockets were cut out with a special tool. The larger heads had the ears applied and the smaller heads had the ear included into the cast (mold). The heads were then baked for 27 hours at a very high temperature. When cool, the heads were rubbed down with sandpaper until smooth and polished and were ready for painting.

Two coats of pale pink were applied and allowed to dry in special driers, then the cheeks, the lips, eyebrows, eyelashes and nostrils were painted. The heads were again fired for seven hours at a much lower temperature. After cooling the heads were ready for the eyes.

Twenty young women make the eyes, but only after five years of apprenticeship. Mon. Jumeau only took in orphans and trained them for this meticulous work. He boarded these orphans for the training period until they became proficient and then they were on their own like any other employee. The eyes were made from sticks of colored glass for the pupil and iris and inserted into the white enamel eye. When it had cooled, it was fired for several hours to make it unbreakable. The eyes are inserted into place and fixed with a coating of wax, then a layer of plaster.

The bodies of these Bébés were made of sheets of thick grey paper soaked in paste and forced into cast iron moulds. The backs and fronts are moulded separately, and when dried 24 to 48 hours, are glued together. The cups of the joints, which are small rings of metal, wood or cardboard are put into place. This work was done by housewives who learned the work at the factory under skilled supervision and after training were given moulds, paper and paste to make whatever limbs that were her specialty, at home. When the parts of the body were glued and the joints were in place the body was ready for painting. A thick coat of white paint was first applied and allowed to dry. Next they sanded to remove all roughness and surplus paint. Then five coats of pink paint and one of varnish was applied and dried. The bodies were then sent to the assembly room where the elastic was run through the limbs and fastened to metal hooks and then the head was placed onto the body. The head was then wigged. Mom. Jumeau used both natural (human) and Tibetan goat for his dolls wigs. The wigs were nailed to a cork insert into the crown of the head.

Mme. Jumeau (Mrs. Jumeau) took over from this point and dressed the dolls in exquisite taste and colors. All materials, laces and braids came directly from the factories of France. The costumes were designed by women and if their designs were chosen by Mme. Jumeau, they were given an order for a certain number of costumes, which they sewed in their own homes.

In 1875 Jumeau produced an 18" walking doll with a rare body. This body was a flat piece of wood to which the arms and legs were attached with metal hinges. At the top of the wood block are fastened four round discs of wood onto which the bisque shoulder head rested. The body, arms and legs were first wrapped with tow, which is coarse and broken parts of flax or hemp, then with lamb's wool. This was covered with stockinette to the wrists where the bisque hands joined it. The legs were covered with stockinette to the knees only where the beautiful bisque legs and detailed feet joined it. The legs swing from the hips both forward and backward and also sideways. There is no walking mechanism.

The success of the Jumeau factory was phenomenal during the 1880's, and before the 1900's many French houses were unable to compete with Germany and Jumeau and were absorbed by the Jumeau Bébé Company, which became a monopoly. It is known that at least one German house merged with them and 1914 the Jumeau Company was turned into a stock company with most of the stock Germany owned. The Director was German (Fleischmann of Fleischmann and Blodel).

The German ownership reflected into the dolls heads as the molding of the heads became slightly heavier around the jaws and under the chin.

The Twentieth Century Jumeau is not as well proportioned as the earlier ones. The bisque is coarser and has higher color.

Records show that in 1881 Jumeau made 85,000 Bebes. In 1883, 115,000 Bébés and in 1884 production totaled 220,000. There were 17 sizes of heads in all and from 600 to 700 of each size was manufactured.

It is known that as late as 1897 there were fashion dolls which were sent to England, Germany and Spain. It is also known that an almost lifesize child with a bisque head was made by Jumeau during short revival around 1938. The last year in which Jumeau made heads and dolls was 1946.

The merger of the French Houses was in 1899 and was called Société Française de Fabrication de Bébés et Jouets...translated: Corporation of French Manufacturers of Dolls and Toys. Some of the other companies were Bru, Rabery and Delphieu, Pintel and Godehaux, Jullien and Danel and Company.

At the start of World War 1, the Director of the S.F.B.J. group was deported as an alien and his holding was sequestered by the French Government.

A rumor circulated in 1964 that the Jumeau company had stored away 20,000 heads in their Paris factory to be released in 1980 (the reason for this date unknown). These heads were to be marked with the "J" which, while used occasionally, were never a Jumeau registered trademark. Both Andre Girard and Jean Moynet of the Jumeau Factory say these must be counterfeit (if they appear). The close of S.F.B.J. came in the mid 1950's when the old factory was taken over by a firm that makes fountain pens with ball points. They used the S.F.B.J. initials on their products.

The symbol of the bee was used in honor of Napoleon 111 and Empress Eugenie of the Second Empire. This symbol of the bee is found on Jumeau shoes and some dolls bear a bee image made into earrings.

Jumeau--21" Long face or Cody Jumeau. Applied ears. Closed mouth. Is wearing original dress only. Marks: 10, on head. (Courtesy Helen Draves) Y-Z

Jumeau--14½" Socket head on composition/ wood body. Open/closed mouth. Pierced ears. Marks: Depose E 5 J. (Courtesy Kimport Dolls) Q-S

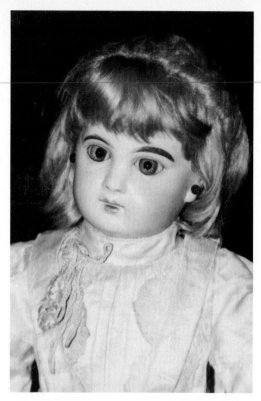

Jumeau--15" Socket head on jointed composition/wood body. Open/closed mouth. Pierced ears. All original (full length view, see color section). Hair in original set. Marks: E 6 J., on head. Jumeau/Medaille D'or/Paris, on body. The eyes on this doll are so "deep" the pupils seem to enlarge. (Author) Q-S

Jumeau--Shows original clothes of E.J. Paper tag on front says Bébé Jumeau.

Jumeau--25" Socket head with applied ears. Maché/composition and wood body. Open/closed mouth. Marks: Depose/Tete Jumeau/BTE SGDG/12/P8. (Courtesy Helen Draves) M-O

Jumeau--14" Socket head on jointed composition/wood body. Open mouth and pierced ears. (Courtesy Grace Ochsner) H-I

KAMMER & RINEHARDT

Kammer and Rinehardt, the largest doll factory in Germany, was organized in 1886 by Franz Reinhardt, a young salesman and Ernst Kammer, an expert molder and skilled workman. In 1908 this company hired an artist in Berlin to make the head of a six week old baby. This mold is now known as the "Kaiser Baby". Kammer and Rinehardt also made character dolls named "Marie" (101), Gretchen (114) and Hans (boy 114) that were molded from Herr Reinhardt's nephew.

After Kammer's death in 1901, Kammer and Reinhardt bought out a rival factory after the death of it's founder, Heinrich Handwerck. Later Kammer and Reinhardt combined with the factory of Simon and Halbig.

The following are some of the Kammer and Reinhardt mold numbers: 17, 18, 20, 21, 22, 23, 25, 26, 28, 30, 32, 35, 35½) celluloid 36, 38, 39, 40, 42, 43, 45, 48, 50, 53, 55, 56, 58, 60, 62, 65 (celluloid), 67, 68, 70, 73, 75, 76, 80, 85, 100, 101, 101X, 107, 112X, 114, 115, 115A, 116, 116A, 117, 117A, 117N, 118, 118A, 119, 121, 122, 124, 126, 127, 128, 131, 138, 195, 200, 214, 225 (Celluloid), 246, 247, 255 (celluloid), 321 (celluloid), 402, 403, 442, 717 (celluloid), 728 (celluloid), 835 Majestic.

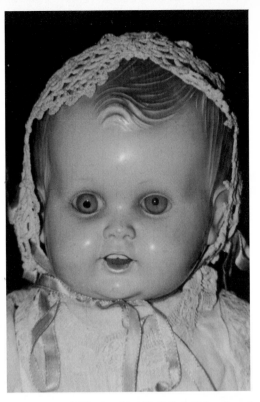

Kammer and Rinehardt--13" Celluloid head and 5 piece body. Bent baby legs. Open mouth/2 upper teeth. Set eyes. Marks: K ✡ R/ 32½. (Courtesy Helen Draves) B-C

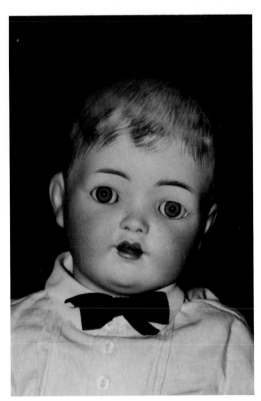

Kammer and Rinehardt--15" Socket head on fully jointed composition/wood body. Molded brush stroke hair. Sleep eyes. Open mouth with 2 upper teeth. Marks: Germany/Simon Halbig/K ✡ R/36. (Courtesy Jane Alton) G-I

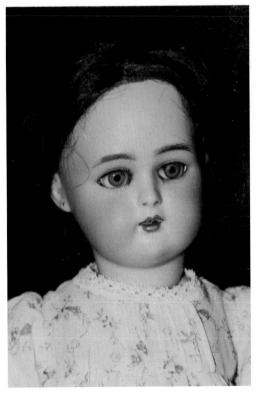

Kammer and Rinehardt--16½" Socket head on fully jointed composition body. Sleep eyes. Pierced ears and open mouth. Marks: Simon Halbig/K ✡ R 43. (Courtesy Kathy Walter) C-D

135

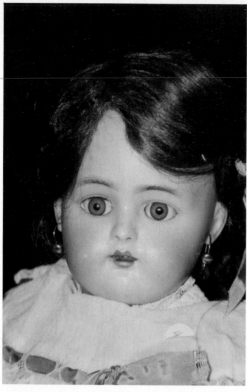

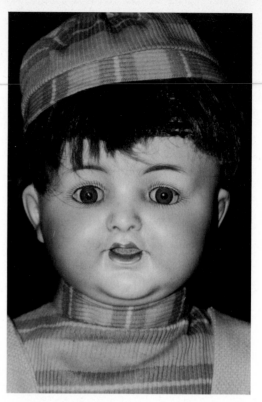

Kammer and Rinehardt--16" Socket head on composition body with full joints. Open mouth, pierced ears and sleep eyes. Marks: Simon Halbig/K ✡ R. (Courtesy Kimport Dolls) C-D

Kammer and Rinehardt--23" Socket head on composition toddler body. Sleep eyes. Open mouth. Marks: K ✡ R/Simon and Halbig. (Courtesy Helen Draves) E-G

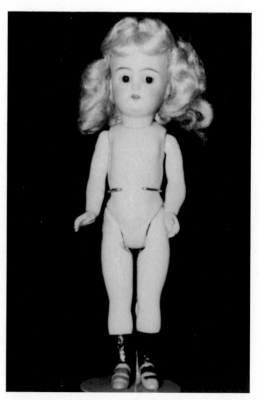

Kammer and Rinehardt--5" Socket head on 5 piece composition/maché body. Open/closed mouth. Sleep eyes. Molded on shoes and socks. Marks: K ✡ R. (Courtesy Helen Draves) A-B

Kammer and Rinehardt--10" Solid composition body with painted on two strap shoes and black hose. Set brown eyes. Pierced ears and open mouth. Marks: S&H/K ✡ R. (Courtesy Kimport Dolls) C-D

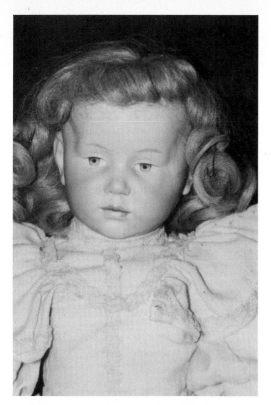

Kammer and Rinehardt--20" Marie. Socket head
on fully jointed composition body. Painted blue
eyes. Closed pouty mouth. Marks: K ✡ R/101.
(Courtesy Jane Alton) S-T

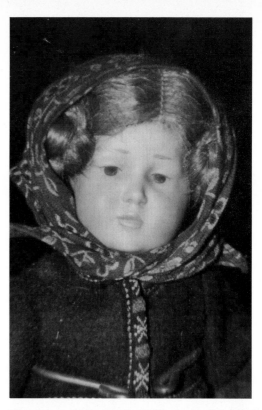

Kammer and Rinehardt--6" Marie. Socket head
on 5 piece composition/maché body. Painted
brown eyes. Closed pouty mouth. Original
clothes. Marks: K ✡ R/101. (Courtesy Jane
Alton) K-M

Kammer and Rinehardt--6" Peter. Socket head
on composition/maché 5 piece body. Painted
blue eyes. Closed pouty mouth. Marks: K
✡ R/101. Original Clothes. (Courtesy Jane
Alton) K-M

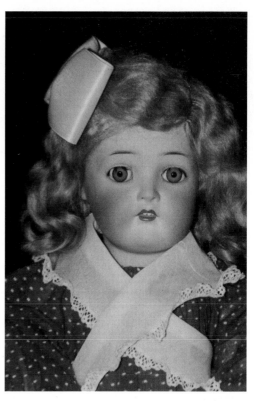

Kammer and Rinehardt--23" Socket head on
"flapper" type composition body. Knee joints
high on legs to allow for shorter dress lengths.
Sleep eyes/lashes. Open mouth. Marks:
K ✡ R/Simon Halbig/403. (Courtesy Julia
Rogers) E-F

137

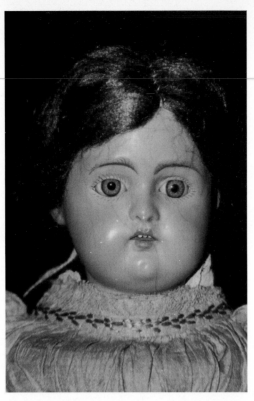

Kammer and Rinehardt--14½" Celluloid head on
fully jointed composition body. Blue sleep eyes.
Open mouth. Ca. 1912. Marks: K ✡ R/406/39.
$135.00. (Courtesy Kimport Dolls) B-C

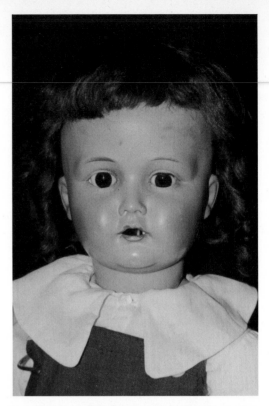

Kammer and Rinehardt--28" Celluloid Socket
head on beautiful toddler body. Rubber hands.
Open mouth (teeth missing). Sleep eyes. Marks
K ✡ R/717. This is the celluloid version of the
117. (Courtesy Kimport Dolls) F-H

Kammer and Rinehardt--19" Celluloid head on
fully jointed composition body. Set blue
eyes/lashes. Open mouth. Marks: K ✡ R/50-
717/Germany. A version of the 117 mold.
(Courtesy Julia Rogers) F-H

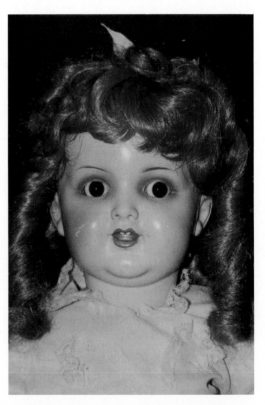

Kammer and Rinehardt--19" Celluloid head on 5
piece composition body. Flirty eyes. Open
mouth. Marks: K ✡ R/828/7/Germany/43/46.
(Courtesy Kimport Dolls) D-E

KESTNER

Johannes Daniel Kestner was the founder of the Waltershausen doll industry by making doll bodies by lathe in 1804 after first making button and slates of pápier maché on these same lathes.

The Kestner company was also one of the few German companies that made entire dolls. The very early Kestners were on kid or muslin bodies with heads of mache and had wooden limbs. In 1860 they had purchased a porcelain factory in Ohrdruf, Thur and began making their own china and bisque heads. Kestner worked also in wax, celluloid, cardboard and leather.

The majority of Kestner dolls have excellent quality bisque and at some point in time, they became very "Frenchy" looking in relation to the heavy feathered eyebrows but the heads almost always kept the heavier jaw area look and the German double chin.

It was in 1895 when Kestner began using his famous trademark of the crown and streamers that he registered in Germany and U.S. in 1896. German magazines and press stories began about the Kestner company being the "King" and soon this huge operating doll manufacturer was referred to as "King Kestner".

Most Kestner dolls are marked with a letter and a number, for example B-6, 0-18, G-11, etc., and some carry a mould number along with these. At times the J.D.K. is incised also. Kestner's most often found heads are mould number 154 and 171.

Sample marks: Made in Germany F½, 10½   B Made in 6 Germany   J.D.K. 167

The following are some of Kestner's mould numbers: 117, 127, 129, 137, 141, 142, 143, 146, 148, 150, 151, 152, 154, 155, 156, 158, 160, 161, 162, 164, 166, 167, 168, 169, 171, 172, 174, 180, 182, 186, 187, 189, 190, 195, 196, 200 (celluloid), 102, (celluloid), 211, 214, 215, 216, 217, 220, 221, 226, 234, 235, 237, 241, 243, 245, 247, 249, 257, 260, 261, 262, 264, 272, 319, 518, 639, 920, 1040, 1070, 1080, 1914.

Sample Marks	Made in F½ Germany 10½	B Made in 6 Germany	J.D.K. 167

Kestner--15" Oriental socket head on composition/wood body. Concave top to head with 3 holes. Full painted closed mouth with upper lip painted lines extended. Marks: 220. Ears pierced into lobes. (Courtesy Helen Draves) K-L

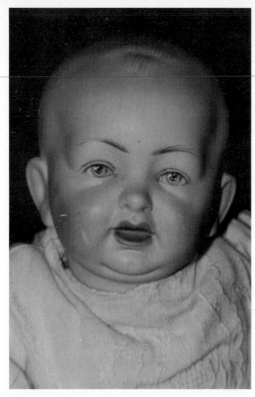

Kestner--11" Socket head on 5 piece bent leg baby body. Full open/closed mouth. Intaglio painted eyes. Marks: 142/J.D.K. (Courtesy Helen Draves) H-I

Kestner--20½" Shoulder head on kid body with bisque forearms. Sleep eyes, open mouth, Marks: 8/148/Made in Germany. (Courtesy Kathy Walter) D-E

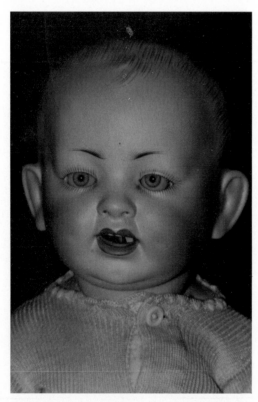

Kestner--15" Socket head on 5 piece bent leg baby body. Open mouth with two upper teeth. Grey sleep eyes. Marks: 151/7. (Courtesy Helen Draves) E-F

Kestner--9" Twins. All original. Socket heads. Bent leg babies. Open mouths. Sleep eyes. Marks: Made in Germany/152. (Courtesy Jane Alton) B-C

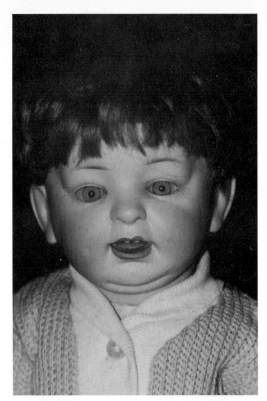

Kestner--16" Socket head on 5 piece composition bent leg baby body. Open mouth with four upper teeth. Blue sleep eyes. Marks: 152/LW and Co. in Square./7. (Courtesy Jane Alton) D-E

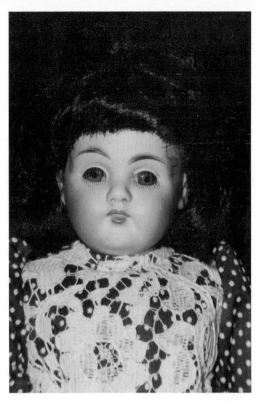

Kestner--This and the following two photos point out the variances used by the same maker on the same mould. This doll is 12½" tall shoulder head on kid body. Marks: Dep 154.1 and she has "fly a way" eyebrows, open mouth with set in teeth and painted lashes below the eyes only. (Courtesy Kathy Walter) D-E

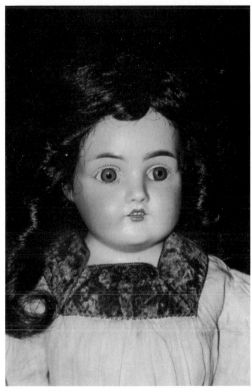

Kestner--This second photo is marked: 5 3/4 154 Dep. and is 17" tall shoulder head on kid body with bisque forearms. She has molded in teeth, lashes above and below the eyes and very heavy brows. (Courtesy Kathy Walter) D-E

Kestner--This third photo is marked Dep 154 13 and is 26" tall with a kid body. She also has painted lashes below the eyes only but more "standard" painted eyebrows and set in teeth. (Courtesy Kathy Walter) D-E

Kestner--14½" Googly. Socket head on fully jointed composition/wood body. Open/closed "watermelon" smile mouth. Marks: 165. (Courtesy Kimport Dolls) Z-+

Kestner--13½" Socket head on fully jointed composition/wood body. Sleep eyes. Open mouth. Pull string talker, says Mama and Papa. Marks: A made in 5/Germany/167. Original clothes, except belt ribbon. (Courtesy Kimport Dolls) C-D

Kestner--12½" Ball head (bald) on kid/cloth "fashion" type body. Closed mouth. Set eyes. Pierced ears. Marks: 172. This is a known Kestner number. (Courtesy Kathy Walter) E-F

Kestner--18" Socket head. Fully jointed composition body. Open mouth. Sleep eyes. Marks: J.D.K. 192. The mould number 192 heads were also made for Juneau and are on a Jumeau marked bodies. Ca. 1890. H-I

Kestner--23" Shoulder plate head with open mouth and fur inset eyebrows. Painted lashes below eyes only. Marks: 11 Dep 195. (Courtesy Helen Draves) D-E

Kestner--11" Pink stuffed gause body/muslin legs/¼ arms. Compo. lower arms/red outlined fingers. Open mouth/two lower teeth. Blue glass sleep eyes. Painted hair. Composition head. "Natural Baby" made by Kestner in 1912. Marks: 211-0/Germany. Second one marked: Germany/J.D.K./211. $100.00. (Courtesy Raiden)

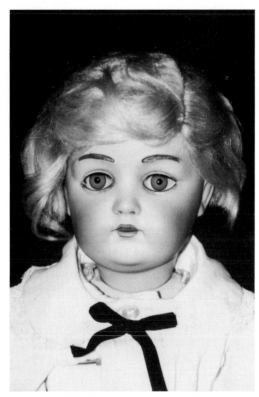

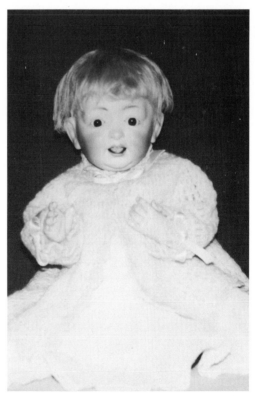

Kestner--21" Socket head. Fully jointed composition body. Fur inset eyebrows. Open mouth. Marks: E Made in 9/Germany/JDK/215. (Courtesy Jay Minter) D-E

Kestner--14" Socket head on 5 piece bent leg baby body. Open mouth. Marks: G Made in 11/Germany J.D.K. 220 (or 226). (Courtesy Mary Partridge) F-G

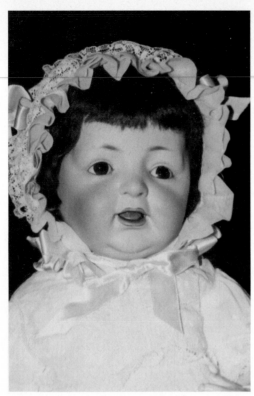

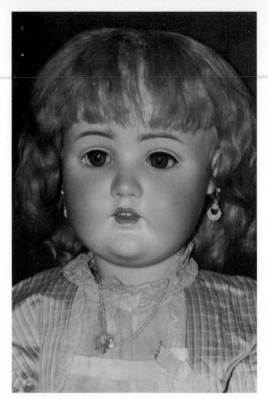

Kestner--18" Socket head on 5 piece composition bent baby leg body. Open mouth with molded tongue. Set brown eyes. Marks: J.D.K./236. (Courtesy Kimport Dolls) F-G

Kestner--38" Socket head on fully jointed composition/wood body. Sleep eyes/lashes. Open mouth and Pierced ears. Marks: C.T.C./Catterfelder/Puppenfabrik/264/8. Made by Kestner for Carl Trautman of Catterfelder. (Courtesy Helen Draves) I-J

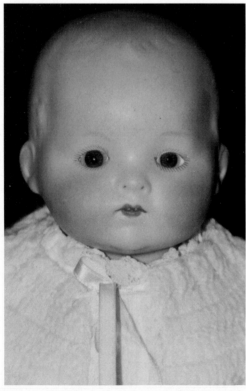

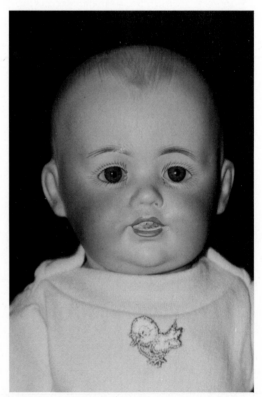

144

Kestner--15" Flanged neck on cloth body with composition arms. Inset glass eyes. Open/closed mouth with two painted upper teeth. Marks: Germany/Century Doll. Made by Kestner for Century Doll Co. (Courtesy Grace Ochsner) D-E

Kestner--13" Socket head on 5 piece bent leg baby body. Dimples. Open mouth/2 upper teeth. Brush stroke hair. Marks: J.D.K./Made in Germany. (Courtesy Helen Draves) C-D

18" Shoulder head on kid body with bisque
forearms. Marks: Horseshoe/backward EK/
HCH 4 H. Made by Heinrich Handwerck.
(Courtesy Kathy Walter)

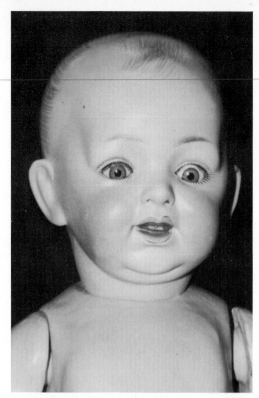

Kestner--15" Socket head on 5 piece composition bent leg baby body. Sleep eyes. Open mouth with 2 painted teeth. Marks: J.D.K./12/Made In Germany. (Courtesy Kimport Dolls) E-F

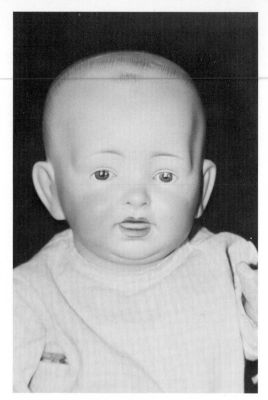

Kestner--12" Socket head on 5 piece bent leg baby body. Brown sleep eyes. Open/closed mouth. Marks: J.D.K./Germany. (Courtesy Kimport Dolls) G-H

Kestner--20½" Bisque swivel head on shoulder plate. Kid body with bisque forearms. Closed mouth. Set brown eyes. Marks: 10, on neck. Possible Kestner. (Courtesy Kathy Walter) J-K

Kestner--14" Turned shoulder head. Closed mouth. Set eyes. Marks: Scroll F-5/J.D.K. (Courtesy Helen Draves) F-G

Kestner--13" Socket head on fully jointed composition body. Open mouth with two teeth. Set eyes. Marks: B Made in 6/Germany. (Courtesy Kathy Walter) D-E

Kestner--16" Turned shoulder head. Closed mouth. Cloth body with bisque forearms. Light brown decal type eyebrows. Marks: B Germany 7/J.D.K. Eyes appear to have been set or replaced. F-G

Kestner--17" Shoulder head on kid body with bisque forearms. Sleep eyes, open mouth and unpierced ears. Marks: B Germany 6. (Courtesy Kathy Walter) F-G

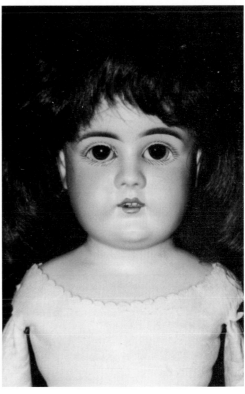

Kestner--18½" Shoulder head on kid body with bisque forearms. Sleep eyes. Open mouth with molded teeth. Marks: 7½/B Germany. (Courtesy Kimport Dolls) B-C

147

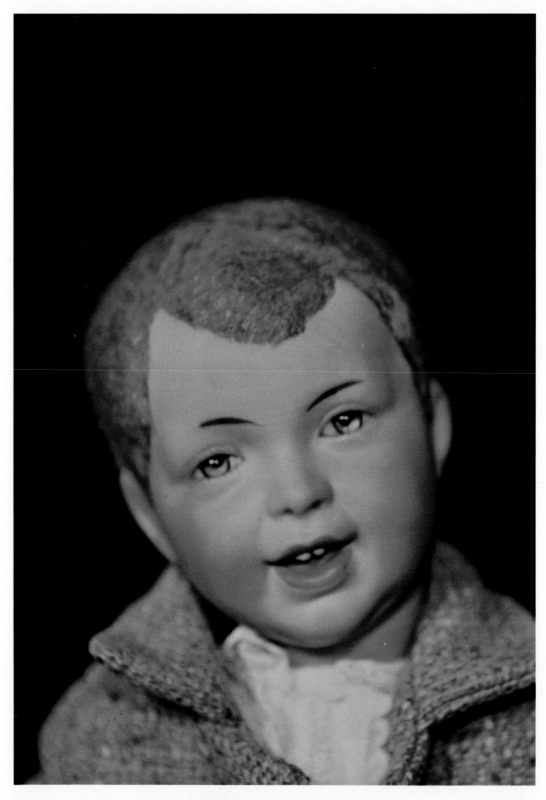

14½" Socket head. Open/closed mouth with 2
teeth. Flocked hair (original). Blue glass eyes.
Marks(S.F.B.J./235. (Courtesy Jeanne Gregg)

7½" Bonn doll of all bisque.See All Bisque
Section for full description. (Courtesy Kathy
Walter)

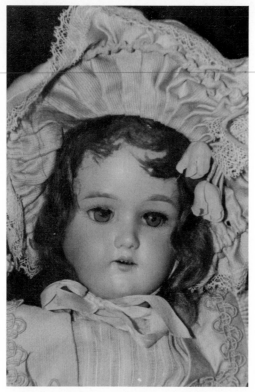

Kestner--17" Socket head on "stick" leg fully jointed composition body. Straight wrists. Sleep eyes/lashes. Open mouth. Original. Marks: C/1. (Courtesy Kimport Dolls) B-C

Kestner--Shows original clothes on Kestner. 17"

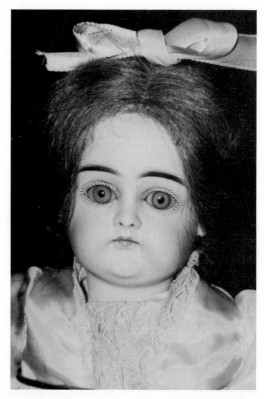

Kestner--12" Socket head on fully jointed composition body. Sleep eyes. Open mouth. Marks: C-5X. B-C

Kestner--15" Socket head. Closed mouth. Marks: D Made in 8/Germany. This doll is shown in Series 1, page 172. We re-shot her so that you can see the detail around the eyes. (Courtesy Jay Minter) J-K

KLEY & HAHN

Kley & Hahn operated from a porcelain factory in Ohrdruf (Germany). This company operated from 1895 to 1929.

Some of the Kley and Hahn characters are extremely fine dolls and very difficult to locate to add to a collection. These are the children with closed, open/closed mouth and painted eyes. Sample marks:

K & H   K&H
             WALKURE

The following are some of their mould numbers: 50, 52, 76, 130, 132, 133, 138, 142, 143, 150, 158, 160, 162, 176, 169, 176, 220, 250, 266, 282, 350, 520, 523, 525, 526, 549, 680, 1600, 2200 Walkure.

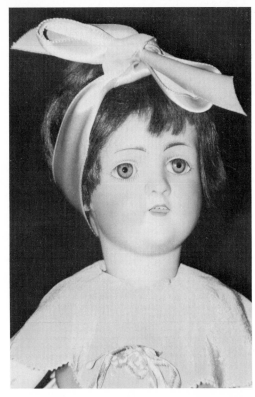

Kley and Hahn--14" Socket head on fully jointed composition/wood "flapper" body with knee jointed high on legs so the doll can wear shorter dress styles. Open mouth/teeth. Sleep eyes/lashes. Marks: Walkure/Germany/o/ 39. Original clothes (Except hair ribbon). Original wig. (Courtesy Helen Faford) C-D

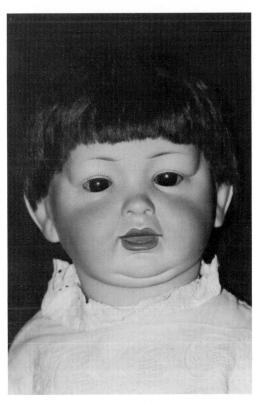

Kley and Hahn--20" Socket head on 5 piece bent leg baby body. Sleep eyes. Open/closed mouth. Open crown/wig. Marks: 130/11. (Courtesy Helen Draves) E-F

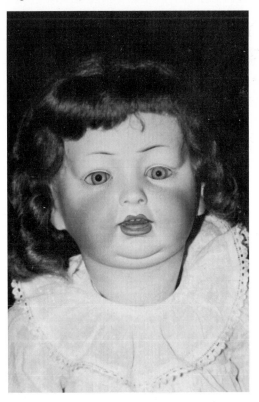

Kley and Hahn--18" Socket head on 5 piece composition bent leg baby body. Pale blue sleep eyes. Open mouth/upper teeth. Marks: Made in Germany/132. (Courtesy Kimport Dolls) E-F

151

26" Armand Marseille "My Dream Baby" made for Arranbee Doll Co. The 341 mold numbers have closed mouths and the 351 mold numbers have open mouths. Old toy courtesy Ralph Minter. (Courtesy Jay Minter)

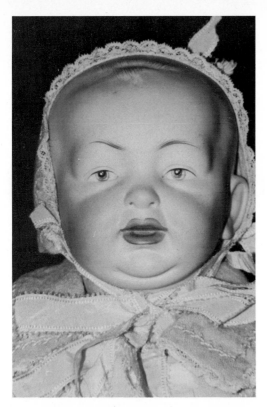

Kley and Hahn--15" Socket head on 5 piece bent leg baby body. Intaglio painted eyes. Open/closed mouth. Marks: 142. (Courtesy Kimport Dolls) G-H

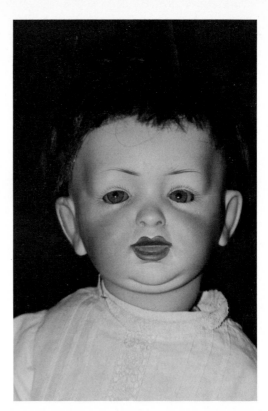

Kley and Hahn--13" Socket head on bent leg composition baby body. Sleep eyes. Open crown/wig. Open/closed mouth. Marks: 150/4. (Courtesy Helen Draves) F-G

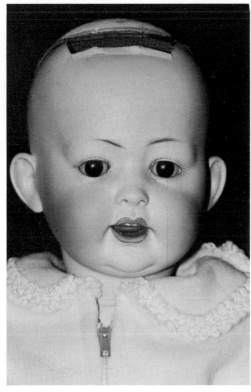

Kley and Hahn--20" Socket head on fully jointed composition toddler body. Cut out in head is for cryer mechanism. Open mouth with molded tongue and painted upper teeth. Sleep eyes. Very protruding ears. Marks: K&H /Germany/ 162-12. (Courtesy Jane Alton) F-G

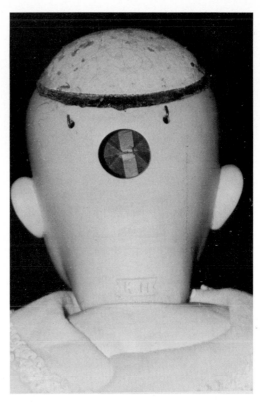

Kley and Hahn--Shows the cut outs for the cryer mechanism and how it is held in on the 20" toddler.

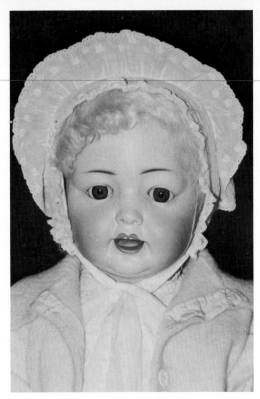

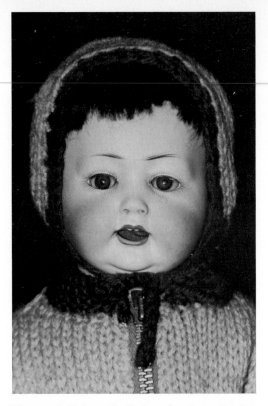

Kley and Hahn--24" Socket head on 5 piece composition bent leg baby body. Open mouth with molded tongue/2 painted upper teeth. Sleep eyes. Open crown/original wig. Marks: K & H/Germany/167-17. (Courtesy Grace Ochsner) I-J

Kley and Hahn--12" Socket head on 5 piece composition baby body. Open mouth with "tremble" tongue and 2 painted upper teeth. Sleep eyes. Open crown/wig. Marks: ⊂ K & H ⊃/Germany/176-4. (Courtesy Jane Alton) F-G

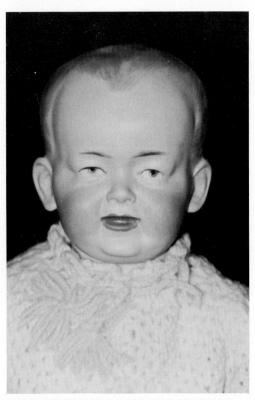

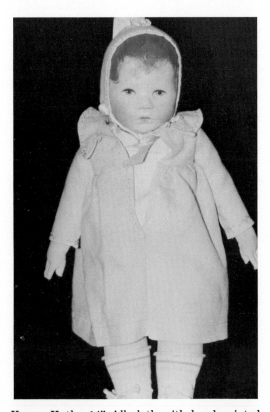

Kley and Hahn--13" Socket head on 5 piece bent leg composition baby body. Open/closed mouth with molded tongue. Intaglio eyes. Bald spot on top back of brush stroked hair. Marks: Germany/ ⊂ K & H ⊃ /525/4. (Courtesy Kimport Dolls) H-J

Kruse, Kathe--14" All cloth with hand painted (oil) features. Original clothes. $125.00. (Courtesy Grace Ochsner)

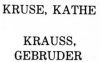

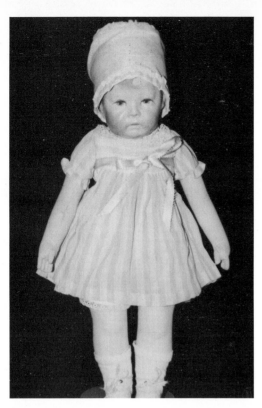

Kruse, Kathe--16" All cloth with pin jointed arms and legs. Oil painted features. All original. $135.00. (Courtesy Jay Minter)

Kruse, Kathe--22" Stuffed and molded felt. Painted features. Made by Kathe Kruse. Ca. 1940's. $85.00. (Courtesy Kimport Dolls)

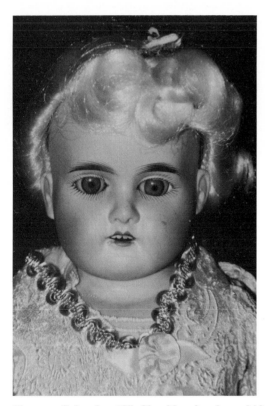

Krauss, Gebruder--20" Shoulder head on kid body with bisque forearms. Sleep eyes. Open mouth. Marks: 238/GBR 170 K/O. The Krauss Brothers were in business from 1863 to 1921 in Germany. (Courtesy Helen Draves) B-C

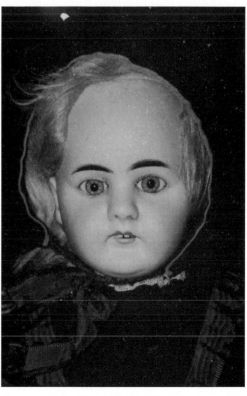

Krauss, Gebruder--23" Shoulder head on kid body with bisque forearms. Open mouth. Set eyes. Solid dome ball head. Marks: 61-285. (Courtesy Helen Draves) B-C

155

FASHION DOLLS

The terms "fashion dolls" is a term that should be restricted to those dolls used for transmitting fashions from shop to customer or from country to country. It actually limits "real" fashion dolls to before the 19th Century, for the coming of ladies fashion magazines (about 1775), the need for fashion dolls disappeared. But, who knows for sure!! There is an article in the September, 1944 Antiques magazine by Imogene Anderson and Ruth Cannon that is titled "Dolls as Purveyors of Fashion" where it is said that fashion dolls were being sent to America as late as 1826 (documented).

The main thing is that there are certain dolls that collectors refer to as "Fashion Dolls", "Lady Types", "Style Dolls", "Dressmaker Doll" and once a term or terms meet wide acceptance, it is most difficult to change.

The first fashion dolls were thought to have been life size and most likely made to represent the lady to whom they were being sent. Charles VI had a wardrobe sent to the Queen of England (refer to Series 1, page 1) and a century later a fantastic doll was ordered by Anne of Brittany and given to Queen Isabella of Spain. In the salon of an early French novelist stood two dressed dolls: "La Grande Pandora" in a stunning costume of the latest fashion and "La Petite Pandora" dressed negligee featuring stylish lingerie. Henry IV of France sent his fiance, Marie de Medici an entire group of dolls showing the latest fashions of Paris. The more famous Catherine de Medici was rumored to have had 16 of her fashion dolls dressed in mourning at the death of her husband, the King.

With the coming of the "Golden Age of Dolls" 1860 to 1890, dolls dressed in the mode of the times and smaller in form came upon the scene and we see no reason for regarding these dolls as having any other purpose than play toys. To try to reverse a term I am calling this section "Ladies of Fashion".

Ladies of Fashion--12" Shoulder head on kid body with bisque forearms. Painted eyes, closed mouth and caracul wig. Wooden box with 5 dress changes. Marks: Aux Infants Sages/Benon and Cie/Passage Jouffroy/Paris/Commison Exportation/1865, on trunk. M-N-Complete

Bru--11" Fashion. Bisque swivel head on bisque shoulder plate. Closed mouth. Large set eyes with black eye liner. Ears pierced into head. Original wig. Kid body with bisque lower arms. Marks: Circle-Dot. (Courtesy Kimport Dolls) Z-+

Ladies of Fashion--18" Shoulder head, closed mouth. Kid over wood fully articulated body, with the upper body maché covered with kid. Marks: E G/32. Made/and or repaired by E. Gesland. See photo of undressed doll in Body Section. (Courtesy Jay Minter) T-U

Ladies of Fashion--Shows full length view of 18" E.G. See full nude photo of her in Body Section. (Courtesy Jay Minter)

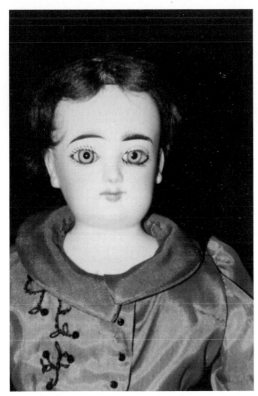

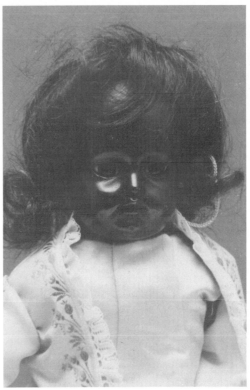

Ladies of Fashion--14" Shoulder head on all kid body with all kid limbs. Pierced ears, closed mouth and original wig. Marks: ⬭ Made by Widow Darnella Delfour 1877-1881. (Courtesy Kimport Dolls) I-K

Ladies of Fashion--12½" This doll is so black that we photographed 4 times with various lighting and this was best we could do. Bisque swivel head on bisque shoulder plate. Closed mouth. Pierced ears. Set eyes. Black all kid body. Marks: F 3 G, on head and F G on shoulder plate. (Courtesy Kimport Dolls) R-S

157

Ladies of Fashion--15" Shoulder head on all kid body. Painted eyes. Closed mouth. Unpierced ears. Marks: F.G. (Courtesy Kimport Dolls) J-K

Ladies of Fashion--13" Swivel shoulder head on shoulder plate. Closed mouth, pierced ears, inset eyes. Made by Jumeau. (Courtesy Jay Minter) I-K

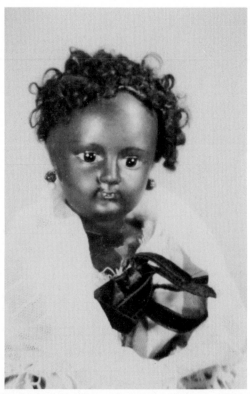

Ladies of Fashion--14" Negro fashion. Adult black kid body with wired kid fingers. Closed mouth, inset eyes and pierced ears. Original red/white stripped heavy cotton dress, white lace shawl and lambs wool wig. Marked Jumeau. (Courtesy Kimport Dolls) L-M

Ladies of Fashion--21" Jumeau. All kid body, set eyes and closed mouth. (Courtesy Helen Draves) K-M

Ladies of Fashion--19" Swivel shoulder head on shoulder plate. All kid with bisque forearms. Original, except jewelry. Head by Jumeau. Seal: (Courtesy Helen Draves) K-M

Ladies of Fashion--22" Swivel head on bisque shoulder plate. Kid body with bisque forearms. Marks: 6, on head and shoulder plate. Stamp on body: (Courtesy Kathy Walter) Q-R

Ladies of Fashion--17½" Swivel shoulder head on bisque shoulder plate. Full wood articulated body. See photo of body in Body Section. Ca. 1870's. Closed mouth, unpierced ears and inset vivid blue eyes. Marks: S-T

Ladies of Fashion--13" Swivel head on shoulder plate. Full articulated abody of kid and wood. Marks: 2., on head. Seal: Ca. 1865-73. K-L

159

Ladies of Fashion--22" Kid body with bisque
forearms. Swivel head on bisque shoulder plate.
Inset eyes. Closed mouth. Molded breasts.
Marks: None. (Courtesy Kimport Dolls) M-O

Ladies of Fashion--20" Bald (ball) shoulder head.
Blue lined eyes. Closed mouth. Kid body. Marks:
None. (Courtesy Helen Draves) I-K

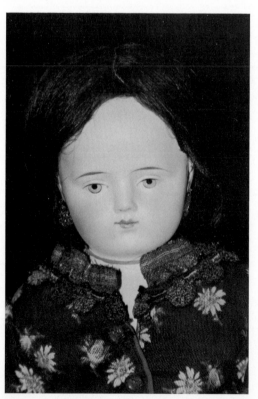

160

Ladies of Fashion--7" Ivory and composition.
Feet attached to music box. Original. Tag: Au
Nain Bleu/406 Rue St Honore/Paris. Made by
Edouard Chauviere Ca. 1890's. $125.00.
(Courtesy Marge Miesinger)

Ladies of Fashion--17" "Huret Type". Bald (ball)
head with wig. Painted blue eyes. Closed mouth.
Kid body with metal jointed shoulders. Shoulder
head. Pierced ears into head. (Courtesy Kimport
Dolls) J-K

LADIES OF FASHION DOLLS

One of the most desirable "Ladies of Fashion" is the Huret and thanks to a little book published in 1868 by M. Henri Nicolle entitled "Les Jouets" we have some interesting information on the Huret dolls.

Mlle. Calixto Huret made "luxury" dolls during her time. The first address listed in French Directoris is 2 Boulevard des Italiens. In February 1851 she was granted a fifteen year patent for a jointed doll body made of gutta-percha. In relation to these bodies M. Nicolle mentions the "I'Isle Adam factory" and says why the Huret dolls were expensive and their production limited to only 1200 to 1500 dolls a year was that the natives who shipped the gutta-percha from Ceylon added to its high cost by also including heavy rocks and dirt. As M. Nicolle says "This proves that as far as one may go one will always find people who know how to take advantage of business matters."

M. Nicolle also tells us that first astrakan (caricul) fur was used for the wigs but for the part one could only use the middle of the animal's back, so that this was discarded in favor of Tibetan goat hair.

He tells us that "The originator of the doll, being a woman, suggested that the child should receive her doll naked, so she could learn how to dress her herself, but since children are not always skillful enough to do a good job, their mothers claimed clothes that could be put on easily, and so a new industry sprang up, employing workers who specialized in doll clothes, for regular seamstresses often refuse to work on such small handwork. This new trade pays pretty well,

from 3 to 4 francs a day and is located in the quarters of Choiseul Street, where several doll manufacturers have made a fortune."

"If nothing else is going on, the young doll-lady receives her friends in the parlor, which is furnished according to her size. Tea is served in small dishes. But when night comes, her hair is taken care of, she puts on a long nightie and her cradle has all the finery of a lacy pillowcase, nor does it lack a quilted cover, with muslin curtains, lined in pink on the outside, which can be drawn so the little dolls may go to sleep right away. Everything is, of course, first class. Should the young lady travel, she will be provided with suitcase containing several compartments and a pocket-book."

Many of these Huret dolls had a fantastic wardrobe and some little trunks include such items as their own calling cards, tiny mirrors, jewelry and even a toothbrush.

Mlle. Huret advised that any doll who was "injured" be returned to her and the part repaired and in one case, according to M. Nicolle, a little girl sitting next to a stove wanted to warm her doll's feet and put her toes next to the open flame. The gutta-percha melted and the foot grew longer and longer. The doll was returned to Mlle. Huret and shortly there arrived a letter from the little girl asking for a progress report on the recovery of her "child".

From 1865 to 1870 Mlle. Huret is listed at 22 Boulevard Montmartre. Huret used metal hands on lady dolls with wood bodies and these are marked with the address 68 rue de la Boetie.

Ladies of Fashion--Shows mark on Huret: Brevet D Iny S.G.D.G./ Maison Huret/Boulevard Montmartre, 22/Paris/9 and seal: Head of man in center, around the outside: Exposition Universals Bebe. Inside seal: Napoleon..rest is unreadable.

Ladies of Fashion--14" Huret. Shoulder head with kid body and Gutta Percha arms and legs. Painted eyes. Closed mouth. Original clothes and hat. Also has hat box (wooden). Marks: See following picture. (Courtesy Kimport Dolls)

Z+

Lanternier, A.--15" French character Toto. Socket head on fully jointed composition/wood body. Open/closed mouth with 2 upper teeth. Marks: Fabrication/Française, in square/Toto Al and Cie/Limoges. (Courtesy Grace Ochsner) H-I

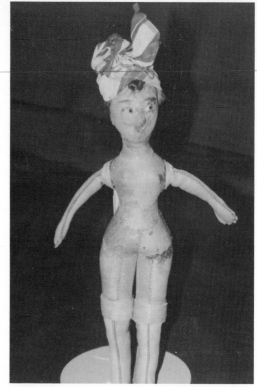

Leather Dolls--11" All leather doll. Inset brown glass eyes. Applied ears. Molded bust. Circular ribbing on arms and legs may be later repair areas. No marks; $75.00. (Courtesy Grace Ochsner)

LEATHER

Although kid was used for doll bodies well over one hundred years, it was not until Lucretia E. Stone, in Decatur, Ill. obtained a patent for a doll head that pressed leather reinforced (inside) with plaster was used. The following year (1866) Frank E. Darrow of Bristol, Conn. made dolls heads of rawhide. Few Darrow dolls remain as their manufacture was short lived as the factory rats liked them as well as the rawhide belts Darrows partner, John A. Way, decided they should also produce. They were "eaten" out of business and by 1877 were bankrupt.

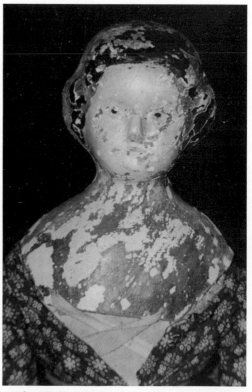

Leather Dolls--17" Rawhide doll with cloth body and leather arms and boots. Almost all the paint has flacked from the cold pressed rawhide. Eyes were painted. Made by Franklin Darrow. Ca. 1866. $875.00. (Courtesy Kimport Dolls)

LENCI

The following was an AP release from Turin, Italy in 1938. "Out of a war mother's loneliness has grown one of the world's foremost doll factories.

Santa Claus himself could be proud of a plant like Madame Lenci's here. Her name, by the way, is really not Lenci at all, although her dolls are known that way on six continents. She is Signora Elena Konig di Scavini, the latter being her husband's name. "Lenci" was just a pet name for her and folks called her first dolls "Lenci" and the name stuck.

A born artist, she developed a passion for dolls and designed beautiful clothes for them. Trips to Austria and Germany inspired her to try more varied costumes.

All this was for fun until her husband, an Italian aviator, went to war. While he was gone, her only child died. Sorrowing and lonely, she turned to the making of dolls, partly to keep busy and partly to support herself.

Soon she needed outside help, mostly women and girls who worked for her in their own homes. Today (1930's) her picturesque factory employs 360 workers and she maintains a sales exposition in the heart of Turin which is a first rate tourist attraction.

Orders now come to her for dolls for the world's great. Queen Elena of Italy buys them for gifts from the royal family. A doll was made to order last year for the Queen of England. Crown Prince Umberto has bought enough of her creations to open a small museum if he so desired.

One of Madame Lenci's most famous orders was from IL Duce (Mussolini) for four figures to be used as gifts to Japan. They were dressed in costumes distinctive of Rome, Sardinia, Lombardy and Piedmont. Mussolini had others made for his grandchildren.

Madame Lenci makes two kinds of dolls, one in ceramics and the other in cloth. The latter, when painted in flesh tones and provided with real hair, have an extremely natural appearance."

Lenci--14" Called "Northern" Lenci because she has pale blue painted eyes and blonde floss hair. Original. Lenci tag on front. $135.00. (Courtesy Jay Minter)

Lenci--12" Small Lenci child that is all original. Brown painted eyes to side with brown mohair wig. $125.00. (Courtesy Grace Ochsner)

163

Lenci--15" All original Lenci with large painted
brown eyes, and mohair wig. $135.00. (Courtesy
Helen Draves)

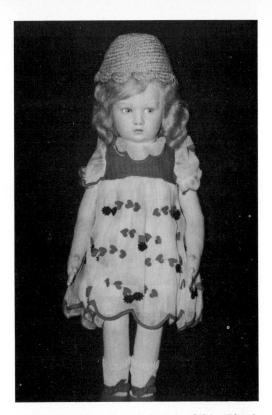

Lenci--18" Lenci Portrait child of 1935. All original. Painted brown eyes and brown mohair in twin braids. $165.00. (Courtesy Kimport Dolls)

Lenci--17" All original Lenci child. Blonde mohair and blue eyes to side. $155.00. (Courtesy Jay Minter)

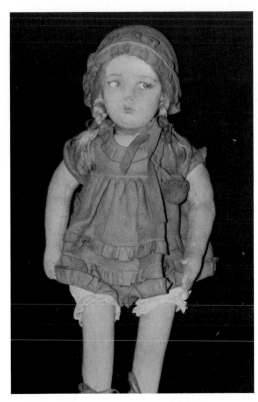

Lenci--21" All original Lenci child. Very pouty expression. Painted blue eyes to side and pale blonde mohair. $140.00. (Courtesy Helen Draves)

Lenci--27½" All felt including clothes. Original. Black floss hair. $135.00. (Courtesy Alice Capps)

165

Lenci--14" All original Lenci young girl. Painted
brown eyes. Mohair wig. $125.00. (Courtesy
Kimport Dolls)

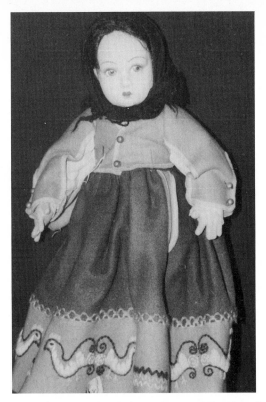

Lenci--14" Called Southern Lenci. All original with tags. Brown painted eyes and brown mohair. $125.00. (Courtesy Jay Minter)

Lenci--9" All original Lenci boy. Blue eyes to side. Open/closed mouth. $95.00. (Courtesy Jay Minter)

Lenci--20" All original Lenci child. Painted brown eyes to the front and tightly curled mohair. $140.00. (Courtesy Kimport Dolls)

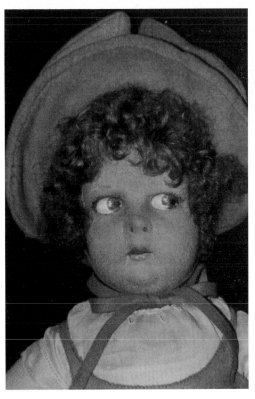

Lenci--17" All original Lenci with brown painted eyes and tightly curled mohair wig. $145.00. (Courtesy Helen Draves)

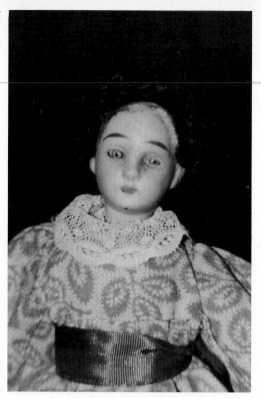

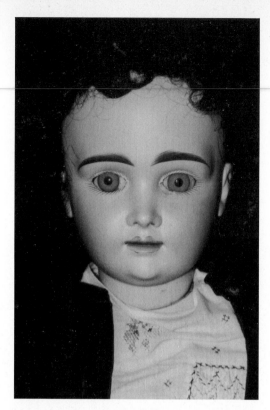

Manufacturer Unknown--7" Socket head on 5 piece composition/maché body. Closed mouth, inset eyes. Marks: None. (Courtesy Helen Draves) B-C

Manufacturer Unknown--23" Swivel shoulder head on bisque shoulder plate. Sleep eyes, open/closed mouth and unpierced ears. Marks: 14, on head. (Courtesy Helen Draves) L-M

168

Manufacturer Unknown--18" Socket head on fully jointed composition/wood body. Pierced ears. Closed mouth. Marks: 182/12. 182 is a known Kestner number. (Courtesy Jay Minter) L-M

Manufacturer Unknown--23" Socket head on marked Schmitt body, jointed but with straight wrists. Unlined sleep eyes. Full closed mouth, unpierced ears and very "square" ridge nose. (Author) N-O

Manufacturer Unknown--27" Socket head on
fully jointed composition/wood body. Body is
marked: Jumeau. Head is almost certain made
in Germany. Closed mouth, double chin with
dimple, pierced ears. Marks: Dep./12, on head.
(Courtesy Helen Draves) M-N

169

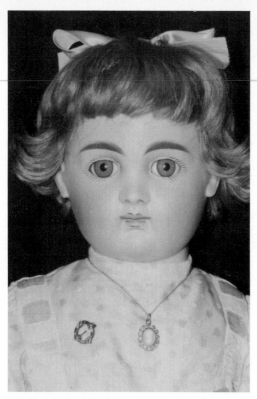

Manufacturer Unknown--24" Socket head on fully jointed composition body. Closed mouth, sleep eyes and unpierced ears. Marks: 15, on head. (Courtesy Helen Draves) L-M

Manufacturer Unknown--9" Socket ball (bald) head on fully jointed body. Closed mouth, glass eyes and unpierced ears. Marks: (|D) /x, on side of neck. (Courtesy Helen Draves) B-C

Manufacturer Unknown--29" Socket head on a Schmitt (French) jointed and marked body. Open mouth. Marks: 199-15/Germany. Both **Gebruder Knoch and Hienrich Handwerck** used this mold number. (Courtesy Grace Ochsner) K-L

Manufacturer Unknown--23" Socket head on composition/wood fully jointed body. Pierced ears, open/closed mouth and set eyes. Marks: Paris/8. (Courtesy Kimport Dolls) S-T

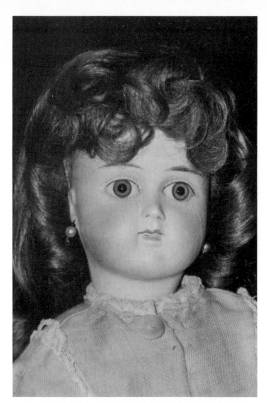

Manufacturer Unknown--22" Swivel head on bisque shoulder plate. Kid body with bisque forearms. Open crown/wig. Black lined eyes. Ears pierced into head. Open/closed mouth. Marks: 911 ✕ 3. (Courtesy Kimport Dolls) K-L

Manufacturer Unknown--22" Turned shoulder head. Double chin, full closed mouth, decal type eyebrows. No marks; (Courtesy Kathy Walter) F-G

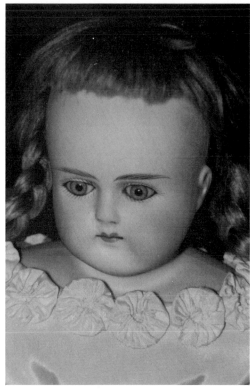

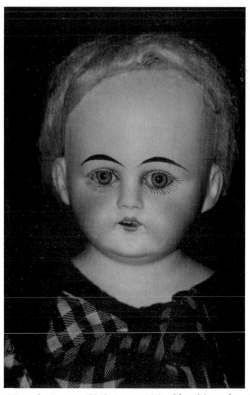

Manufacturer Unknown--14" Turned shoulder head on kid body with bisque forearms. Ball (bald) head, full closed mouth, decal type eyebrows and unpierced ears. (Courtesy Helen Draves) F-H

Manufacturer Unknown--18" Shoulder head slightly turned with ball (bald) head. Open mouth, set eyes, unpierced ears and single stroke eyebrows. Marks: Made in Germany/SP 2. (Courtesy Helen Draves) D-E

171

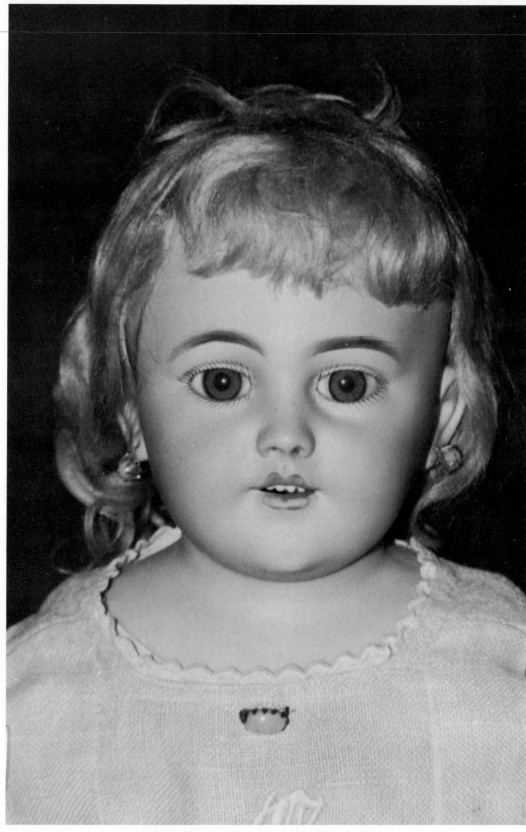

Manufacturer Unknown--26" Shoulder head on
kid body with bisque forearms. Open mouth, set
eyes and pierced ears. Marks: 11½. (Courtesy
Helen Draves) E-F

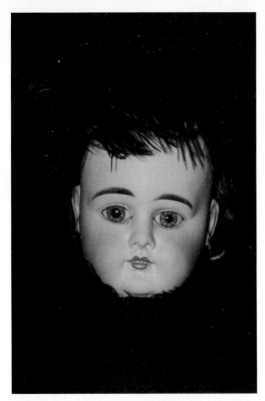

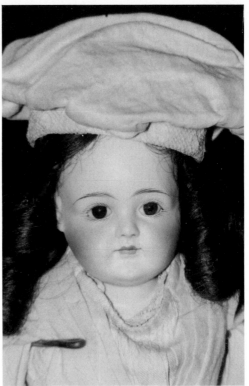

Manufacturer Unknown--22" Shoulder head on kid body with bisque forearms. Open mouth, pierced ears and unusual lined eyes. Marks: ⅁ (Courtesy Helen Draves) C-D

Manufacturer Unknown--15" Slightly turned shoulder head on kid body with bisque forearms. Full closed mouth, slight double chin and decal type eyebrows. Marks: 4½. (Courtesy Helen Draves) F-G

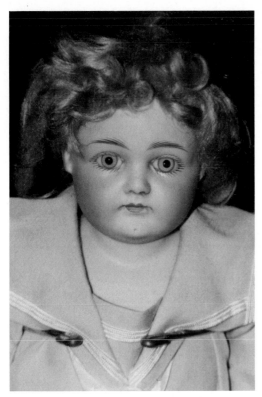

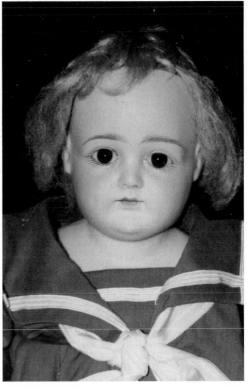

Manufacturer Unknown--18" Turned shoulder head with decal eyebrows. Full closed mouth, dimpled chin and slight double chin. Kid body with bisque forearms. Marks: 5, high on back of head. (Courtesy Helen Draves) F-G

Manufacturer Unknown--17" This doll is exactly like last doll shown except with dark eyes and a light cheek dimple. Marks: same: 5 high on head. (Courtesy Helen Draves) F-G

173

Manufacturer Unknown--14" Swivel shoulder head on bisque shoulder plate. Sleep black pupiless eyes and full closed mouth. Small unpierced ears and slight double chin. Marks: None. (Courtesy Helen Draves) G-H

Manufacturer Unknown--20" Shoulder head with set black pupiless eyes and full closed mouth. Decal type eyebrows, small unpierced ears and very slight double chin. Original wig and clothes. Marks: 8. (Courtesy Helen Draves) F-G

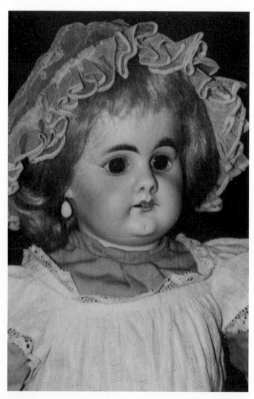

Manufacturer Unknown--18" Socket head on composition jointed body with straight wrists. Open mouth, pierced ears set eyes and very pugged nose. Marks: 300/9. (Courtesy Kathy Walter) D-E

Manufacturer Unknown--8" All composition and jointed only at the shoulders. Painted features and shoes/socks. Red mohair wig. Original. Tag: Unbreakable/Made In/U.S.A.. Other tag: Betty. $65.00. (Courtesy Kimport Dolls)

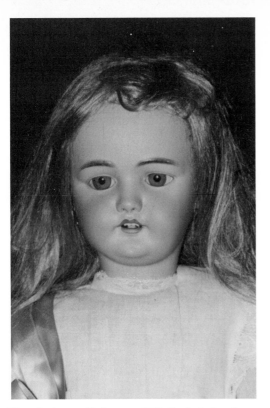

Manufacturer Unknown--33" Socket head on fully jointed composition body. Molded eyebrows, open mouth and pierced ears. Marks: Germany/15. (Courtesy Helen Draves) E-F

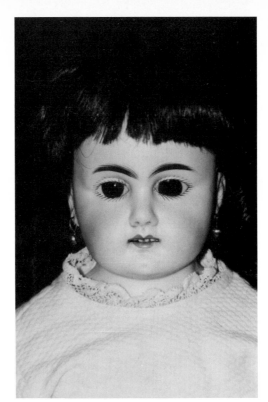

Manufacturer Unknown--19" Shoulder ball (Bald) head with kid body and bisque forearms. Open mouth, pierced ears and set eyes. Marks: 10-27, on head. Seal on body: Our Kiddy, in an oval. (Courtesy Kimport Dolls) C-D

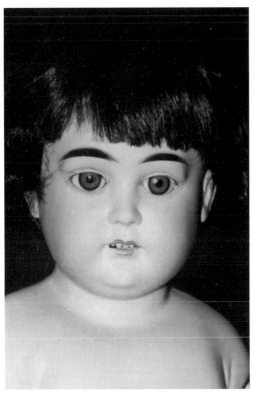

Manufacturer Unknown--21" Turned shoulder head. Set eyes, unpierced ears, open mouth with only middle of lower lip painted. Kid body with bisque forearms. Marks: 2015 ⚓ 6. (Courtesy Kimport Dolls) C-D

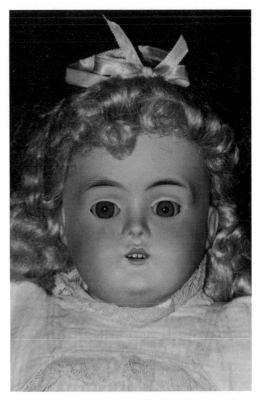

Manufacturer Unknown--23" Shoulder head on kid body with bisque forearms. Sleep eyes, open mouth and very unusual molding around eyes. Marks: △ (Courtesy Helen Draves) C-D

175

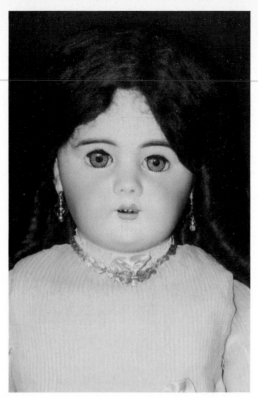

Manufacturer Unknown--31" Socket head on fully jointed composition body. Sleep eyes, open mouth and pierced ears. Marks: Dep. (Courtesy Helen Draves) D-E

Manufacturer Unknown--9" Socket head on fully jointed composition/maché body. Open mouth. Marks: ✕ 11/Made In Germany/193/14/0/ Dep. (Courtesy Helen Draves) B-C

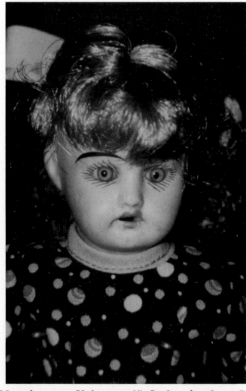

Manufacturer Unknown--9" Socket head on 5 piece composition body. Painted on shoes and socks. Open mouth. Marks: Germany/and what looks like M-Ola. (Courtesy Cecelia Eades) A-B

Manufacturer Unknown--7" Socket head on 5 piece maché body. Open mouth. Original. Marks: M 14/0. (Courtesy Helen Draves) A-B

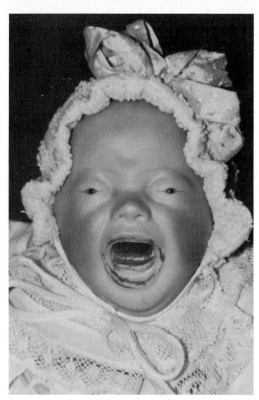

Manufacturer Unknown--12" Bisque head with tiny inset blue glass eyes. Open/closed mouth. Cloth body with celluloid hands. Marks: 255/ *ℱ* /O1C. (Courtesy Helen Draves) M-O

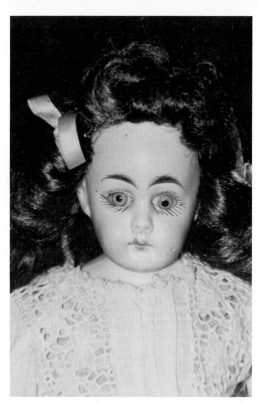

Manufacturer Unknown--13" Ball (bald) head with one hole. Shoulder head on kid body with bisque forearms. Closed mouth. Marks: 9, on head. (Courtesy Helen Draves) B-C

Manufacturer Unknown--7" Socket head on 5 piece composition body. Open mouth. Marks: 3. (Courtesy Jay Minter) A-B

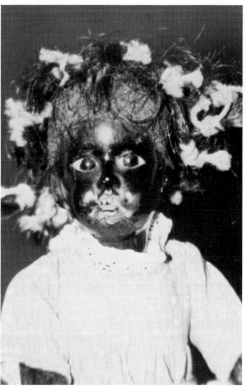

Manufacturer Unknown--7" Black bisque head on 5 piece maché body. Set glass eyes, open mouth and original wig and clothes. Marks: None. (Courtesy Kimport Dolls) B-C

177

Manufacturer Unknown--8" Socket head on maché 5 piece body. Painted on shoes and socks. Open mouth. Marks: None. (Courtesy Kimport Dolls) B-C

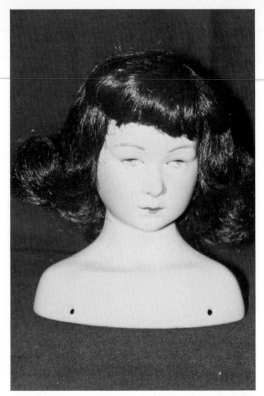

Manufacturer Unknown--4" tall head. Ball (bald) head with painted blue/green eyes. Closed mouth. Marks: F.3. $100.00. (Courtesy Kimport Dolls)

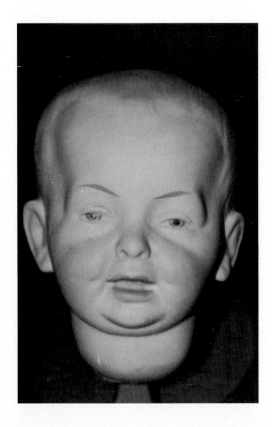

178   Manufacturer Unknown--12" Circumference. Open/closed mouth and painted blue eyes. Brush stroke brown hair. Marks: F 8/0. $65.00. (Courtesy Helen Draves)

Manufacturer Unknown--15" Socket head on fully jointed composition body. Closed mouth and inset glass eyes. Marks: None. (Courtesy Grace Ochsner) K-L

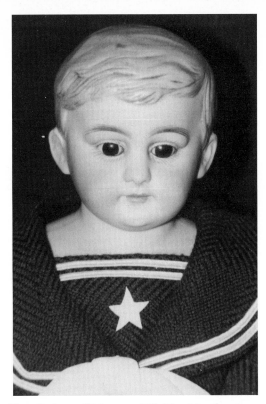

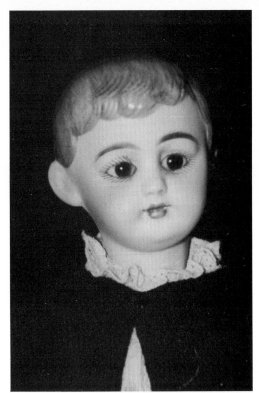

Manufacturer Unknown--16" Shoulder head on kid body with muslin legs and bisque forearms. Inset glass eyes, closed mouth and molded very light brown hair. This doll is often referred to as both Tommy Tucker and American Schoolboy. (Courtesy Helen Draves) G-H

Manufacturer Unknown--9½" Socket head on fully jointed composition body. Inset brown eyes, closed mouth and molded dark blonde hair. Marks: 1, on head. (Courtesy Kimport Dolls) F-G

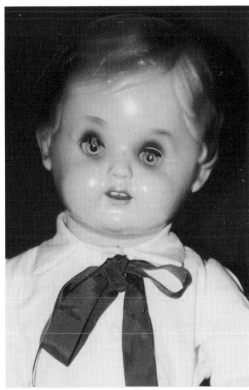

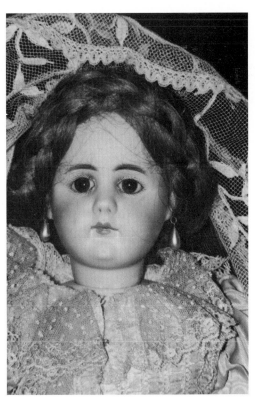

Manufacturer Unknown--16" 5 piece composition body. Head is a pottery type material and looks like "Can't Break Em" composition. Molded hair and open mouth/2 teeth. The eyes are very pale blue/lashes. Marks: None. $85.00. (Courtesy Pat Raiden)

Manufacturer Unknown--17" All original Bride. Full closed mouth, pierced ears. Shoulder (swivel) head on bisque shoulder plate. Kid body with bisque forearms. Ca. 1880. Marks: GK/32.26. 26, on shoulder plate. (Courtesy Kimport Dolls) K-L

179

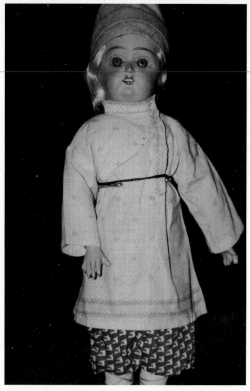

Manufacturer Unknown--14½" Russian bisque of 1930's using German mold. Socket head on fully jointed composition body. Original peasant costume. (Courtesy Kimport Dolls) A-B

Manufacturer Unknown-6" Socket head on 5 piece composition body. Set eyes, open mouth and original costume. Marks: Italy/4/0. (Courtesy Kimport Dolls) C-D

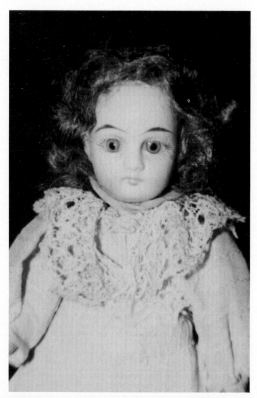

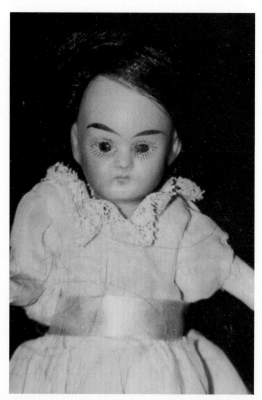

Manufacturer Unknown--5½" Swivel head on 5 piece maché body. Set eyes, closed mouth and one stroke eyebrows. Painted on shoes and socks. Marks: None. (Courtesy Kimport Dolls) C-D

Manufacturer Unknown--6" Socket head on 5 piece maché body. Set eyes, open mouth. Marks: 2/0. (Courtesy Helen Draves) B-C

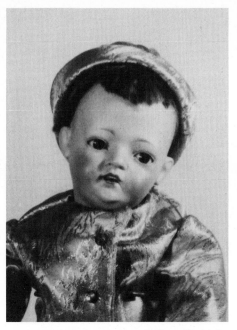

Manufacturer Unknown--24" Socket head. Open mouth/3 upper teeth. Pierced ears. Marks: 19 79 Dep. This may be a Heinrich Handwerck doll as they used mold number 79. (Courtesy Jessie Smith) E-F

Manufacturer Unknown--18" Character with unusual molding. Open/closed mouth on fully jointed composition/wood body. Marks: 191. This mold number was used by Simon and Halbig on dolls made for both Kammer and Rinehardt and C. M. Bergmann and also by Louis Amberg for a baby. (Courtesy R. H. Stevens)

Manufacturer Unknown--23" Bald (ball) head with set eyes, closed mouth and pierced ears. Shoulder head on kid body with bisque forearms. Has tiny waist. (Courtesy R.H. Stevens) F-H

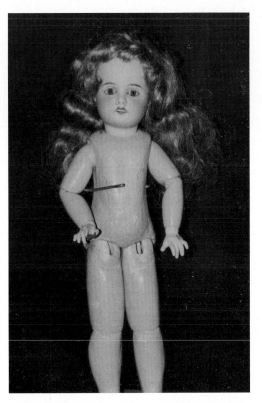

Manufacturer Unknown--14" French Oriental. Sleep eyes, open mouth on 5 piece composition body with painted on red shoes. Ticket on underskirt: Abraham and Strauss/D8404. This was a New York Dept. Store. (Courtesy Kimport Dolls) M-O

Manufacturer Unknown--15" Socket head on heavy French body that is maché and wood. Open mouth, pierced ears and set eyes. Ca. 1900. Marks: Mon Cheri/L G/Paris. (Courtesy Kimport Dolls) H-I

181

May Frères and Cie--25" Socket head on fully jointed composition/wood body. Closed mouth. Very deep paperweight set eyes. Marks: M. Ca. 1890. Called Bebe Mascotte. (Courtesy Grace Ochsner) P-Q

Mechanical--16" A Theroude mechanical walker of French Patent of 1840 Represents Opera singer Marqurita in the Jewel Song. Maché head with bamboo teeth, in open mouth. Original. See following photo. (Courtesy Kimport Dolls) Z-+

Mechanical--The three wheeled patent of 16" A. Theroude Walker/

Mechanical--10½" Autoperipatetikos. Patented July 15, 1861. See following photo for walking mechanism. China head. Hairdo with a snood and white ruff and cluster of grapes. (Courtesy Kimports) N-O

Mechanical--Shows the walking mechanism for the Autoperipatetikos. The doll was made with china, maché and untinted bisque heads. Patented by Enoch Rice Morrison in England and America.

Mechanical--11" George Hawkins walker. Rag composition head. Pewter hands with wood torso and pewter feet. Moving metal legs. Label on head: X.L.C.R./Doll Head/Pat. Sept. 8, 1868. Carriage is marked Goodwin patent date 1867-1868. (Courtesy Kimport Dolls) R-S

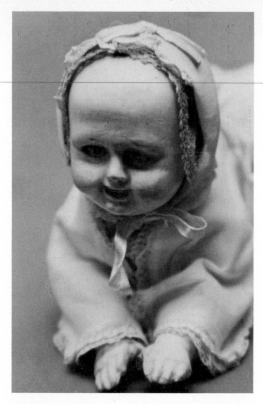

Mechanical--11" Robert J. Clay creeping baby advertised as "The Wonderful Creeping Baby" Patented March 1871. Head and limbs are wax over maché. Has clock like mechanism that is key wound. It crawls in a realistic manner. (Courtesy Kimport Dolls) L-M

Mechanical--15" Jumeau mechanical. Raises and lowers both arms and head. Hold Ivory covered book of Fairy Tales (in French) and waves fan with other hand. Key wind with music box in base. Fully marked. (Courtesy Kimport Dolls) X-Y

Mechanical--20" Mechanical standing on music box. She waves fan and moves longettes up to head. Unmarked. Open mouth. (Courtesy Helen Draves) M-O

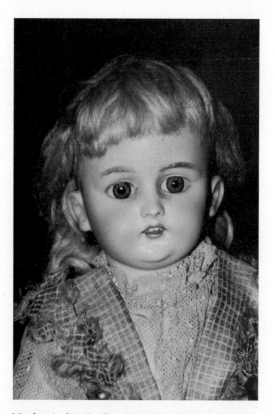

Mechanical--18" Ferdinand Imhof walker. 2 wheels under each foot/shoes non-removable. Keywind. Has German and French patents. Marks: S&C/Germany/5. Molded brows, open mouth. Made for Sannier and Caut on Imhof patent. Head most likely made by Simon and Halbig. (Courtesy Kimport Dolls) L-M

Mechanical--14" Jumeau key wind walker. Maché body, pierced ears, closed mouth and large set brown eyes. All original dress and pin. Marks: Tete Jumeau/4. (Courtesy Jeanne Gregg) Q-R

Mechanical--23" Mechanical Steiner (Jules Nochols). Socket head with composition upper and lower torso, also lower leg and all of arms. Twill covered sections of hips and upper legs. Crys, kicks and turns head as it cries. Keywind. Set eyes and two rows teeth. (Courtesy Helen Draves) P-Q

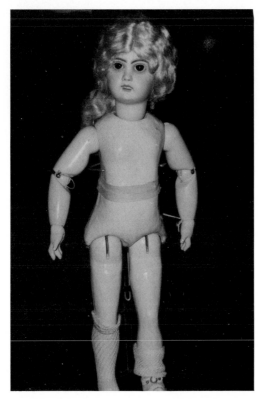

Mechanical--22" Jumeau that walks, cries with each step, turns her head and throws a kiss. Pierced ears, sleep eyes and open mouth. Tete Jumeau on head and Jumeau on body. (Courtesy Kimport Dolls) K-L

Mechanical--12" Jester. Shoulder head with inset blue eyes. Closed mouth. Ivory handle that is a whistle. By moving Jester back and forth there is a "whipping" sound. Pierced ears. Shoulder marked F.G. (Courtesy Kimport) E-F

185

Mechanical--17½" Socket head. Mechanical windup walker with flirty eyes. Pierced ears. Open mouth. Marks: S & H/7½. (Courtesy Jeanne Gregg) M-N

Mechanical--12" and 7" bisque heads. Inset blue glass eyes/lashes. Small one has metal hands. Keywind. Doll walks and pulls cart. Marks: SFBJ/301/Paris. (Courtesy Kimport Dolls) S-T

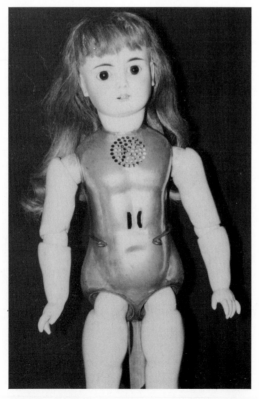

Mechanical--24" Edison Patent Doll. Patent dates: 1878-79. Composition/wood body limbs with all tin torso. Bisque head is marked: 224. Also used was the Simon and Halbig head number 719 with open mouth. (Courtesy Kimport) K-L

Mechanical--8" Clown with bisque head/hat. Wood arms and legs. Bellows in stomach. When pressed arms come together. Has wood paddle in hand. Original. (Courtesy Grace Ochsner) C-D

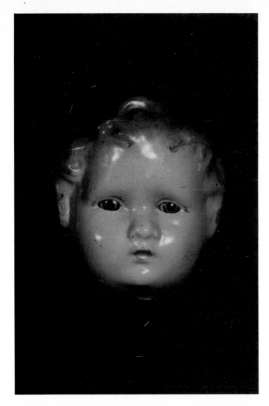

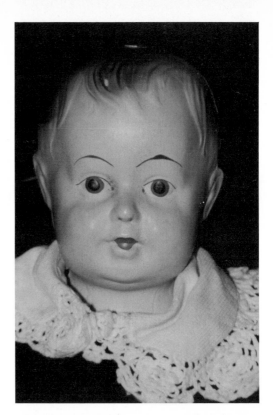

Metal--19" Metal shoulder head with cloth body and wire pinned arms and legs of composition. Sleep, flirty tin eyes. Molded hair with hole for ribbon. Marks: None. $125.00. (Courtesy Bessie Greeno)

Metal--16" Metal head with painted features. Molded hair. Closed mouth. Cloth body with composition arms. Marks: None. $87.50. (Courtesy Helen Draves)

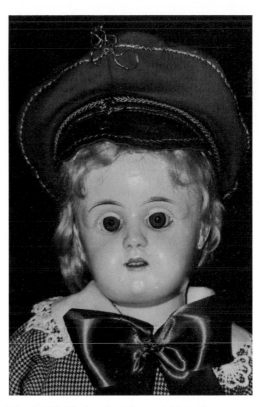

Metal--19" Brass head. Flange neck on cloth body with metal hands. Original. Marks: Unable to make our marks. $95.00. (Courtesy Helen Draves)

Metal--20" Tin head with inset blue glass eyes. Open mouth and crown. Original wig. Ears are applied after the head was put together. Fully jointed German composition/wood body. Marks: None. $87.50. (Courtesy Kimport)

187

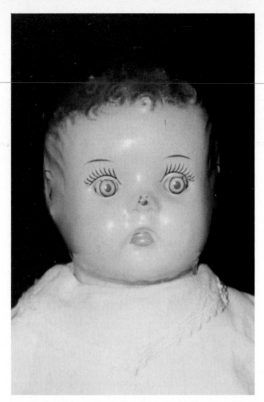

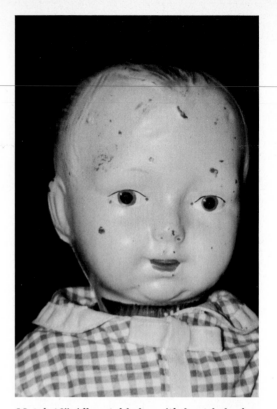

Metal--16" Tin head baby. Molded hair. Large sleep eyes. Ears are painted. Cloth body with composition limbs. Marks: None. $75.00. (Courtesy Kimport)

Metal--16" All metal baby with bent baby legs. Painted eyes. Closed mouth. All joints are spring strung. Marks: None. $110.00. (Courtesy Kimport)

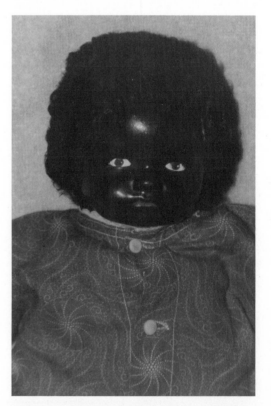

188

Metal--15" Metal baby. Cloth body with one piece head and shoulderplate. One sew hole front and back. Inset glass eyes. Molded yellow blonde hair. Marks: None. Has been repainted. $75.00. (Courtesy Bessie Greeno)

Metal--14" Metal head baby. Brown cloth body with metal lower legs. Composition hands. Sleep tin eyes. Replaced lamb's wool wig. Marks: None. $125.00. (Courtesy Bessie Greeno)

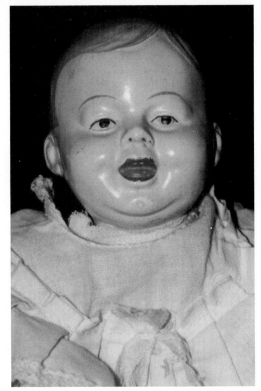

Metal--7" Heavy metal head with painted eyes, molded yellow hair and open/closed mouth with painted teeth. Lower arms are metal and upper cloth. Cloth covered squeeze box for body. No legs. $65.00. (Courtesy Kimport Dolls)

Moss, Leo--Leo Moss made his dolls during the late 1800's and the early 1900's. He was a Black man that lived in Macon, Georgia. He made his living as a handy man and by making the dolls. This extremely talented man would be commissioned by a childs parents to create a doll and would do so with the result that the doll bore a striking resemblance to the child. Mr. Moss made both black and white dolls.

The Moss dolls have heads that are individually molded of páper maché and the bodies were mainly purchased from a white toy supplier.

The dealer from whom Mr. Moss bought parts did not feel that there was a market for his dolls in the North and never purchased any from him but a few were exported to Europe.

During the very early 1900's Mr. Moss's wife left taking their baby with her. It is a rumor that he made a tear in the eyes of all his dolls thereafter.

He died in 1932 and was buried a pauper without a headstone.

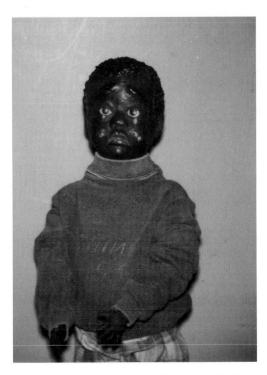

Moss, Leo--24" With painted eyes and three molded tears on the cheeks. Composition jointed body. (Courtesy Ralph Griffith Doll Museum)

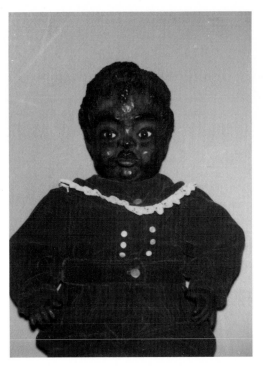

Moss, Leo--25" Toddler type baby. Glass eyes. Cloth body with composition arms and legs. (Courtesy Ralph Griffith Doll Museum)

Moss, Leo--Shows a large Moss baby with glass
eyes and closed mouth. The standing girl is 20"
tall and has an open mouth with painted teeth.
She also has glass eyes. L-+

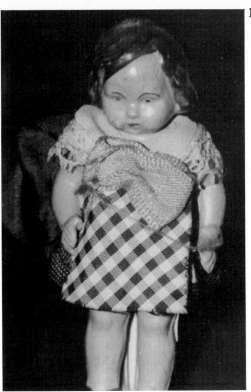

Painted Bisque--4" Painted bisque with one piece body and head. Painted features. All original. Painted on shoes and socks. $25.00. (Courtesy Marge Meisinger)

Painted Bisque--4" Painted bisque that is jointed at the shoulders only. Painted features and shoes. Side part molded hair. Pouty. Marks: None. $18.00. (Courtesy Helen Draves)

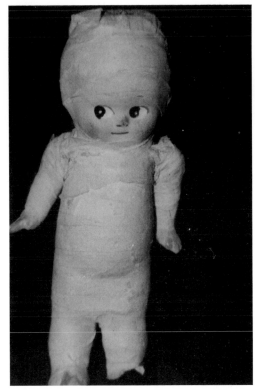

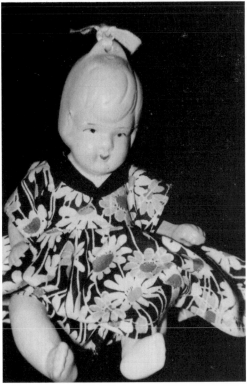

Painted Bisque--5" Painted bisque with jointed shoulders only. Painted on shoes. "Plaster" bandages were applied and these were used as a table favor for a benefit by the "Mothers of World War I". Marks: Germany. $18.00. (Courtesy Maxine Heitt)

Painted Bisque--5" Painted bisque with one piece body and head. Pin jointed arms and legs. Molded hole in hair for ribbon. Bend baby legs. Marks: None. $6.00. (Courtesy Helen Draves)

Painted Bisque--7" Painted bisque with one piece body and head. Molded on red tam to side of head. Painted features and shoes and socks. Marks: Made In/Occupied/Japan. $9.00. (Courtesy Maxine Heitt)

Painted Bisque--8" Painted bisque with painted features, shoes and socks and one piece body and head. Marks: Made In/Japan/S1095. $12.00. (Courtesy Maxine Heitt)

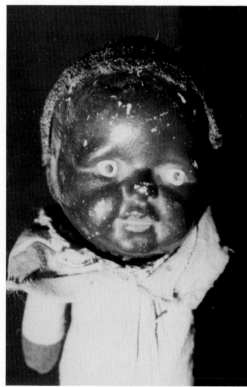

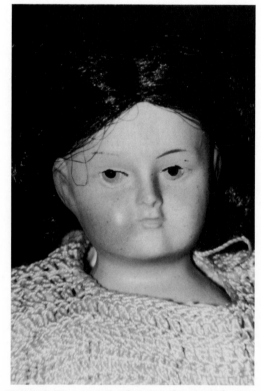

192

Painted Bisque--7½" Painted black bisque. Flange type neck. Old cloth body with darker cloth "handa". Painted features. Hair is rubber. Marks: 101 $35.00. (Courtesy Kimport)

Painted Bisque--11" Flat top head with two stringing holes. Painted bisque shoulder head. Cloth body with painted bisque forearms. Painted eyes and closed mouth. Marks: M & S/Paris. $95.00. (Courtesy Kimport)

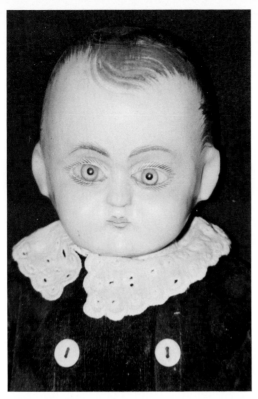

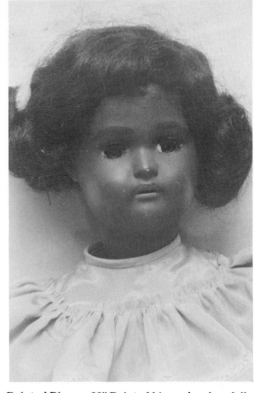

Painted Bisque--17" Painted bisque socket head on fully jointed composition body. Set pale blue eyes. Closed mouth. Brush stroke hair. Marks: None. $225.00. (Courtesy Jane Alton)

Painted Bisque--23" Painted bisque head on fully jointed composition body. Molded and painted eyebrows. Sleep eyes. Open mouth/4 teeth. Marks: Has the unidentified mark found on many black and brown dolls: 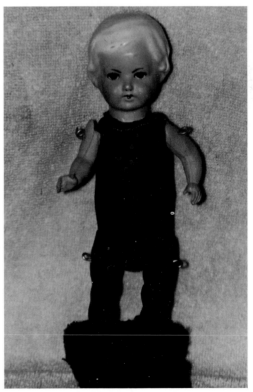... $145.00. (Courtesy Ruth Clarke)

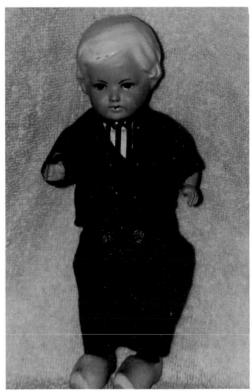

Painted Bisque--8½" Painted bisque head with blue decal eyes. White painted hair. Excelsoir stuffed body with wire pinned composition arms. Glued on wooden shoes. Plasterlike painted black legs. Marks: $85.00. (Courtesy Frances and Mary Jane Anicello)

Painted Bisque--Shows body, arms and legs of painted bisque.

193

Painted Bisque--11½" Googly boy novelty doll. Has molded pushed in face with impish smile. Has white plaster like body and painted bisque like arms and legs. Open crown. Flirty blue glass "googly" eyes. Staples on mohair wig and clothes. Marks: None. $110.00. (Courtesy Frances Anicello)

Pápier Maché--30" French maché of 1830. Inset pupiless eyes. Wig over painted hair. Cloth body with leather arms. Doll is stuffed with dried rose pedals and spices. Old beautiful clothing. Doll is reported to be from Queen Victoria's collection and a true fashion doll. $1,250.00. (Courtesy Kimport Dolls)

Pápier Maché--14" "'Lacquer Head" of the 1840's. Cloth body with wooden limbs. $695.00. (Courtesy Kimport Dolls)

Pápier Maché--23", 12" and 5" machés. All with wood limbs. Tall one has feathered hair and is dated between 1845 and 1860. Undressed one is dated same period. (Courtesy Helen Draves)

194

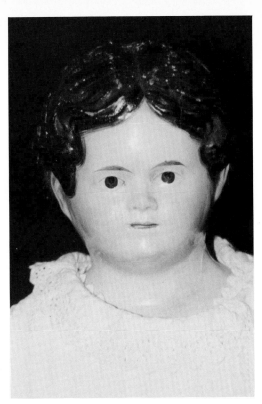

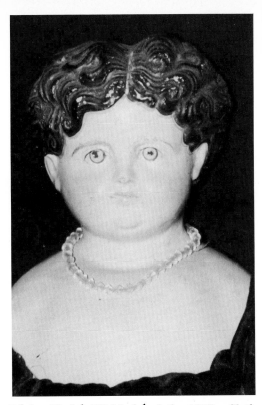

Pápier Maché--23" Maché of the 1850's. Brown painted eyes. Cloth body with leather arms. (Courtesy Helen Draves) G-H

Pápier Maché--23" Maché of the 1850's. Cloth body with leather limbs. (Courtesy Jane Alton) G-H

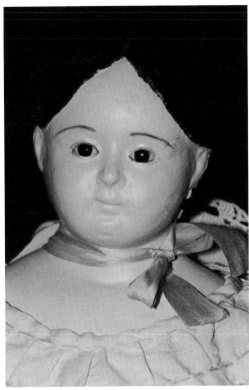

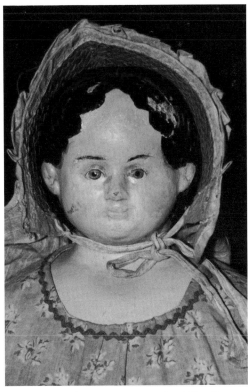

Pápier Maché--29" Greiner maché of 1858. Inset black glass eyes. Repainted. Original body. (Courtesy Helen Draves) F-G

Pápier Maché--26" Greiner of 1858. Stamp: Greiner's/Improved/Patent Heads/Pat. March 30th '58. (Courtesy Helen Draves) F-G

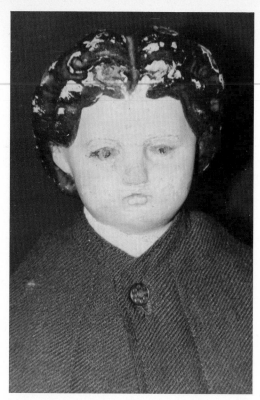

Pápier Maché--32" Black hair maché with blue painted eyes. Cloth body with leather arms. Can't make out stamp on body. (Courtesy Helen Draves) G-H

Pápier Maché--22" Maché with black hair and painted blue eyes. Cloth body with wooden limbs. Stamp on original body but unable to read. (Courtesy Helen Draves) F-G

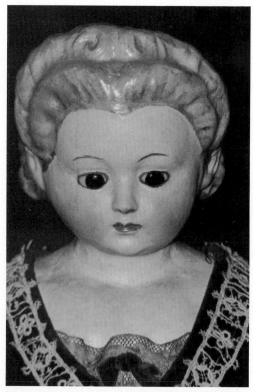

196

Pápier Maché--27" maché with molded band in hair. Glass inset eyes. Closed mouth. Cloth body with mache limbs. Repainted. (Courtesy Helen Draves) D-E

Pápier Maché--30" Blonde maché with blue eyes and very deep (long) shoulder plate. Cloth body with leather arms. (Courtesy Helen Draves) G-I

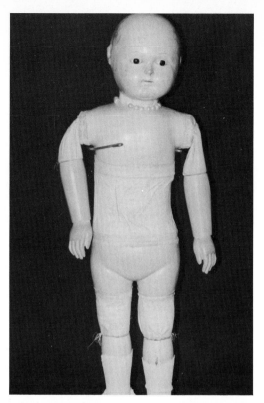

Pápier Maché--26" Maché of the Motschmann type. Body of wood and twill. Glass eyes and brush painted curls around base of head. (Courtesy Helen Draves) F-G

Pápier Maché--14½" Maché of 1880. Blonde molded hair with blue ribbon. Cloth body with composition limbs. (Courtesy Kimport Dolls) C-D

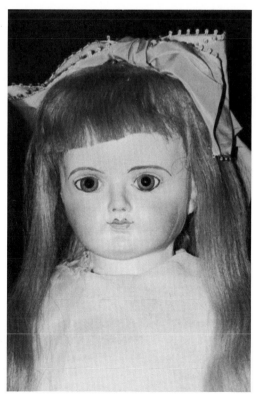

Pápier Maché--26" Maché head on cloth excelsior filled body with composition arms and legs. Large blue glass eyes with pink wash over eyes. Marks: J/JParis. (Author) D-E

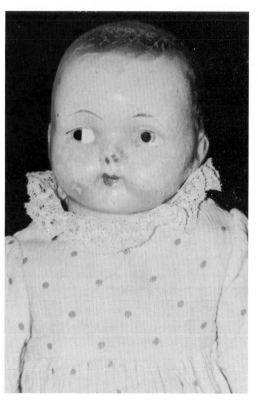

Pápier Maché--10" Maché head with cloth body and limbs. Excelsior filled. Pin jointed limbs. Painted blue eyes. Childhood doll of Frances Patterson Johnson. Marks: None. $65.00. (Courtesy Maxine Heitt)

197

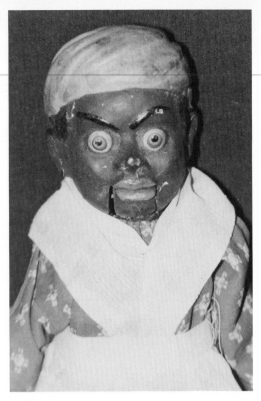

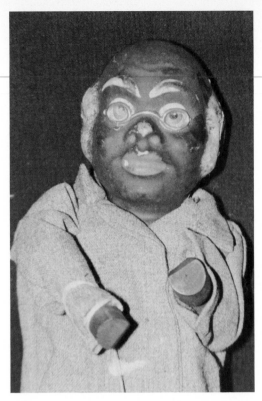

Pápier Maché--12" Maché puppet, Bellows in stomach area operate mouth. Inset glass eyes. $125.00. (Courtesy Helen Draves)

Pápier Maché--10" Maché with molded on glasses. Bellows in stomach area when pressed move wooden arms. $125.00. (Courtesy Helen Draves)

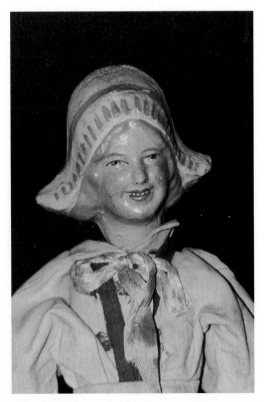

Pápier Maché--13" Puppet with maché head and wood body and limbs. $85.00. (Courtesy Helen Draves)

Pápier Maché--26" Maché head Santa Claus. Beautiful detail of painted features. (Courtesy Grace Ochsner) D-F

198

PARIAN

Parian was at first entirely white and was made to imitate the white marble which was found on the Isle of Paros in Greece and that is why it is called Parian (paros).

Parian was made at several potteries in Hanley, England. The Trent Works, which began manufacturing in 1859 made a cheaper grade of Parian (figures, vases, and busts) and they were not marked. The first parian was invented by William Taylor Copeland (England) in 1846, but the largest manufacturers of Parian, in England, was John Bevington at the Kensington Works during the latter part of the 19th Century and Turner and Wood at Stroke-upon-Trent (1850). The United States Pottery in Benninton, Vermont was the first Parian manufacturer in America (1847) and it is not known if they made doll heads.

Parian itself, is a special hard, clear paste, white and unglazed. The finest has a soft and very smooth feel and was an excellent medium to obtain detail. Choice Parian dolls are a work of art and have fine delicate features. It was easier to get detail into parian than china although some china molds were poured in parian, but detail was added to the molds and to the head after the parian had "set up".

Parian heads were also made in Europe from 1850 to 1880, although the majority of them were made in the 1870's and 1880's. Fine early heads were made in the Dresden potteries from 1850 to 1860. There were French parian heads and many of these have cameo perfect features.

In parian there was every imaginable thing applied to heads and shirt tops, from flowers, snoods, ruffles, feathers, plumes, ribbons, etc. Many have inset glass eyes. Most are blonde (golden) and only rarely do you find one with black hair. Parian dolls came with kid or cloth bodies and had kid or bisque limbs.

If parian dolls are marked, the marks are generally found on the inside of the shoulder plate.

Parian--9" Rare black hair parian. Brush marks at temples, molded in hair band and pierced ears. Cloth body with leather arms. $375.00. (Courtesy Kimport Dolls)

Parian--12" Parian with glazed black hairdo. Molded in ribbon and shirt top and collar. Braids around bun tied with a ribbon in back of hairdo. Marks: 8532 🍀 $795.00. (Courtesy Helen Draves)

199

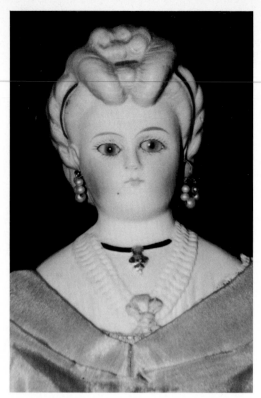

Parian--15" Parian with blonde hairdo and molded in blue ribbon. Pierced ears. Decorated shoulder with necklace and gold medallion. Inset glass eyes. Cloth body with parian limbs. $795.00. (Courtesy Kimport Dolls)

Parian--15" Parian with light brown molded hairdo. Inset glass eyes, pierced ears with full ears exposed. Cloth body with parian limbs. $675.00. (Courtesy Kimport Dolls)

Parian--18½" Dresden Parian. Light brown hair molded in short crispy curls. Elaborate molded on Dresden flowers. Cloth body with parian limbs. $895.00. (Courtesy Kimport Dolls)

Parian--17" Parian with pierced ears, blue band and rose luster bow. Lavender ruchiang on shoulder with molded pearl necklace. Cloth body with parian arms. $895.00. (Courtesy Kimport Dolls)

Parian--18½" Parian with elaborate curls and applied decoration both in hairdo and on shoulder. Pierced ears. $875.00. (Courtesy Kimport Dolls)

Parian--14" Parian of the "Dolly Madison" style. Molded in blue with gold trim ribbon. Glass inset eyes. $795.00. (Courtesy Helen Draves)

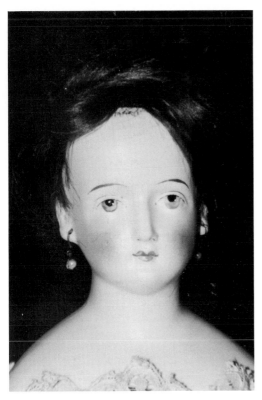

Parian--18" Bald parian with wig. Pierced ears and molded painted eyes. Cloth body with parian arms. $650.00. (Courtesy Kimport Dolls)

Parian--12" Parian with "Eugenie" braids, luster plumes and snood. Blue enamel eyes. $595.00. (Courtesy Kimport Dolls)

Parian--23" "Dagmar" parian with light brown hair. Molded in bow same color as hair. Molded on shirtwaist top (this one has been repaired). Cloth body with leather arms. $325.00. (Courtesy Kimport Dolls)

Parian--15½" Parian with rare inset Tiara of metal. Brown molded hair and molded scarf around shoulders. Pierced ears. Cloth body with parian arms. $495.00. (Courtesy Kimport)

Parian--26" "Dolly Madison" parian with molded blonde hair and molded in bright blue ribbon. Cloth body with parian arms. $650.00. (Courtesy Kimport Dolls)

Parian--23" Parian with pierced ears and rare hairdo with curls on forehead. Applied flowers and leaves with black ribbon and bows. $595.00. (Courtesy Kimport Dolls)

Parian--19" Parian with applied wreath of Dresden flowers, blue luster ribbon with tassel. Cloth body with parian limbs. $895.00. (Courtesy Kimport Dolls)

Parian--10½" High hair parian. Cloth body with parian limbs. $295.00. (Courtesy Kimport Dolls)

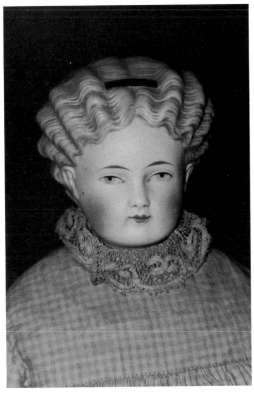

Parian--16" Parian with wrapped braids in back and blue band through hairdo. Full ears show. Cloth body with parian limbs. $695.00. (Courtesy Jean Anderson)

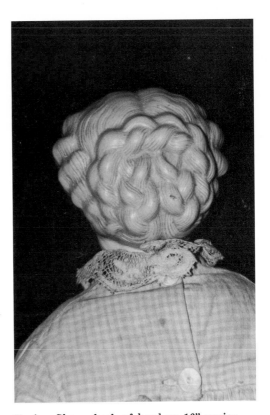

Parian--Shows back of head on 16" parian.

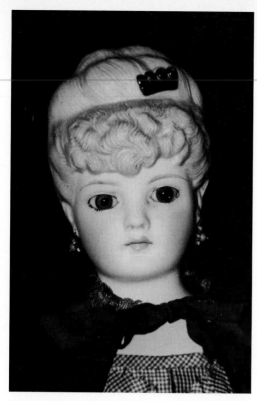

Parian--18½" Parian with blonde molded curls and black comb. Brown glass inset eyes. Pierced ears. Cloth body with leather arms. $495.00. (Courtesy Kimport Dolls)

Parian--18" Blonde parian with unusual applied scarf on decorated shoulders. Inset glass eyes. Pierced ears. Marks: 151-4. $695.00. (Courtesy Kimport Dolls)

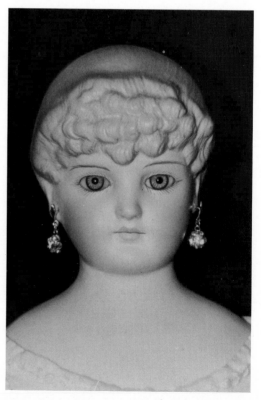

Parian--17" Parian with inset glass eyes, gray plumes and black comb. Pierced ears. Applied collar and rose. Marks: 144-3. $595.00. (Courtesy Kimport Dolls)

Parian--19½" Glass eyed Parian. Pierced ears. Blonde hair. $495.00. (Courtesy Kimport Dolls)

Parian--10½" Blonde parian with molded long curls down back of head and neck. Pierced ears. Molded large bow in center of hairdo that is painted same color as hair. Kid body with leather arms. $375.00. (Courtesy Kimport Dolls)

Parian--13½" Parian of 1860. Cloth body with leather arms. $300.00. (Courtesy Kimport Dolls)

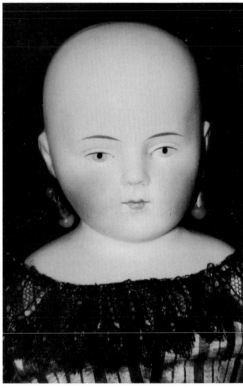

Parian--23" Parian with turned shoulder, pierced ears and inset glass eyes. Blonde with ribbons and bows in back of hairdo. Cloth body with parian limbs. $875.00. (Courtesy Kimport Dolls)

Parian--18" Bald parian with pierced ears. Kid body with parian forearms. $695.00. (Courtesy Kimport Dolls)

Parian--15" Parian with blonde short, center part hairdo. Full ears are exposed. Cloth body with parian arms. $375.00. (Courtesy Helen Draves)

Parian--15½" Parian child with slightly turned shoulder head. Molded in ribbon and fully exposed ears. Detailed shoulders. Cloth body with parian limbs. $475.00. (Courtesy Kimport Dolls)

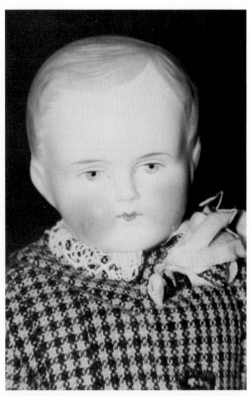

Parian--12" Parian boy. Side part blonde molded hair. Turned shoulder head. Cloth body with bisque forearms. $500.00. (Courtesy Kimport Dolls)

Parian--25" Blonde parian with slightly turned shoulder head. Inset glass eyes. Kid body with parian forearms. $475.00. (Courtesy Helen Draves)

Parian--11" Parian Bonnet Sailor Style. Molded on dress top. Cloth body with parian limbs. $475.00. (Courtesy Kimport Dolls)

Parian--16" Bonnet parian. Cloth body with parian limbs. $395.00. (Courtesy Helen Draves)

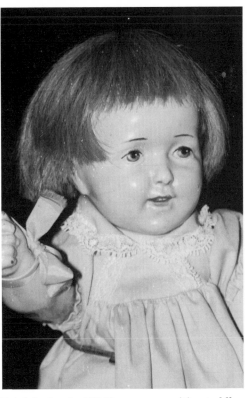

Pennsylvania Soap Co.--4" Smiling soap doll made by the Pennsylvania Soap Co. Marks: Penna. Soap Co./Lancaster/Pa. $10.00. (Courtesy Grace Ochsner)

Raleigh, Jessie--13" Heavy composition toddler. Painted brown eyes. Open/closed mouth with two painted teeth. $100.00. (Courtesy Grace Ochsner)

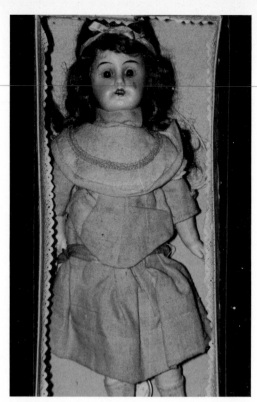

Rauenstein--11" Socket head. Open mouth.
Jointed composition body with straight wrists.
All original in box. Marks: Made in
Germany/ ⨍ o. 2/A/ ⨯. (Courtesy Helen
Draves) A-B

Rauenstein--9" Socket head with sleep eyes and
open mouth. Fully jointed composition body.
Marks: ⨯ /R-N. (Courtesy Helen Draves)
A-B

Reinecke, Otto--13" Socket head on fully jointed
composition body. Sleep eyes and unpierced
ears. Open mouth. Marks: Trebor/Germany/22/
P 7/0M. $150.00. (Courtesy Kimport Dolls)
A-B

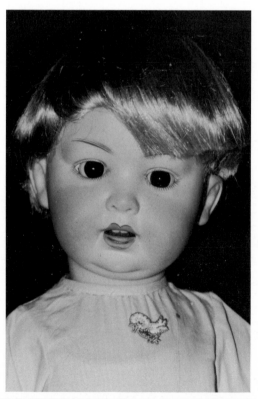

Reinecke, Otto--18" Sleep eyes, dimples and
open mouth with two upper teeth and molded
tongue. 5 piece bent leg baby body. Marks:
PM/914/8. Ca. 1910. (Courtesy Helen Draves)
C-D

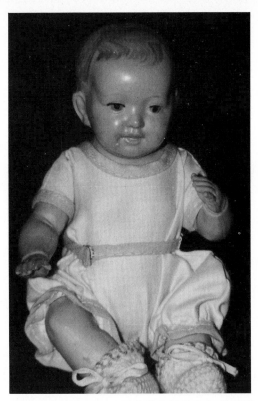

Rheinische Gumme Und Celluloid Fabric Co.--6" All one piece celluloid. Painted blue eyes. Open/closed mouth with molded tongue. Dimples. Ca. 1928. Marks: Turtlemark, in diamond/17. $12.00. (Courtesy Frances and Mary Jane Anicello)

Rheinische Gumme und Celluloid Fabric Co.--7" All celluloid baby with one piece body and head. All original. Marks: Turtlemark/Schulz-Mark/18/Germany. $35.00. (Courtesy Helen Draves)

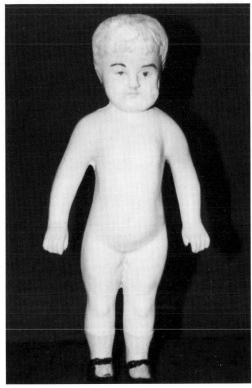

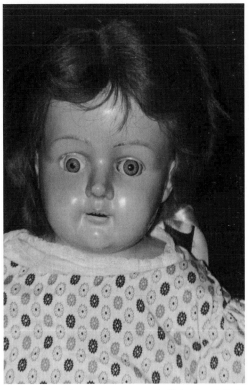

Rheinische Gumme Und Celluloid Fabric Co.--7¼" All celluloid "frozen" type. Molded on shoes and socks. Marks: Turtlemark. $20.00. (Courtesy Kimport Dolls)

Rheinische Gumme Und Celluloid Fabric Co.--27" Celluloid head (shoulder head) on cloth body. Set glass eyes and open mouth. Marks: Turtlemark/No. 20. $87.00. (Courtesy Helen Draves)

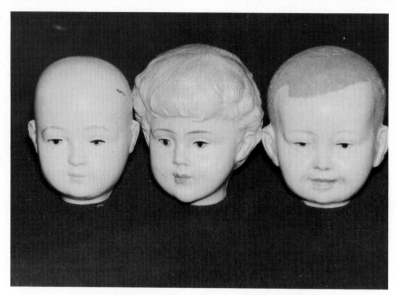

Rheinische Gumme Und Celluloid Fabric Co.--9"
tall all celluloid doll with interchangeable heads.
All have painted eyes, one takes wig, and boy
has flocked hair. There was also a Cats head
with the set. Marks: Turtle Mark/Schultz-
marke/24/Germany/D.R.G.M./447323. $95.00
complete. (Courtesy Kimport Dolls)

Rubber--5" All rubber and molded in one piece.
Marks: None. $25.00. (Courtesy Helen Draves)

Rubber--6" All rubber and molded in one piece.
Marks: Gyr Co. Made by Goodyear Rubber
Company. $45.00. (Courtesy Helen Draves)

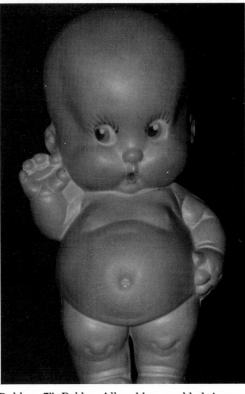

Rubber--7" Baldy. All rubber molded in one piece. Painted blue eyes. Marks: Seiberling Latex Products/Made In USA/Baldy/56. $15.00. (Courtesy Elaine Kaminsky)

BRUNO SCHMIDT

Schmidt, Bruno--Bruno Schmidt manufactured dolls from 1900 into the 1930's. He operated from Walterhausen, Thur. He not only worked in porcelain but also pápier maché and celluloid. His trademarks all include hearts and he registered Mein Goldhertz (My Golden Heart) in 1904 and the BSW in a heart this same year. Other years they registered hearts were: 1908, 1910 and 1915. Sample marks: ♡ ♡ ♥ Some of Bruno Schmidt's mold numbers: 204, 529, 2048, 2072, 2094, 2096, 2097.

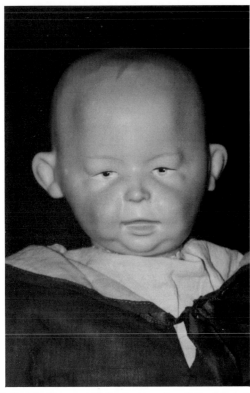

Schmidt, Bruno--15" Socket head on fully jointed composition body. Painted eyes. Open/closed mouth. Large ears. Marks: BSW. (Courtesy Kimport Dolls) K-L

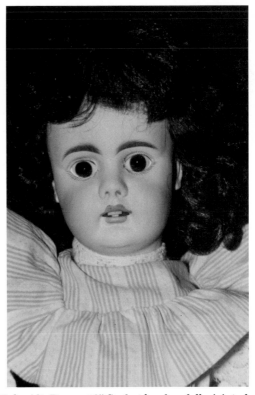

Schmidt, Bruno--19" Socket head on fully jointed composition body, with straight wrists. Open mouth. Eyes have been re-set. Marks: 204, on head. (Courtesy Kimport Dolls) C-D

211

Schmitt and Fils--16" on jointed composition/
wood Schmitt body with straight wrists. Pink
wash over eyes. Closed mouth. Pierced ears.
These early Schmitt and Fils are often
unmarked and are referred to as "Portrait
Jumeaus" as they bear a strong resemblance to
Jumeau dolls. The typical Schmitt body can be
marked, or the head or both. (Author) T-U

SCHOENAU & HOFFMEISTER

Schoenau and Hoffmeister--Schoenau and Hoffmeister entered the doll field late in 1901 and their factory was in Bavaria. The factory was called "Porzellanfabric Burggrub" and this is so marked on some of their dolls. Sample mark: ☆ Following are some of their mold numbers: 21, 169, 170, 769, 900, 914, 1800, 1906, 1909, 1923, 4000, 4500, 4900, 5000, 5300, 5500, 5700, Hanna.

Schoenau and Hoffmeister--16" Socket head on 5 piece bent leg baby body. Sleep eye/lashes. Open mouth with two upper teeth. Marks: Porzellenfabric-Burggrub/169/3//x0 Germany. (Courtesy Kathy Walter) E-F

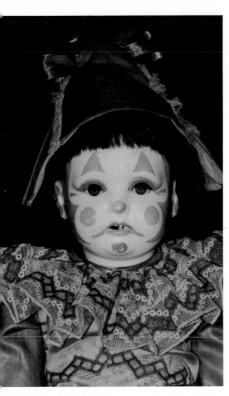

Schoenau and Hoffmeister--26½" Socket head on fully jointed composition body. Sleep eyes. All original. Marks: S ☆ H/1 -4/Germany. (Courtesy Kimport Dolls) I-J

Schoenau and Hoffmeister--12" Socket head on fully jointed composition body. Sleep eyes/lashes. Open mouth. All original in original box. Marks: S ☆ H/1909/6/0/ Germany. (Courtesy Helen Draves) B-C

Schoenau & Hoffmeister--17½" Socket head on jointed composition body with straight wrists. Sleep eyes. Open mouth. Marks: S ☆ H/1909/2. (Courtesy Kathy Walter) C-D

213

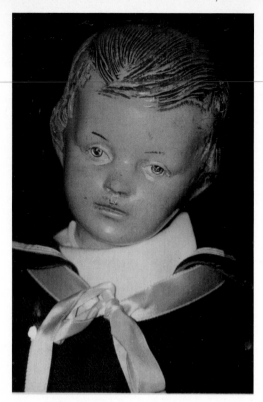

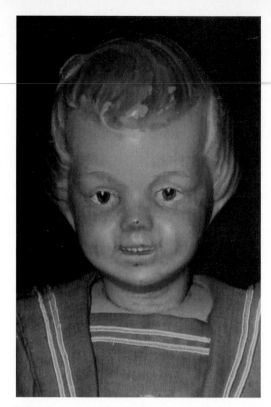

Schoenhut--19" Boy with sculptured, carved hair. (Courtesy Jay Minter)

Schoenhut--17" All wood with carved hair and ribbon. Painted blue eyes. Open/closed mouth with painted teeth. Marks: seal-see introduction. (Courtesy Helen Draves)

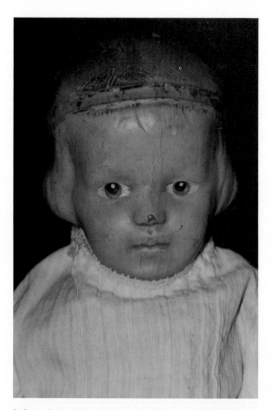

Schoenhut--14½" All wood. Painted brown eyes. Open/closed mouth with painted upper teeth. Original wig. Marks: seal-see introduction. (Courtesy Julia Rogers)

Schoenhut--17" All wood with carved hair with head band. Painted eyes. Closed mouth. Marks: Seal-see introduction. (Courtesy Helen Draves)

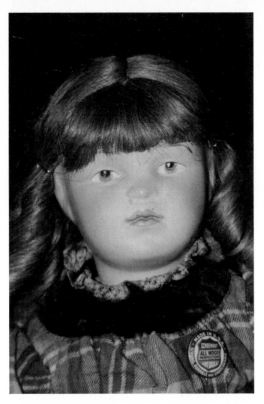

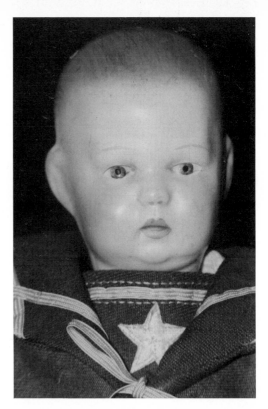

Schoenhut--22" All original girl. Blue eyes. Has never been played with. Original Pin.

Schoenhut--14" All wood. Brush stroke hair. Painted blue eyes. Closed mouth. Marks: seal-- see introduction. (Courtesy Helen Draves)

Wood--12 "Clo and Harry Pinn" Wood block body. Jointed neck. Clothes pin arms and legs. Jointed knees, hips and shoulders. Yarn hair. Painted features. Marks: Patent Pending/1936/ Tm St. Paul, Minn. Made by Schoenhut. $20.00 each. (Courtesy Mary Partridge)

Wood--8½" "Beauty Pinn" 7 5" "Baby Pinn" Beauty/jointed neck, hips, shoulders. Clothes pin arms/legs are straight. Baby/one piece body and head, straight arms/legs but jointed at hips/ shoulders. Painted pale blue feet with pink trim. Original. No marks on Baby. Beauty is marked same as Clo and Harry Pinn. Made by Schoenhut 1936. $20.00. (Courtesy Mary Partridge)

Schoenhut--Circus wagon with rubber wheels.
(Courtesy Susan Manos)

Schoenhut--This is the clown from the 1952
Devlon Circus)

Schoenhut--Camels with glass eyes. (Courtesy
Susan Manos)

Schoenhut--Top to bottom left side, Cat with glass eyes, Ruffled Poodle with glass eyes, glass eye Cow from storyland set, Horse with saddle for performer. Top to bottom right side, glass eye Donkey, glass eye Buffalo, Lion carved mane and painted eyes, glass eye Elephant, Horse with attached saddle and painted eyes. (All courtesy Susan Manos)

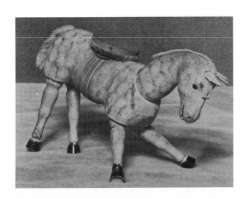

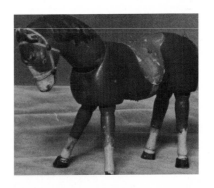

217

SCHUETZMEISTER & QUENDT

Schuetzmeister and Quendt--Schuetzmeister and Quendt was one of the doll companies that only operated a few years and these years were 1893 to 1898. Theri factory was located at Boilstadt, Thur. Sample marks:

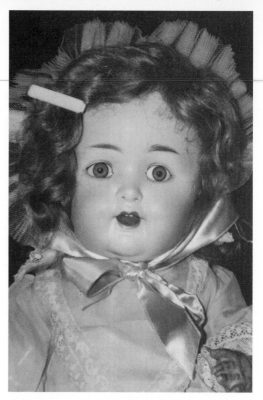

Schuetzmeister and Quendt--17" Socket head on 5 piece bent leg baby body. Sleep eyes. Open mouth with two upper teeth. Marks: ◯ / Germany. (Courtesy Jay Minter) D-E ◯

Schuetzmeister and Quendt--9" Socket head on 5 piece solid composition body. Ball (bald) head with two stringing holes. Came with wardrobe and trunk. Set glass eyes and closed mouth. Marks: SQ 20 (or 39). (Courtesy Kimport Dolls) I-J

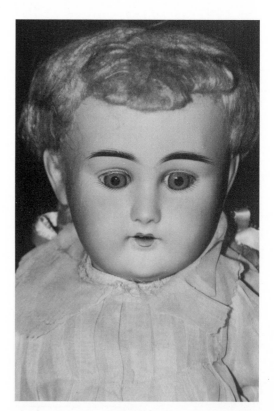

Schuetzmeister and Quendt--21" Socket head on fully jointed composition body. Sleep eyes. Open mouth. Original. Marks: SQ /101/Dep./10. (Courtesy Helen Draves) E-F

218

SIMON & HALBIG

Some of the finest quality German dolls came from the Simon and Halbig factory which was located at Grafenhain near Ohrdruf, Thur. The dates for Simon and Halibg are vague but they began sometime in the late 1860's or early 1870's and ran until the mid 1930's.

Simon and Halbig made many heads for the French trade and as yet there has been no proof that there was a connection with P. Simon of Paris who handled German heads.

Simon and Halbig made every conceivable type heads, entire dolls, all bisque dolls, flange necked dolls, lady and "doll house" dolls, shoulder heads, turned shoulder heads and socket heads. They were one of the few manufacturers that made entire dolls.

Some Simon and Halbig dolls have molded hair and untinted bisque and quite a few have been found with "ball (bald) heads and in 1890 they obtained patents for movable eyes. One was a wire, with a loop, through a hole in the back of the head and later it was a wire with a handle to make eyes movable from right to left. They made dolls for many companies and were a big supplier to Kammer and Reinhardt but also made dolls for Fleischmann and Blodel, Gimbel Bros., C.M. Bergmann, Jumeau, Cuno and Otto Dressel, Bawo and Dotter, Hamberger and Co., George Borgfelt and Co., etc.

It was in 1895 Simon left the firm (retired or deceased) and Carl Halbig took over as a single owner. There are dolls with just the Carl Halbig that have been reported. Carl Halbig did not register "S and H" until 1905. Before then the dolls were marked with just SH or the full name Simon and Halbig. The most often found mold number is #1079. The following are sample marks and some of the mold numbers:

		Halbig	1030
C.M. Bergmann	S and H		
Simon and Halbig	1079	K ✡ R	Jumeau (body)
		Germany	

50, 76, 100, 120, 122, 126, 139, 151, 156, 191, 282, 382, 403, 409, 461, 530, 540, 550, 570, 576, 600, 616, 709, 719, 739, 759, 769, 905, 909, 929, 939, 940, 941, 945, 949, 950, 960, 969, 970, 979, 1000, 1008, 1009, 1009N, 1010, 1019, 1039, 1040, 1059, 1060, 1069, 1070, 1075, 1078, 1079, 1080, 1099, 1109, 1129, 1159, 1160, 1169, 1170, 1199, 1242, 1248, 1249, 1250, 1260, 1269, 1279, 1280, 1290, 1294, 1296, 1299, 1301, 1303, 1305, 1329, 1348, 1349, 1358, 1368, 1388, 1469, 1488, 1498, 1616, 1848, 1900, Baby Blanche, Ericka, Jutta, Santa, IV.

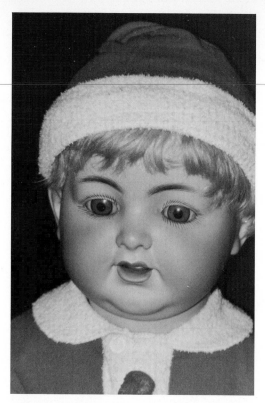

Simon and Halbig--14" Brown socket head on brown fully jointed body. Open mouth. Marks: 50 9/0/5/Made in Germany. Second one marked 50 9/0/S.H./Germany. (Courtesy Jane Alton) C-D

Simon and Halbig--23" Socket head on 5 piece bent leg baby body. Tremble tongue. Sleep eyes. Open mouth. Marks: Simon Halbig/126. (Courtesy Helen Draves) E-F

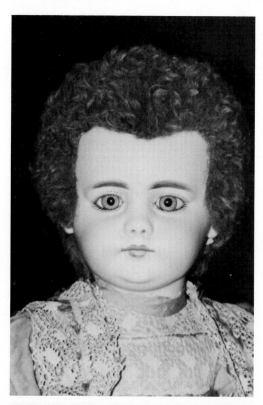

Simon and Halbig--14" Twins Socket head with shapely 5 piece bodies. All original. Teddies of silk crepe, stockings, garters and patent shoes. Original box marked 1/12 doz. 2/382/33/Made in Germany. Childhood dolls of Jennie Gregg and sister. (Courtesy Jeanne Gregg) C-D

Simon and Halbig--18" Socket head on jointed composition body with straight wrists. Ball (bald) head. Closed mouth. Ears pierced above earlobe into head. Wood block on body side inside neck with composition applied around it. Marks: S 11 H 719 Dep. high on head. (Author) G-H

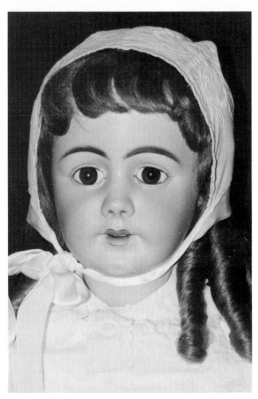

Simon and Halbig--36" Socket head on fully jointed composition body. Open mouth. Marks: S 17 3/4 H/939/Dep. (Courtesy Helen Draves) I-J

Simon and Halbig--25" Socket head on fully jointed composition body. Set eyes. Open/closed mouth. Marks: S 13H/939. (Courtesy Helen Draves) K-L

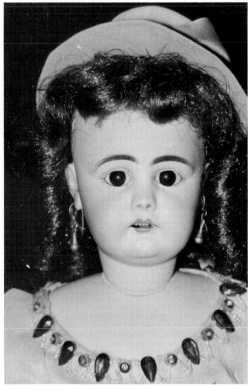

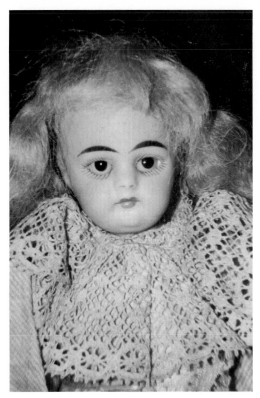

Simon and Halbig--18" Swivel head on bisque shoulder plate. Open mouth. Pierced ears. Marks: S 9 H/949. (Courtesy Helen Draves) E-F

Simon and Halbig--8" Shoulder head on cloth body with bisque arms. Sleep eyes and closed mouth. Marks: SH 4/0 950. (Courtesy Kimport Dolls) D-E

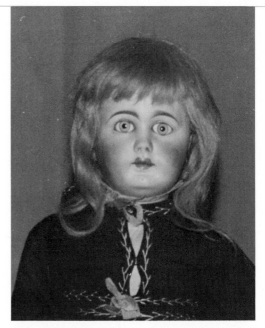

Simon and Halbig--21" Twins Socket heads on jointed bodies with straight wrists. All original. This was set of three, see 4 photos of sister (dressed and undressed) in Series 1, page 198. Marks: 1009 No. 8/Dep. (Courtesy Helen Draves) H-I

Simon and Halbig--18½" Socket head. Closed mouth, blue paperweight eyes, straight wrists and original mohair wig. Marks: 1009x. We have placed this doll under Simon and Halbig only because the mold number 1009 is theirs. (Courtesy Jeannie Gregg) K-L

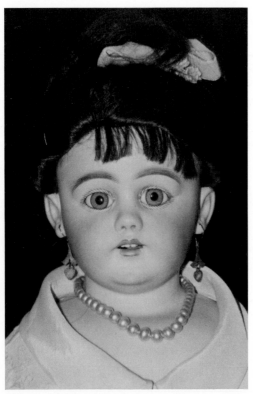

Simon and Halbig--26" Shoulder head on adult type kid body with bisque forearms. Open mouth. Pierced ears. Marks: S 12 H/1010 Dep. (Courtesy Grace Ochsner) E-F

Simon and Halbig--19½" Shoulder head on kid body with bisque forearms. Almost black set eyes. Pierced ears. Open mouth. Marks: S 7 H 1010 Dep. (Courtesy Kathy Walter) D-E

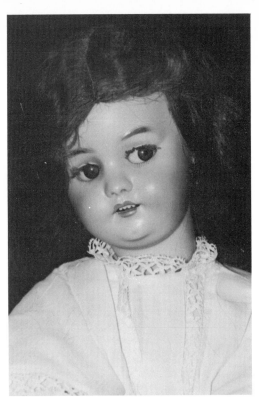

Simon and Halbig--20" Socket head on fully jointed composition/wood body. Molded brows and flirty sleep eyes with lashes. Open mouth. Marks: 1039/Simon and Halbig/S & H/10. (Courtesy Helen Draves) D-E

Simon and Halbig--16" Hindu brown socket hed on fully jointed brown composition body. Very large sleep brown eyes. Open mouth. Pierced ears. Original. Marks: SH 1039/6 Dep. (Courtesy Kimport Dolls) I-J

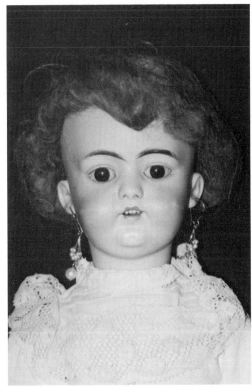

Simon and Halbig--17" Socket head. Sleep eyes, open mouth and pierced ears. Marks: SH 1075 Dep/7/Germany. (Courtesy Helen Draves)D-E

Simon and Halbig--32" Socket head on fully jointed composition body. Sleep eyes/lashes and painted lashes under only. Open mouth. Marks: 1078/Simon and Halbig/S & H/7. (Courtesy Jay Minter) F-H

223

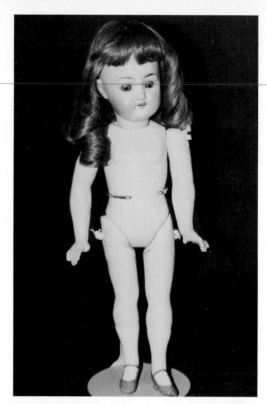

Simon and Halbig--10" Socket head on 5 piece composition body. Molded on heeled shoes. Sleep eyes. Open mouth. Marks: 1078/Simon and Halbig/S & H. (Courtesy Kathy Walter) C-D

Simon and Halbig--Shows body of 10" S & H 1078.

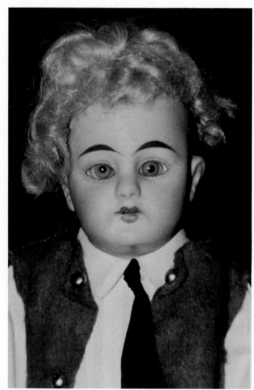

224

Simon and Halbig--8" Socket head on 5 piece composition body with painted on socks and boots. Sleep eyes. Open mouth. Original clothes. Marks: 1079 2/0/Dep/S & H. (Courtesy Helen Draves) A-B

Simon and Halbig--18" Turned shoulder head with two sew holes front and back. Kid body with bisque forearms. Open mouth with molded teeth. Marks: Germany/Simon and Halbig/ 1080-S & H 7. (Courtesy Jay Minter) E-F

Simon and Halbig--22" Turned shoulder head. Set eyes and closed mouth. Many are unmarked and others: S & H 1081, etc. (Courtesy Jane Alton) F-G

Simon and Halbig--13" Socket head with olive skin tones on same color fully jointed composition body. Almond shaped sleep eyes. Open mouth. Marks: SH 1129/Dep/3/Germany. (Courtesy Kimport Dolls) L-M

Simon and Halbig--25" Swivel shoulder head on bisque shoulder plate. Adult figure kid body with bisque forearms. Open mouth and pierced ears. Marks: 1159/Germany/Simon and Halbig/S & H/9½. (Courtesy Helen Draves) J-K

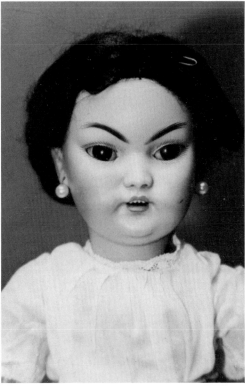

Simon and Halbig--15" Oriental socket head on fully jointed body. Sleep eyes and open mouth. Pierced ears. Marks: SH 1199/Germany/Dep./6. (Courtesy Kimport Dolls) M-N

225

Société
Francaise de
Fabrication de
Bébés et Jouets
(S.F.B.J.)

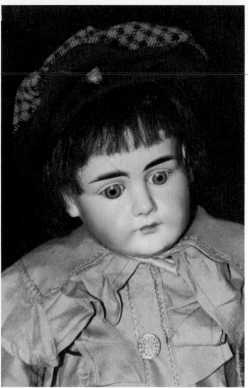

Simon and Halbig--24" Shoulder head on kid
body with bisque forearms. Open mouth. Set
eyes. Marks: 1260 Germany Dep ℔ 12.
(Courtesy Kathy Walter) E-F

SOCIÉTÉ FRANÇAISE
de BÉBÉS et JOUETS

Société Française de Bébés et Jouets
(S.F.B.J.)--This society was formed in 1899 and
was made up of many of the French doll makers
including Jumeau, Bru, Jullien and Danel and
Cie. The Director was Herr. Fleischmann of
Fleischmann and Blodel. They used the initials
S.F.B.J. The character dolls made by them are
some of the highest priced and seemly most
desirable dolls to add to a collection.

Sample Marks: Depose
S.F.B.J.

The following are some of their mold numbers:
21, 25, 30, 30.4, 32, 60, 215, 226, 227, 228, 229,
230, 233, 234, 235, 236, 237, 238, 239, 245, 246,
247, 251, 252, 255, 257, 301, 1123.

Société Francaise de Fabrication de Bébés et
Jouets--12" Shoulder head on excelsior filled
body with composition limbs. Painted eyes.
Molded open/closed mouth. All original. Marks:
SFBJ/60/Paris. (Courtesy Helen Draves) C-D

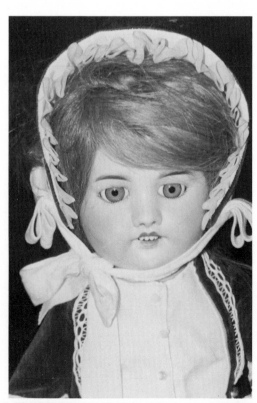

Société Française de Fabrication de Bébés et
Jouets--18" Socket head on fully jointed body.
Sleep eyes and open mouth. Marks: SFBJ/60.
(Courtesy Grace Ochsner) E-F

226

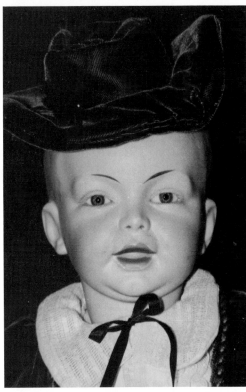

Société Française de Fabrication de Bébés et Jouets--20" Socket head on fully jointed body. Solid head with light brushed hair. Open/closed mouth. Inset blue eyes. Marks: SFBJ 226. (Courtesy Grace Ochsner) O-P

Société Française de Fabrication de Bébés et Jouets--14" Socket head on fully jointed body. Open/closed mouth with two teeth. Laughing mouth design. Blue inset glass eyes. Blonde real fur hair (flocked). Marks: SFBJ 235/Paris/4. (Courtesy Jeannie Gregg) N-O

Société Française de Fabrication de Bébés et Jouets--14" Socket head on full jointed body. Inset eyes. Closed mouth. Marks: SFBJ/239/Paris. Designed by Poulbot and called "Street Urchin". (Courtesy Kimport Dolls) Z-+

Société Française de Fabrication de Bébés et Jouets--7" "Twirp" head on 5 piece maché body. Marks: SFBJ/247. (Courtesy Kimport Dolls) N-O

227

STANFUSS,
KARL

STEINER,
EDMUND

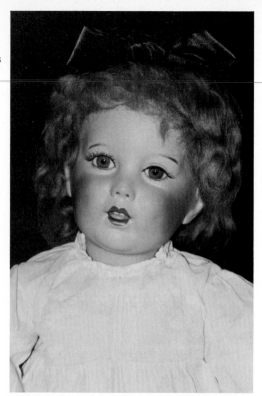

Société Francaise de Fabrication de Bébés et Jouets--25" Socket head on full jointed toddler body. Open mouth with molded tongue. Marks: 22/SFBJ/251/Paris. (Courtesy Jay Minter) N-O

Stanfuss, Karl--23" Metal head on cloth body and wood half arms with sewn on leather boots. Painted eyes and open/closed mouth. Marks: 6¼/Germany, on back. Juno, on front. $95.00. (Courtesy Bessie Greeno)

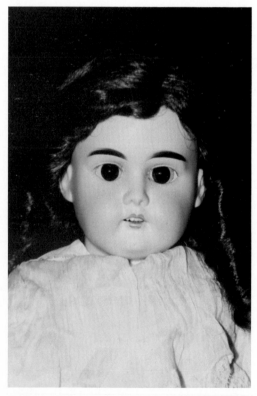

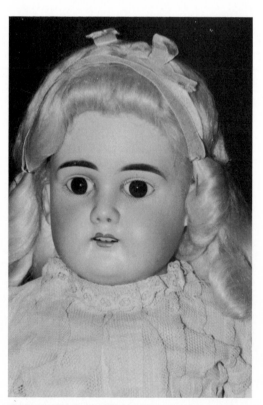

Steiner, Edmund Ulrich--21½" Shoulder head on kid body with bisque lower arms. Open mouth. Marks: ⟨EUS⟩/Made in Germany. (Courtesy Kimport Dolls) C-D

Steiner, Edmund Ulrich--24" Shoulder head on kid body with bisque arms. Open mouth. Marks: ⟨EUS⟩/Made in Germany. (Courtesy Helen Draves) D-E

228

HERMANN STEINER

Steiner, Hermann--Hermann Steiner did not enter the doll field until after World War 1 (1921) and made dolls at Neustadt, near Colburg and Sonneberg. Sample marks: |S|)S(The following are some of Herm Steiner's mold numbers: 45, 75, 128, 133, 134, 140, 141, 145, 401, 947, 4015, 4016, 95464 (this is a registration number incised on some dolls)

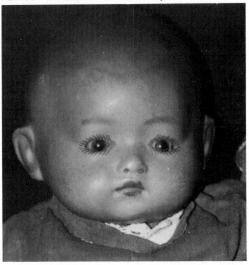

Steiner, Herm--12" Brown bisque baby. Sleep eyes and closed mouth. Marks: 11/ |S| Germany. (Courtesy Helen Draves) D-E

Steiner, Herm--19" Black composition. Set eyes. Open/closed mouth with painted upper teeth. Marks:)S(/134. (Courtesy Kimport Dolls) D-E

Steiner, Jules Nichols--10" Socket head on crude 5 piece maché body. Set eyes. Closed mouth. Marks: Steiner/Paris/FR-A-3. (Courtesy Kimport Dolls) J-K

Steiner, Jules Nichols--25" Socket head. Closed mouth. Pierced ears. Marks: A 17/Paris, on head. Le Parisian SGDG/stamp in red on body. (Courtesy Kimport Dolls) S-U

229

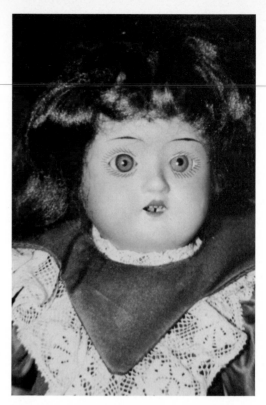

Sterling Doll Co.--28" "Eddie Cantor" Composition head and feet. Cloth body and arms with felt hands. Original clown costume. Also came dressed as football player and minstrel. Called the "Many characters of Eddie Cantor." Marks: Sterling/Doll Co. $95.00. (Courtesy Helen Draves)

Strobel and Wilkens--9" Bisque socket head on 5 piece composition body. Open mouth. Set eyes and unpierced ears. Marks: Ⓢ /Made in Germany. (Courtesy Kimport Dolls) A-B

SWAINE & CO.

Swaine and Co.--operated from 1854 to 1918 at Huttensteinach (North Koppelsdorf) Thur. By 1921 the remains of the company joined Schoenau to become Gebruder Schoenau, Swaine and Co. and manufactured bathroom fixtures.

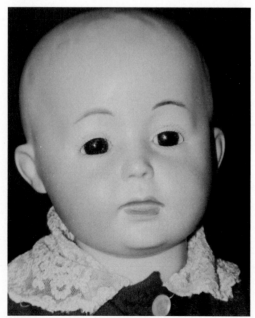

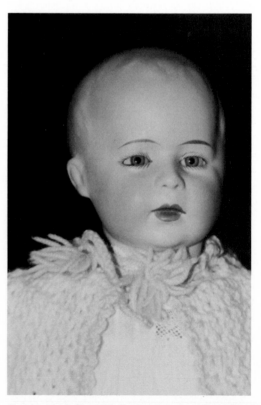

230

Swaine and Co.--22" Lori Baby. Socket head on toddler body. Open/closed mouth. Marks: D/Lori/1. (Courtesy Grace Ochsner) I-J

Swaine and Co.--13" Socket head on bent leg 5 piece baby body. Sleep blue eyes. Open/closed mouth. Marks: D1/3 and seal (Courtesy Kimport Dolls) G-H

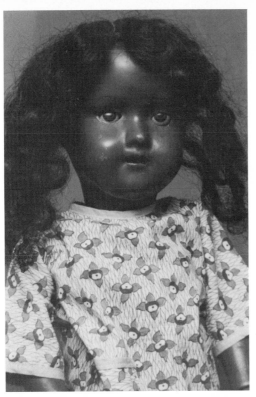

Trego--18½" Painted bisque head on fully jointed composition body. Sleep eyes and open mouth. Marks: Trego, in square/Made in USA. (Courtesy Alice Capps) B-C

Union Nationale Inter-Syndicali--11½" Court Jester with bisque on 5 piece maché body. Open mouth. Original. Marks: Unis/France, in oval. 71/49/60. (Courtesy Kimport Dolls) F-G

Union Nationale Inter-Syndicali--15" Socket head on fully jointed composition body. Open mouth. Set eyes. Marks: 70/Unis France, in oval 149/60. (Courtesy Kathy Walter) D-E

Verlingue, J. 13" Shoulder head on cloth body with bisque arms and legs. Closed mouth and painted brown eyes. Marks: J. anchor V. (Courtesy Grace Ochsner) D-E

231

Wagner and Zelzsche--14" Turned shoulder head on kid body with bisque forearms. Open mouth. Marks: 4 Wagner and Zelysche are known for flat under side of eyebrows and eyebrows being very close to eyes. (Courtesy Helen Draves) D-E

Wagner and Zelzsche--19" Turned shoulder head. Kid with bisque forearms. Open mouth. Marks: W & Z (Very scrolled)/9. (Courtesy Helen Draves) E-F

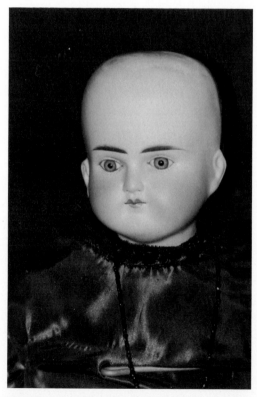

232

Wagner and Zelzsche--22" Turned shoulder head on kid body with bisque forearms. Open mouth. Marks: 1123 K (or X) 8. (Courtesy Helen Draves) E-F

Wagner and Zelzsche--23" Turned shoulder head. Tight closed mouth. Ball (bald) head. Marks: Wagner and Zelzsche, in a scroll. (Courtesy Helen Draves) F-G

Wagner and Zelzsche--27" Turned shoulder head on kid body with bisque forearms. Marks: 10, high on head. (Courtesy Helen Draves) F-G

Wagner and Zelzsche--29" Turned shoulder head on kid body with bisque forearms. Set eyes and open mouth. Marks: Made in/Germany/K-13. (Courtesy Helen Draves) G-H

Wax--21" Pressed wax baby with cloth body and pressed wax limbs. Inset glass eyes. Closed mouth. $350.00. (Courtesy Helen Draves)

Wax--14" Wax with set blue eyes. Closed mouth. Pierced ears. Cloth body with wax limbs. $225.00. (Courtesy Helen Draves)

233

Wax--16" Wax of 1875 with rare sleep eyes. Closed mouth. Cloth body with wax limbs. $275.00. (Courtesy Kimport Dolls)

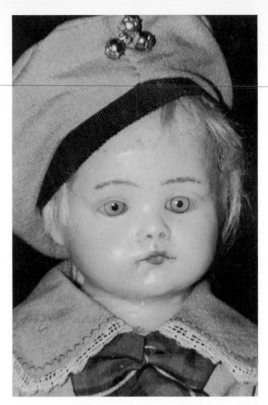

Wax--14" Poured wax with wax limbs and cloth body. Inset blue eyes. Pouty mouth. Open crown/wig. $225.00. (Courtesy Kimport Dolls)

Wax--28" Poured wax with inset blue glass eyes. Closed mouth. Cloth body with poured wax limbs. $325.00. (Courtesy Helen Draves)

Wax--8½" Pumpkin head wax with molded on snood. Inset glass eyes. Old cloth body (enigma) with arms and legs of wood. Painted on orange shoes. Squeeker box in stomach. $150.00. (Courtesy Kimport Dolls)

234

Wax--20" Wax over maché with inset glass eyes. Closed mouth. Original wig and clothes. Cloth body with wax limbs. $250.00. (Courtesy Helen Draves)

Wax--24" Wax over maché with molded bow and very detailed hairdo. Large glass inset eyes. Closed mouth smile. Cloth body with wax limbs. $300.00. (Courtesy Helen Draves)

Wax--21" Wax over maché with molded hair band. Glass inset eyes. Closed mouth. $225.00. (Courtesy Jane Alton)

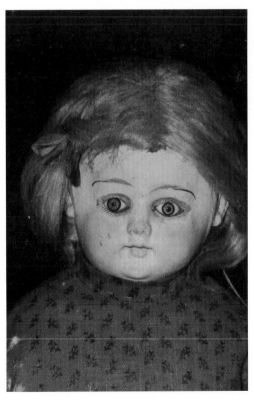

Wax--22" Wax over maché with inset glass eyes. Closed mouth. Cloth body with mache limbs. $185.00. (Courtesy Helen Draves)

Wax--13" Wax over maché with cloth body and wax limbs. Inset glass eyes. Open mouth. Original. $235.00. (Courtesy Helen Draves)

Wax--20" Wax over maché with cloth body and maché limbs. Inset glass eyes. Closed mouth. $200.00. (Courtesy Helen Draves)

Wax--6" Wax over maché. Glass inset eyes. Original. $165.00. (Courtesy Jane Alton)

Wax--10" Wax over maché with inset glass eyes. Closed mouth. Molded hairdo. Original. $175.00. (Courtesy Helen Draves)

Wax--8½" Wax fashion. Wax over maché of the pin cushion or "half doll" type. Mounted on wooden base. Original. $95.00. (Courtesy Helen Draves)

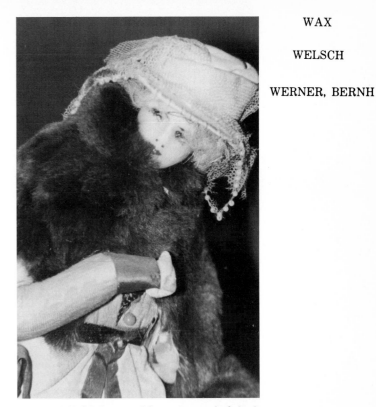

Wax--12" Molded wax with armiture/cloth body and limbs. Original. $65.00. (Courtesy Helen Draves)

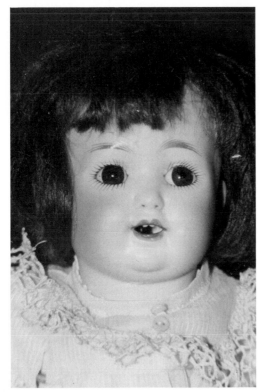

Welsch and Co.--14" Socket head on bent leg baby body. Open mouth with two upper teeth. Large sleep eyes. Marks: 201/W and Co./Thuringia/2. (Courtesy Kimport Dolls) C-D

Werner, Bernh--7" Socket head on maché body with straight legs and arms. Open mouth/teeth. Marks: W B/121/19/0 Z. A-B

237

White Bisque--6" White bisque bonnet doll. Cloth body with white bisque limbs and glazed black shoes. Marks: Germany. $260.00. (Courtesy Helen Draves)

White Bisque--7" White bisque bonnet shoulder head on cloth body with white bisque limbs. Black glazed hair. $185.00. (Courtesy Helen Draves)

White Bisque--9 3/4" White bisque with molded on "Jockey" cap and shirt and collar. Cloth body with china limbs. $185.00. (Courtesy Helen Draves)

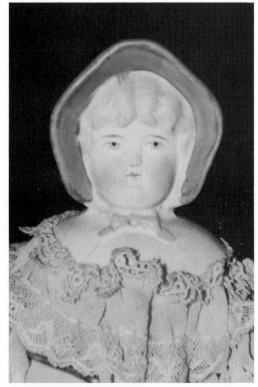

White Bisque--10" White bisque bonnet shoulder head with cloth body and white bisque limbs. $175.00. (Courtesy Helen Draves)

White Bisque--10" White bisque bonnet shoulder head on cloth body with white bisque limbs. $260.00. (Courtesy Helen Draves)

White Bisque--12" White bisque bonnet shoulder head. Cloth body with white bisque limbs. This same bonnet head can be seen in the 7" version in the All Bisque section. $165.00. (Courtesy Helen Draves)

White Bisque--12" White bisque with molded large bow and collar. Cloth body with white bisque limbs. $240.00. (Courtesy Helen Draves)

White Bisque--13" White bisque bonnet shoulder head with applied necklace and with two sew holes front and back. Cloth body with white bisque limbs. $285.00. (Courtesy Grace Ochsner)

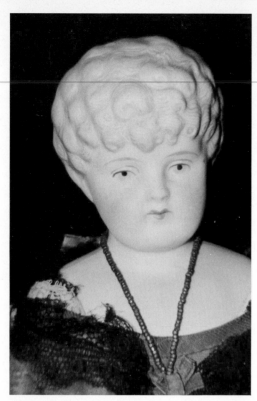

White Bisque--13" White bisque with molded blonde hair. Cloth body with white bisque arms and legs. Marks: 1. $250.00. (Courtesy Helen Draves)

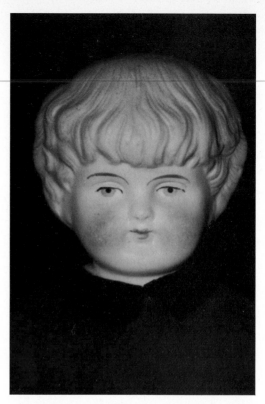

White Bisque--18" White bisque shoulder head on cloth body with white bisque limbs. $195.00. (Courtesy Helen Draves)

Wood--22" Queen Anne. Ca. 1680. Inset glass eyes. Cloth arms and legs. $2,250.00. (Courtesy Kimport Dolls)

Wood--13½" English wood. Applied leather ears. Red painted torso. $350.00. (Courtesy Kimport Dolls)

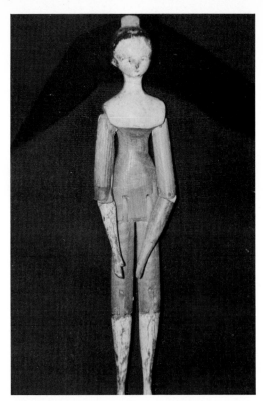

Wood--9" Peg wood with molded hair and comb. $450.00. (Courtesy Kimport Dolls)

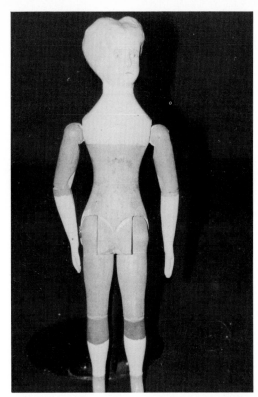

Wood--11½" All wood with pewter hands and feet. Mason and Taylor/Springfield. Patented 1881. $595.00. (Courtesy Kimport Dolls)

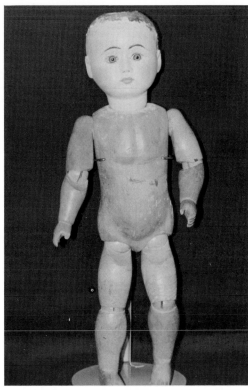

Wood--18" beautifully done wood body of French origin. Head is all wood that is painted. One large hole in top of head. Inset glass eyes. Closed mouth. Unable to read seal on upper chest. $695.00.

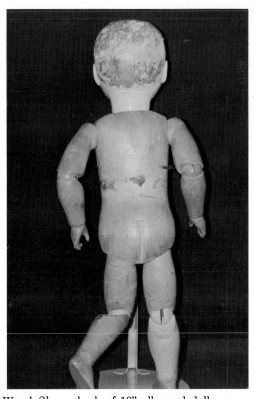

Wood--Shows back of 18" all wood doll.

241

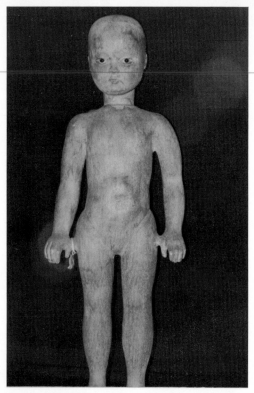

Wood--20" All one piece wood. Inset glass eyes. Marks: None. $495.00. (Courtesy Helen Draves)

Wood--6½" All wood and completely jointed. A very tiny perfect figure. $200.00. (Courtesy Helen Draves)

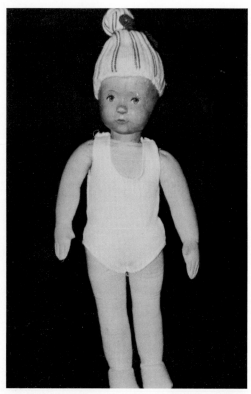

Wood--13" Tightly stuffed with wool dust body and limbs. Wood head. Disc jointed hips and stitch jointed arms. Flax hair glued on under cap. Painted blue eyes. Marks: None. $65.00. (Courtesy Ellie Haynes)

Wood--6" All wood with jointed hips and shoulders. Spoon hands with thumb detail. Painted features. Original. $3.00. (Courtesy Mary Partridge)

242

Wood--23" Wajang Koolit Shadow puppet. These were made for hundreds of years of water buffalo hides and wood. All wood with cloth clothing. $50.00. (Courtesy Jay Minter)

Wood--23" Wajang Koolit Shadow puppet. $50.00. (Courtesy Jay Minter)

Wood--4½" Boy and Girl. This view shows the clothes which are original. (Courtesy Frances and Mary Jane Anicello)

Wood--4½" All wood. Painted features. Cloth upper ¾ arms. Wood peg jointed hips/legs. Legs carved in one piece. Painted on shoes. Marks: None. $5.00. (Courtesy Frances and Mary Jane Anicello)

INDEX

Numbers Index

Dates

Letters and Symbols